Hélène Cixous

Twayne's World Authors Series
French Literature

David O'Connell, Editor
Georgia State University

TWAS 860

HÉLÈNE CIXOUS
Photo © Martine Franck / Magnum Photos

Hélène Cixous

Lynn Kettler Penrod

University of Alberta

Twayne Publishers
An Imprint of Simon & Schuster Macmillan
New York

Prentice Hall International
London • Mexico City • New Delhi • Singapore • Sydney • Toronto

Twayne's World Authors Series No. 860

Hélène Cixous
Lynn Kettler Penrod

Twayne Publishers
An Imprint of Simon & Schuster Macmillan
1633 Broadway
New York, New York 10019

Library of Congress Cataloging-in-Publication Data

Penrod, Lynn, 1946–
Hélène Cixous / Lynn Penrod.
p. cm. — (Twayne's world authors series; TWAS 860)
Includes bibliographical references and index.
ISBN 0-8057-8284-2
1. Cixous, Hélène, 1937– —Criticism and interpretation. I. Title. II. Series: Twayne's world authors series; TWAS 860.
PX2663.I9Zi 1996
848'.91409—dc20 95–34509
CIP

The paper used in this publication meets the minimum requirements of American National Standard for Information Sciences—Permanence of Paper for Printed Library Materials, ANSI Z39.48-1984.∞™

10 9 8 7 6 5 4 3 2 1 (hc)
10 9 8 7 6 5 4 3 2 1 (pb)

Printed in the United States of America.

For Sacha, Nessa, and Jenny

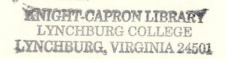

Contents

Preface

Writing an English-language introductory volume on the works of Hélène Cixous is, to put it mildly, a daunting task, not to say an impossible one. Yet at the same time such a project is incredibly enticing and tempting, presenting a challenge that many veteran, or even neophyte, readers of Cixous might well be inclined to accept. Indeed, Nicole Ward Jouve would seem to speak for many of those readers when she describes this admittedly contradictory position: "The crippling combination of hubris and self-doubt in my make-up makes me want to do the big thing: produce an account of the whole of Hélène Cixous's work. Immediately I want to say that this is of course impossible and in any case I'm not up to it. A characteristic female manoeuvre and one that Hélène Cixous herself has steadily avoided. Indeed, her whole work urges us to avoid it. Do not dream, then retreat. Act. Go through the gate. Do not hang around it, fashioning ghostly guardians out of your dreams and fears."[1]

So let us imagine, then, that the reader-critic of Hélène Cixous does open the gate and go through, does attempt, albeit in a mediating way and from a position one step removed from Cixous's writing, to in turn "write against the wall," to "produce an account of the whole of Hélène Cixous's work." What basic problems does such a reader-critic encounter in attempting to introduce the work of Hélène Cixous? For the reader-critic writing such a book destined for an English-language audience, these would appear to derive from two fundamental sources: (1) from basic problems involving translation and accessibility to texts and (2) from problems involving the major theoretical shifts that have occurred within literary studies over the past 20 years, changed ways of thinking about "literature" and about writing *about* literature that can loosely be termed *poststructuralist.*

For a volume in this series—a series that provides "introductions" to the "works" of an acknowledged "world author"—the problems of translation and accessibility become acutely apparent. To date, Cixous, an author who writes in French, is known chiefly to readers in the English-speaking world (even more specifically, perhaps, to a world of readers who are mostly female, mostly "feminist," mostly unilingual English) as the author of two closely related texts that were first published in the mid-1970s and that often appear on reading lists in women's studies courses or in courses on women's writing: "The Laugh of the Medusa" and *The Newly Born Woman.* She is, in rather sharp contrast to Julia Kristeva and Luce Irigaray, the other two members of contemporary French feminism's seemingly inseparable (at least in the minds of most Anglo-American critics) trio, not readily accessible in English translation. Indeed, from 1967 to 1991, although Cixous has produced more than 40 volumes of writing (including literary criticism and theory, essays, novels, short fiction, plays, and "texts"), only a half dozen of these have as yet been translated into English in their entirety. A small number of essays, interviews, and selected anthologized "extracts" completes the English textual corpus. When an author is represented so partially in translation, accounting for "the whole" of her works makes for a strange modality in the critical voice—one that the reader must be careful to listen for.

Of course, it is not necessarily the case that all texts of any author be read preferentially in the original, but for the work of Hélène Cixous, the original French, with its delight in word play and punning, the sheer playfulness of its language, and the poetic and highly metaphoric style that characterizes it, provides a richly fertile textual ground for exploration. Translators, ever keenly aware of the loss of linguistic richness as they attempt border crossings separating one language from another, have had much to mourn when translating Cixous. In the words of one of her translators, Deborah Jenson: "Translating the resonant poetics of Hélène Cixous's work into anything but her particular language—which is not French, not German, but poetry—is a difficult (Promethean?) task in which the reader must participate for full effect."[2]

Although Cixous in English translation has been slow in coming, in the last year alone four new translations have appeared: Cixous's 1983 fiction, *Le Livre de Promethea* (*The Book of Promethea*); a series of seminars Cixous has presented in Paris on the Brazilian writer Clarice Lispector (*Reading with Clarice Lispector*); a volume of selected critical essays by Cixous (*Coming to Writing and Other Essays*); and a volume of readings by Cixous on the poetics of Blanchot, Joyce, Kafka, Kleist, Lispector, and Tsvetaeva (*Readings*). The "difficulty" of translating Cixous is not necessarily insurmountable, and, as we will see, the process of translation itself is often a helpful entry point into a Cixousian text. Indeed, as more translations of Cixous appear—in English, in German, in Italian, in Japanese—the Cixous oeuvre, too, will be both transformed and transmuted as it resonates "poetically" in other languages, in other cultures.

And even with an only partial Cixous oeuvre extant in English, the wonderfully varied and richly evocative texts produced over the course of the past two decades provide an extraordinary reading experience, whether in the original or in translation. Hélène Cixous exemplifies an extraordinarily rich vein of women's writing coming from contemporary France. Her earliest published academic work centered on James Joyce (the subject of her mammoth doctoral disseration, *L'Exil de James Joyce ou l'art du remplacement* [*The Exile of James Joyce*]) and authors as varied as Kleist, Freud, Poe, and the German romantics. Novels, short stories, "fictions," and her now classic essays on *écriture féminine* take their place alongside a solid body of dramatic works (most of which have been produced by her close collaborator, Ariane Mnouchkine, at Paris's Théâtre du Soleil).

Because this volume is addressed for the most part to readers who wish an introduction to the works of Hélène Cixous and who perhaps do not have full bilingual ability to read the texts in the original French, I have chosen to concentrate on those that have been translated into English. Other works by Cixous will be described and discussed as well, but always with the caveat that only short quotations (my own) have been provided, and that, unfortunately for those readers who wish to continue their reading, the entire text may not as yet be available to them. Thus, of necessity all attempts to "interpret" or even "describe" the totality of Hélène Cixous's work will remain partial and will accordingly provide but a preliminary sketch rather than a nuanced portrait.

A second major source of difficulty for the reader-critic of Cixous preparing an introductory English-language volume on her work involves negotiating the rather complex shifts in literary studies that have occurred over the past 20 years and the new ways of thinking about literature and what it means to read and to write. This includes looking at the ways in which these kinds of critical shifts have been imported into Anglo-American critical discussions of literature. What we loosely term *poststructuralist* theory, as it refers to the domains of philosophy or psychoanalysis or the *sciences humaines* in general, is absolutely crucial to an introductory presentation of the work of Hélène Cixous. Of course no introductory volume on Cixous can ever provide an adequate overview of those theoretical discussions even though they actually constitute much of the intertextual ground for virtually all her writing. It is one thing to refer to Jacques Derrida, Jacques Lacan, poststructuralist Freud, Martin Heidegger, Marcel Mauss, Claude Lévi-Strauss, or Immanuel Kant in passing as one discusses a text by Cixous but quite another to expect readers of an "introduction" to have such a complete intellectual "baggage," as the French would say, readily available as they begin to read this book.

Besides theoretical reading as necessary background to making Cixous's acquaintance, the list of Cixous's "grandmother texts" is also a formidable one. Verena Conley lists the following as "decisive readings" (and this list is, like all lists of its kind, partial): Shakespeare, Joyce, the German romantics (especially Heinrich Kleist and Franz Kafka); philosophy (Søren Kierkegaard, Heidegger, and Derrida); Freudian psychoanalysis; the poets (Arthur Rimbaud and Rainer Maria Rilke); the Brazilian writer Clarice Lispector; the Russian poets (Anna Akhmatova, Osip Mandelstam, Marina Tsvetaeva).[3] And after reading Cixous's most recent work, one must also add Thomas Bernhard, the German writer who died in 1989.

The necessity for some rudimentary "theory" and the difficulties that can imply, as well as a need for a rather broad background in a variety of national literatures, is further complicated, in a volume of this nature, by what poststructuralist thought has contributed to the near total breakdown, or at least extensive blurring, of traditional divisions among literary genres—a breakdown that absolutely characterizes Cixous's work from its inception. As Susan Rubin Suleiman notes, "Although H.C.'s formal Bibliography . . . divides 'novels, stories, and fictions' from 'essays, theory, and criticism,' this division strikes me as purely arbitrary—certainly insofar as the works published over the past fifteen years are concerned."[4]

How, then, does the reader-critic compartmentalize the work of Hélène Cixous in order to talk about it in any kind of logical way? Are we talking about creative fiction? theory? autobiography? philosophical writing or commentary? literary interpretative strategies? poetry? All of the above and none of the above. It is quite clear that for Cixous there is as much "theory" in a text marked clearly by the word "novel" on its title page as there is "fiction" or "novel" or "autobiography" in a text that would seem to advertise itself as "theory."

Just as the translation-accessibility problem is negotiable for the careful reader, the theory/fiction problem and the genre-blurring problem are certainly ones that can be successfully dealt with by the alert and patient reader. The reader-critic who is attempting to introduce the work of Cixous, however, constantly feels a certain Catch-22 atmosphere attaching to her work. The critical voice here needs to be clear without being definitive, needs to open the conversation but never close it. The critical voice seeks to explain where possible and to signal important moments and leitmotivs within the text. In introducing the works of Hélène Cixous, the reader-critic can indicate multiple entries into any text; the "ways out" (*sorties*) are sometimes more difficult to locate.

The organization of this book, in keeping with what is admittedly a traditional way of introducing readers to the work of a specific author, is basically chronological. It begins with a brief sketch of Cixous's life and then moves on to a study of her writing, from the earliest published work, a collection of short stories (*Le Prénom de Dieu*), her doctoral thesis on Joyce, and her first novel *Dedans*, all dating from the 1960s, up to her more current work, the fictional texts *Manne* (1988), *Jours de l'an* (1990), and *L'Ange au secret* (1991).

The study of the works has itself been subdivided—arbitrarily but with a sense of wishing to respect Cixous's own formal designations wherever possible—into a chapter on "writing theory," two chapters on "writing fiction," and a chapter on "writing theater." I have respected Cixous's own indications of "genre" even though I wholly agree with Suleiman's view that the boundaries between the works are virtually nonexistent (and this has become even more evident with more recent production). Wherever possible, I have used published translations of cited material. Where a work has not yet appeared in translation, however, the translated passages (for better or for worse) are my own.

A final brief word of advice to those readers who feel fairly comfortable reading French but who may perhaps find many Cixousian texts a bit too linguistically sophisticated or polyvalent for reading with any kind of ease. I would suggest that you read with both English and French texts in front of you whenever possible rather than simply relying on the English translation. At first this technique may appear even more cumbersome than simply looking up every new word in the dictionary, but after a period of adjustment, the rythmn of reading both languages will settle in and, I believe, provide a rich (and fairly "realistic") reading experience of the Cixous oeuvre. Once you have read through the available translated texts in this manner, your ability to tackle works in the original will be much strengthened.

Reading Hélène Cixous is often demanding, more often than not requiring several rereadings. Readers will be constantly aware of numerous allusions to other texts both outside and inside the Cixousian textual universe and to other discourses as well (philosophical, psychoanalytical, anthropological). Readers will also be aware that Cixous writes from within a complex network of postwar contemporary French thought, encompassing most of the ideas made popular in poststructuralist Paris since the mid-1960s. Her own academic training and reading are at times so eclectic and wide-ranging that her reader can become frustrated by the necessity of following obscure and highly eccentric textual tracks that lead along quite labyrinthine trails. Some texts, of course, will be more readily accessible than others; it is the personal, intellectual, and cultural background brought to the text by the reader that will, in the reading of Hélène Cixous, always be the most significant determining factor.

Cixous, however, as a professor in her own seminars, does not demand that novice readers—whether those of Derrida, Clarice Lispector, or, indeed, of Cixous herself—be entirely conversant with a text's allusive genealogy or with the complex network of its ideological or cultural contexts. On the contrary, she consistently encourages a direct textual meeting between reader and writer, no matter what the reader's background or textual community. It is, for Cixous the teacher, only through hands-on contact with the text itself that any "interpretive act" becomes possible. As she describes reading the texts of Clarice Lispector,

> When we read a text, we are either read by the text or we are in the text. Either we tame a text, we ride on it, we roll over it, or we are swallowed up by it, as by a whale. There are thousands of possible relations to a text, and if we are in a nondefensive, nonresisting relationship, we are carried off by the text. This is mainly the way it goes. But then, in order to read, we need to get out of the text. We have to shuttle back and forth incessantly. We have to try all possible relationships with a text. At some point, we have to disengage ourselves from the text as a living ensemble, in order to study its construction, its techniques, and its texture.[5]

The more intellectual baggage readers carry along with them, the more intellectually satisfying their reading experience perhaps will be. But with the texts of Hélène Cixous, one is struck most profoundly by the sensuous feel of the writing itself, by the enormous physical pleasure—a knot in the stomach, a tear in the eye—that the words evoke. Poetic prose, prose poetry, fiction-theory—old terms perhaps, but ones that do still manage to convey some small yet significant sense of Cixous's praxis.

Paul Simon tells us in the song that there "must be fifty ways to leave your lover"; Hélène Cixous reminds us in an analogous way, that "there are fifty possible ways of entering this text, and it is up to the reader to find them. In terms of a quest, we can set out in many different directions. What counts is to find ourselves in the process" (*Readings,* 3).

Acknowledgments

This small book owes some very large debts of gratitude. I should like, first of all, to express my thanks to the University of Alberta's Central Research Fund, its Endowment Fund for the Future, and its Support for the Advancement of Scholarship program for providing both operating and travel grants that allowed me two research trips to Paris, where I had the opportunity to speak with Hélène Cixous, to attend her seminars at the Collège International de Philosophie, and to continue my work on this project. Suffice it to say as well that without the tremendous help from the staff of the University of Alberta Interlibrary Loan division, this book would never have been completed. I also owe a tremendous vote of thanks to all my students in French 490 for their eager reading and questioning of Cixous's work. And, too, I must express my appreciation to all my colleagues at the University of Alberta who have put up with me and my chattering about Cixous with such patience—especially members of the Women's Studies group and graduate students, Françoise Watson and Erika Lefevre. I should like to thank as well David O'Connell, the editor of this series, and the editors at Twayne Publishers for their fine editorial work. But finally, of course, my greatest thanks go to Hélène Cixous, "the author in truth" of so many richly evocative and wonderful texts.

Chronology

1937 Hélène Cixous born 5 June in Oran, Algeria, the daughter of Georges Cixous, a physician, and Eva Klein, a midwife. Family of Georges Cixous are Sephardic Jews (they had lived in Morocco before moving to Algeria); Eva Klein (of Austro-German descent) had emigrated to Algeria from Germany in 1933.

1937–1948 Spends infancy and early childhood in Oran (Algeria, a French colony, is under Vichy government during World War II). As a Jew, is not permitted to attend ordinary school; learns alphabet, reading, and writing with other Jewish children. After the war the Cixous family relocates to Algiers.

1948 Father dies 12 February. Cixous completes secondary school studies at Lycée d'Alger (Algiers).

1956 Beginning of Algerian War. Cixous moves to France and continues her studies, first at Lycée Lakanal in Sceaux (suburb of Paris), then university studies at the Faculté des Lettres (liberal arts), University of Bordeaux. Reads English and American literature.

1957 Obtains *licence-ès-lettres* in English.

1959 Daughter born. Cixous passes the Agrégation d'anglais. At 22, is youngest-ever *agrégée de lettres* in France.

1961 Son born.

1962 Named *assistante* at the Faculté des Lettres, University of Bordeaux.

1965–1967 Works and teaches as *maître assistante* at the Sorbonne (Faculté des Lettres of the Université de Paris).

1967 Begins career as published writer of fiction at the age of 27 with collection of short stories, *Le Prénom de Dieu*; is named *maître de conférence* at Nanterre (another part of the Université de Paris).

1968–1974 Receives *docteur-ès-lettres* (doctoral thesis is on the writings of James Joyce, later published [1969] as *L'Exil de James Joyce ou l'art du remplacement*); becomes *chargée de mission* for setting up an experimental Université de Paris VIII at Vincennes.

1968 Named professor of English literature at Paris VIII–Vincennes (now at Saint-Denis).

1969 First novel, *Dedans,* wins prestigious Prix Médicis; is contributor to numerous periodicals.

1970 *Le Troisième Corps* and *Les Commencements*. With Gérard Genette and Tzvetan Todorov, founds the literary critical journal *Poétique*.

1971 *Un vrai jardin.*

1972 *Neutre* and *La Pupille* (theater text based on *Révolutions pour plus d'un Faust*).

1973 *Portrait du soleil* and *Tombe*. Begins writing about sexual difference.

1974 Founds the Centre de recherches en études féminines at Paris VIII and becomes the center's first director. *Portrait de Dora* premieres; *Prénoms de personne.*

1975 *Portrait du soleil; Révolutions pour plus d'un Faust; Souffles;* "Le Rire de la Méduse"; "Sorties" (in *La Jeune Née* [with Catherine Clément]); *Un K. incompréhensible: Pierre Goldman.*

1976 Begins publishing all work with Editions des femmes in order to show solidarity with the women's movement and her political commitment to women. *Partie*, *Portrait de Dora*, and *LA*.

1977 *L'Arrivante* mounted at the Festival d'Avignon; *Angst; La Venue à l'écriture* (with Annie Leclerc and Madeleine Gagnon). Discovers writing of Brazilian author Clarice Lispector.

1978 *Le Nom d'Oedipe* presented at the Palais des Papes at the Festival Avignon; *Préparatifs de noces au-delà de l'abîme.*

1979 *Vivre l'orange* and *Ananké.*

1980 *Illa.*

1981 *With ou l'art de l'innocence.*

1982 Public reading of *Je me suis arrêtée à un mètre de Jérusalem et c'était le Paradis* at the Jardin d'Hiver. *Limonade tout était si infini.* Discontinues publishing with Editions des femmes in order to enjoy greater poetic freedom.

1983 *Le Livre de Promethea*. Begins collaborative work with Ariane Mnouchkine and the Théâtre du Soleil; produces *L'Histoire terrible mais inachevée de Norodom Sihanouk, roi du Cambodge.*

1984 *La Prise de l'école de Madhubai* (theater).

1985 *L'Histoire terrible mais inachevée de Norodom Sihanouk, roi du Cambodge* mounted by Ariane Mnouchkine at Théâtre du Soleil.

1986 *Pour Nelson Mandela* and *La Bataille d'Arcachon*. After break of two years, resumes publishing with Editions des femmes (*Dedans* is reissued, *LA* as well). Publishes combined theater volume containing *Portrait de Dora* and *La Prise de l'école de Madhubai. Entre l'écriture.*

1987 *L'Indiade ou l'Inde de leurs rêves* (theater). International conference on the work of Cixous—"Hélène Cixous: Chemins d'une écriture"—held at University of Utrecht.

1988 *Manne, aux Mandelstams, aux Mandelas.*

1989 *L'Heure de Clarice Lispector.* International conference on the work of Cixous held at University of Liverpool. *La Nuit miraculeuse* (film production in collaboration with Ariane Mnouchkine).

1990 *Jours de l'an.* "Three Steps on the Ladder of Writing," lectures given at the University of California, Irvine, as the Wellek lectures and part of the International Association of Philosophy and Literature (IAPL). Stops collaborating on regular basis with the Théâtre du Soleil.

1991 *L'Ange au secret* and *On ne part pas, on ne revient pas* (theater). Receives honorary doctor of letters and takes part in international colloquium on "Femmes, Écritures, Sociétés" at Queen's University (Kingston, Ontario, Canada).

1992 *Déluge.* "We Who Are Free, Are We Free?" lecture presented as part of the Oxford Amnesty Lectures. Receives honorary doctor of laws from the University of Alberta and from Cornell University.

1993 *Beethoven à jamais ou l'existence de Dieu*, and *Three Steps on the Ladder of Writing*.

Chapter One
Écriture Féminine: Writing and Life

In the beginning, there is an end. Don't be afraid: it's your death that is dying. Then: all the beginnings. When you have come to the end, only then can Beginning come to you.

Hélène Cixous, "Coming to Writing"

Triply Marginalized

Hélène Cixous was born on 5 June 1937 in Oran, Algeria, the daughter of Georges Cixous, a physician (the family name is pronounced "Siksu"), and Eva Klein Cixous, who was trained as a midwife. Most of Cixous's childhood was spent in the Mediterranean atmosphere of a French colony in North Africa, first in Oran and later in Algiers, as the child of Jewish parents living through the historical and political turbulence of World War II. Her family situation, as well as her place of birth and early formative years, has obviously had a lasting and profound effect on her and her writing.

In an essay describing her own "coming to writing," Cixous says that she had the "luck" to take her first steps "in the blazing hotbed between two holocausts" (*Coming to Writing,* 17), and in interviews over the years she has frequently described herself as "triply marginalized"—as a woman, as a Jew, as an Algerian colonial. Indeed, being a Jewish child in Algeria during the German Occupation of France is certainly a key to many of the major preoccupations of her writing. "My father was a military officer during the war (temporarily, because he was a doctor)," she writes, "so suddenly we were admitted to the only garden in Oran (Oran is a very desert city), that of the Officers' Club. But the place was a hotbed of anti-Semitism. I was three years old, I hadn't the slightest idea that I was Jewish. The other children started attacking me, and I didn't even know what it was to be Jewish, Catholic, and so on" (*Coming to Writing,* xix).

Dr. Georges Cixous, who had been born in Algeria, was technically a French citizen, yet because his family were Sephardic Jews and had lived in Morocco before moving on to Algeria, they still spoke Spanish at home. Cixous has recalled, however, that during the 1930s, at the time of the Popular Front government headed by the Socialists, her father felt both culturally and politically close to France. In 1933 Cixous's mother, Eva Klein, left Germany (after Hitler had come to power), and in 1938 Cixous's maternal grandmother emigrated to Algeria as well. Cixous's grandmother had lived in Alsace prior to World War I and was thus able to leave Germany on the strength of her Franco-German papers. Cixous's Hungarian-Czech maternal grandfather had been killed in 1915 on the Russian front.

By the end of World War II, many members of Cixous's family had been deported. The majority of them died in concentration camps. Cixous's sense of "luck" at being a survivor, even though a survivor "in exile," is another constant theme in her writing. Speaking about various Russian writers and about Clarice Lispector, she explains that exile can be either metaphorical or real, that it can even be double (as in the case of the Russian poet Marina Tsvetaeva or Cixous herself): "There is something of foreignness, a feeling of not being accepted or of being unacceptable, which is particularly insistent when as a woman you suddenly get into that strange country of writing where most inhabitants are men and where the fate of women is still not settled."[1] "So," she concludes, "sometimes you are even a double exile, but I'm not going to be tragic about it because I think it is a source of creation and of symbolic wealth" (12–13).

By 1942, when the young Hélène was ready to begin formal schooling, the political situation of the day made it impossible for a little Jewish girl to go to school. One of Cixous's earliest memories is of going to a house in Oran and sitting in a single room with other children, learning the alphabet, learning to read and write, and all the while listening to the other older children recite their lessons. Even from this very early age, Hélène Cixous decided that whatever work she eventually chose to do in life, it would involve doing something with books. "In Books I became someone," she says. "I was 'at home' there, I found my counterparts in poetry (there were some), I entered into alliances with my paper soulmates, I had brothers, equivalents, substitutes, I was myself their brother or their fraternal sister at will" (*Coming to Writing,* 29).

Growing up in a French colony left its mark on Cixous in many ways. Besides the fact of her Jewishness, there was also the sense of being without a national identity in Algeria: "People said, 'the French,' and I never thought I was French. . . . I felt that I was neither from France nor from Algeria. And in fact, I was from neither" (*Coming to Writing,* xix). Even the very basic question of language was problematic. Both Cixous's mother and her grandmother spoke German at home; thus Hélène's first language (her mother tongue) was German. She has described it as her language of nursery rhymes and songs and later the language of poetry. She began to learn the Arabic and Hebrew languages with her father, yet they were abruptly silenced when her father died. French became the language of school, and later English (as her academic training began to focus on English literature). Yet even this tremendously ambiguous and complex relationship with language itself is described by Cixous in the most positive fashion. It is seen as a source of the creative impulse: "Blessing: my writing stems from two languages, at least. In my tongue, the 'foreign' languages are my sources, my agitations. 'Foreign': the music in me from elsewhere; precious warning: don't forget that all is not here, rejoice in being only a particle, a seed of chance, there is no center of the world, arise, behold the innumerable, listen to the untranslatable" (*Coming to Writing,* 21).

After World War II ended, the Cixous family moved from Oran to Algiers, the capital, where Dr. Cixous resumed his interrupted medical practice, setting it up in an Arab neighborhood. Once again a sense of isolation and alienation become a focus for the young Hélène: "Since I didn't belong to the European community and wasn't admitted into the Arab community, I was between the two, which was extremely painful" (Sudaka, 92). Perhaps the most crucial event in Cixous's formative years was the death of her father on 12 February 1948, when she was not quite 11 years old. This traumatic event would seem to have been a crystalizing moment in her psyche and the source of the majority of her "creative" (as opposed to "academic") writing, from its inception in 1967 through the mid-1970s, when she turned away from her somewhat "narcissistic" mode to a more "feminist" one. Although the family circle included Cixous's brother, mother, and grandmothers, and although the maternal is also deeply implicated in Cixous's works, the daughter's problematic relationship with her absent dead father represents one of the earliest and most reliable points of entry into her work.

The desert landscape of Algeria—seacoast, sun, and sand—is also a key point of reference in all of Cixous's writing, presenting topographical elements of childhood that are used again and again, transformed and constantly undergoing metamorphosis, as the writer moves through time. The wordplay Cixous uses in the autobiographical text *Vivre l'Orange/To Live the Orange* (Vivre l'Oran-je = "I living in Oran") is a small but significant marker of the North African sensibility and sensuality that return repeatedly in Cixous's writing.

On her father's side, Cixous's family had come from very poor, very humble origins. She has told the story of her great-grandmother (Georges Cixous's grandmother), who could not wear the new shoes that had been purchased for her wedding since she had never before worn shoes and they simply hurt her feet too much. Another Cixous family story is one about a single pair of shoes which had to be shared by all the children, which meant that only the child whose turn it was to wear the shoes for that day could go to school. Cixous says that her father and her uncle were really the first in their family to be educated, the first "to benefit from the enormous work of this family where all the children had to try to earn their own living from the age of eight or nine."[2]

From her father's side of the family, Cixous points to a legacy of "their love, their unbounded devotion, devoid of self-interest. A life which had its beauty. What came to me from that world was elementary ritual, cleaning on Fridays, the fact that the door was always open on Fridays, and that beggars used to go in to my paternal grandmother's. All those practices were spontaneous, not calculated or planned. And insofar as what remains of that community is still that way, I loved them then and I still do. It was a gift without strings" (Sudaka, 93).

Indeed, when asked whether she had been conscious of being Jewish, as that autobiographical fact was linked to the historical fact of anti-Semitism, Cixous replied that in a personal way one of the determining elements of her childhood and adolescence was "the fact of being in an atmosphere where the question of antisemitism was always present, in an atmosphere which was truly poisoned by it" (Sudaka, 92).

Living in "a milieu which was exclusively Jewish for the simple reason that Jews were not permitted to enter educational institutions," Cixous had her first "education" in a kind of private school where there were no non-Jews, although she was too young to know this or to understand that this was a result of the historical situation (Sudaka, 92). A few years later, when the Cixous family moved to Algiers and Cixous was attending the *lycée,* she claims she "discovered in a very clear way, there was a 'tacit' *numerus clausus*" and did her high school–level studies without being in a Jewish milieu, which she missed quite a bit (Sudaka, 93). "I felt my difference, my outside alien position, very violently," she says of that time in her life, "and I had no one to share my outsider status" (Sudaka, 93). After the fact, Cixous claims that she is not sorry about this state of affairs ("I'm very happy to have gone through those deserted zones of opposition" [Sudaka, 93]). Her friends were non-Jewish; their parents were anti-Semites.

It was with her arrival in Algiers that Cixous learned about "the hatred and the horror" of the social scene. "That is why I was neither with the Algerian French—and for good reason—nor with the Arabs who were still enemy brothers. There I had the impression of being in a world gone wild, ignorant of what was going on in Europe" (Sudaka, 93). When Cixous left Algeria for France, she found that her situation as a Jew was no longer problematic in the same way. Indeed, in France, being Jewish was not used to classify people according to racial or ethnic backgrounds as had been the case in Algeria. "France was a foreign country for me when I arrived, " says Cixous (Sudaka, 93), and the question of Jewish identity became displaced once she was living there. "When I found out that a certain aunt had died in a concentration camp and that that was part of my history, I did not feel not implicated. How could I not have been, since ever since my earliest childhood, I had thought just the opposite: that is, I had thought what an extraordinary accident had meant that my mother, who had come from Germany, was one of the few people in my family to have stayed alive. I was born in a place where one was part of that war. I identified with the German Jewish community, never with the Algerian Jewish community" (Sudaka, 93).

When she is asked whether the phrase "being a Jewish woman" has a sense for her, however, Cixous has stated quite bluntly that it does not. "In my whole life I've never thought in those terms. I don't like to hear it because it can be the source of every kind of misunderstanding, of falsification. For me, being a woman has a sense: it's even the primary sense. Being a woman determines me absolutely, and among the numerous determinations which I'm made up of, there is the fact that I'm Jewish in origin. It's not a privileged or special factor" (Sudaka, 93).

Hélène Cixous was consistently a very bright student. Leaving Algeria for Paris, she finished her *lycée* work in France, then began her university studies in English, receiving her *licence-ès-lettres* (the equivalent of a B.A.) in English in 1957 from the University of Bordeaux. In 1959 she took the Agrégation d'anglais and became, at the age of 21, France's youngest-ever *agrégée* (in English) and in 1968 France's youngest-ever *docteur-ès-lettres,* at 31.

Cixous had married at a very young age (indeed, some of her early work on Joyce, taken from her doctoral thesis, was actually published under her married name of Hélène Berger and is still listed in Joyce bibliographies). She is the mother of two children: a daughter (born in 1959) and a son (born in 1961), both of whom are now university professors. She was divorced in 1964.

From 1962 until 1964 Cixous worked as an *assistante* at the University of Bordeaux; from 1965 to 1967 she was *maître assistante* at the Sorbonne, completing her doctoral thesis on the works of James Joyce in 1968, under the supervision of Jean-Jacques Mayoux (the thesis was published the same year by Grasset). By 1967–68 Cixous had become *maître de conférence* at the University of Nanterre, the most radical and left-wing of French postsecondary institutions and the scene of much of the student upheavals during the revolutionary events of May 1968. Indeed, the reforms demanded by French university students in 1968, coupled with Cixous's fortuitous posting at Nanterre, resulted in her appointment by the French Ministry of Education as *chargée de mission* for the establishment of the experimental University of Paris VIII at Vincennes (now at Saint-Denis) that same year. Cixous has been professor of English Literature at Paris VIII ever since, still giving her seminars at Paris VIII and at the Collège International de Philosophie. Along with Gérard Genette and Tzvetan Todorov, she founded the critical and theoretical journal *Poétique: Revue de Théorie et Analyse Littéraire* in 1970. She is also director of the Centre de recherches en études féminines (Women's Studies Research Institute), which she founded in 1974 at Paris VIII. This center has provided the first setting of its kind in France for advanced postsecondary research in this area.

Cixous's academic career, theoretical contributions to women's studies, and completmentary careers as "creative writer" and playwright have meant that she has been widely sought after as a visiting professor and lecturer in numerous American universities. She has lectured as well in Canada, England, the Netherlands, Denmark, Austria, and Spain. The subject of an international colloquium ("Hélène Cixous: Chemins d'une écriture") in the Netherlands at the University of Utrecht in the summer of 1987 and another ("The Body and the Text: Hélène Cixous, Reading and Teaching") in England at the University of Liverpool in the spring of 1989, she received an honorary doctor of letters from Canada's Queen's University in 1991 and was honored at Queen's sesquicentennial colloquium, "Femmes, Écritures, Sociétés."

Yet the life of Hélène Cixous, even though under the sign of triple marginalization, has been triply productive. For in addition to her academic career and her professorial activities associated with women's studies and literary studies within the French university system and worldwide, she has also been known, since 1967, as a prolific writer of "creative" works. Her first published fiction was a volume of short stories called *Le Prénom de Dieu*; her first novel, *Dedans,* won the 1969 Prix Médicis; and her output of novels and "texts" has been constant, and an almost yearly event, for the past 25 years. One facet of her textual production, focusing as it does—especially during the early years of her writing career—on an exploration of an inner world, and evolving from readings of Freud and the oneiric (dream-related) text, is intensely intimate in tone, while the complementary facet—much more public in nature—is her career as a playwright. Author of several plays in the 1970s (the most widely known perhaps is *Portrait of Dora,* a reworking of the Freud case study of hysteria), Cixous began collaborating with Ariane Mnouchkine and the Théâtre du Soleil troupe in Paris in the early 1980s and is currently very well known for her epic, Shakespeare-style historical works for the theater, most notably *L'Indiade* (on the independence and partition of India) and *L'Histoire terrible mais inachevée de Norodam Sihanouk, roi du Cambodge.*

Triply marginalized perhaps, as woman, Jew, and colonial, Hélène Cixous has nonetheless transformed these autobiographical facts into a triple writing life: as an academic, as a creative writer, as a playwright.

Speaking and Writing from the Margins

Given that Hélène Cixous has made her home in Paris during the exciting intellectual ferment of the 1970s, most especially during the heyday of the intellectual revolution of first the structuralists and then the post-structuralists Jacques Derrida and Jacques Lacan, it is not surprising that writing from the margins has involved writing from the spaces of post-Freudian psychoanalysis and deconstructionist philosophy.

As May 1968 marked a kind of new beginning for the French feminist movement, it is also interesting to trace Hélène Cixous's involvement in French feminism. Although she is well known to international feminists for her writings on écriture féminine and for her participation in the founding of Editions des femmes, the first feminist publishing house in France, as she herself has said, "In 1968 the women's movement began. I must say that at the time I didn't feel at all involved, the little I had seen of it in my particular turf, university territory, didn't interest me, it seemed hard, violent, aggressive, and I felt no complicity with that kind of discourse. At that point, however, I began to develop my own basis which had to do with texts and touched on sexual difference in literature."[3] Cixous marks this stage of her development at the period in 1972–74; the result was the founding of the Centre d'études féminines, which for Cixous "was a step to get things started, I wanted there to be a place where one could discuss the subject. There was nothing of the sort in the university system, so at least let's talk about it, let's do it. It still exists" (Cixous, 3).

In 1975 Antoinette Fouque, who had been one of the founders of the women's movement in 1968, asked Cixous for a book. "This is how I came to the women's movement and began to discover this world," says Cixous. "There were ideological oppositions that were often poorly thought out. On the one hand there were Antoinette's leanings, which were very articulated and made use of psychoanalysis, and on the other hand there were leanings with social-reformist bases" (Cixous, 3–4). Cixous has said that she would find it dishonest to say that she was in the women's movement, as she got there very late: "I was in complete solidarity with the movement that was emerging, through the influence of Antoinette Fouque in the form of Editions des femmes. I did what I could, which was not much—publish there, be present at demonstrations, but I took no initiative; quite the contrary, I know profoundly what is outside my area. Yet I know the women are part of something absolutely essential for me, which does not mean that I am confined to that world. I think that it must be unenclosed, it should be as free and large as possible" (Cixous, 4).

Cixous's formative years spent in Algeria, combined with her postsecondary academic training within the French system, make her "coming to 'feminism'" (and for Cixous the word feminism must always be signaled with quotation marks) an interesting one. She has described her "political" and "poetical" projects at some length in several interviews, yet she has nonetheless been criticized by many feminists, most particularly Anglo-American feminists, who continue to find her work too "theoretical" and not sufficiently engaged in the day-to-day issues that are of vital concern to women (violence against women, abortion rights, support and custody of children on marital breakdown, and poverty).

The question of "writing as a woman" poses the same kind of problem for Cixous. "One of the dangers, one of the difficulties that women who write have encountered these last two decades consists in having to stand up to the *word* 'woman,' to the word 'feminine,' issuing from critical places."[4]

> For it's true that it's *the woman* in me who writes, not only the poet. . . . But there is one thing that I can't eliminate from my consciousness, and that's misogyny; I've always known that. At those moments I feel solidarity with all efforts, not to force misogyny back—because I've never seen misogyny step back, I have only seen it disguise itself—but in any case to analyze it and try to find the means to respond to it. There is a

> part of me that answers to the name "woman." I would not make use of a sentence like "I'm not a woman, I'm a writer," because not for anything in the world would I say "I'm not a woman." To me that means nothing. Yes, I am a woman. I admit that I don't even know what the utterance "I am not a woman" means when pronounced . . . by a woman? . . . I think that the woman who says "I am not a woman" says so because she feels threatened by the condition of women. She is not alone; we are all threatened by that. (Jardine and Menke, 238, 239)

Given that one of Cixous's major contributions to contemporary theoretical debate has been her ongoing questioning of the status of "the subject" and her persistent efforts to think difference differently from the Western cultural tradition of binary opposition, much of what goes by the designation of "feminist" in France, at least in Cixous's opinion, involves *not* a different way of thinking difference but rather a simple reversal of the binary opposition that keeps woman in the inferior position of lack. Attempts by "feminists" to appropriate the superior position currently occupied by male power or authority does nothing to undo the system we live within. Cixous has most certainly participated "politically" in attempts to make real social conditions better for women, but her own *politique* has generally remained *poétique* in that her writing and teaching, which are concerned with femininity (or better, a system of libidinal economies, both masculine and feminine), seek to subvert the "what is" of culture.

Indeed, Cixous's contribution to French feminism(s) and to feminism in its largest sense must involve the totality of her prodigious production as a writer. Her sense of the necessity for equilibrium between the political and the poetic was perhaps best expressed during a 1982 interview. When the interviewer remarks that the terms *political* and *poetic* of the chiasm—"poetically political, politically poetic" (a phrase often used by Cixous)—are potentially irreconcilable, Cixous responds, "People who are into politics cannot *not* say such things. People who are poets, to use a general term, but who at the same time have a political concern are obligated to say the opposite. For the latter, the poetic must have a political value: of course, it must not be an easy solution. It is not sufficient to write to be poetic. It is true, though, that you have works that think themselves and write themselves poetically without forgetting the political question."[5]

Cixous cites the examples of Clarice Lispector and Kleist—authors who constantly ask questions that are political but are treated poetically. "I try to do the same," she says.

> I would lie if I said that I am a political woman, not at all. In fact, I have to assemble the two words, political and poetic. Not to lie to you, I must confess that I put the accent on poetic. I do it so that the political does not repress, because the political is something cruel and hard and so rigorously real that sometimes I feel like consoling myself by crying and shedding poetic tears. That is why I wrote the text *With ou l'art de l'innocence.* I think that I am constantly guilty, for example, of having the privilege of being able to console myself poetically. Besides, I never console myself; as soon as I console myself, I punish myself. I think that is the paradox and the torment of people who have a calling to write that is stronger than anything else, and who know and do not forget—because most people do forget—that as soon as one writes, one betrays someone or something. (Conley 1984, 139–40)

The Grandmother Texts

Rather than speak of "influences" on her writing, Cixous has often referred to texts that she calls her "grandmother texts": "I forget them in their antiquity. The grandmother texts are the Bibles: the Bible and all the other Bibles, the epics, the texts that are the founders of all literature, from the epic of Gilgamesh, the Iliad, the Odyssey. . . . These texts which I adored as a child have brought an enormous human world into my reach. I put them aside, because what they brought me were human beings more than writing itself" (Cixous, 5). For Cixous, there are also great writers for whom she expresses not only admiration but also love: Shakespeare ("I would be astonished if he were not family to all people who write") and Kafka ("Because he introduced me to a dimension of the soul's combat with death that we don't really have in this culture") (Cixous, 5). Cixous also considers the work of German poets as being among those with which she frequently "keeps company" (Cixous, 6): "Perhaps my maternal tongue is at play in this. Rilke, Hölderlin, and others are texts that are absolutely necessary for me. I admit that they reach me through the song of language" (Cixous, 6). Kleist, too, numbers among her "grandmother texts"—"a man who had such adventurous confidence in what there can be of the best in the soul, the freest, that I venerated him when I was young. I found it admirable that he could desire the spirit of justice in man, the courage, and even the shifting of taboos" (Cixous, 6).

Kafka's contribution to Cixous's literary topography involves "something serious, something which causes literature to situate itself at the last hour of life and death" (Cixous, 5). Yet for Cixous, perhaps the most beautiful poems and the most wonderful texts are those which are separated, freed in some way from their author, "and yet they palpitate with the entire richness of that person" (Cixous, 5). "Personally," she says, "I don't have the courage to write the most delicate poem in the world, the briefest book. With someone like Kafka the most beautiful texts are the ones he didn't write, they are the texts he set down hastily on bits of paper when he was on his deathbed. They were phrases that he addressed to the people standing by him because he could no longer pronounce them, he could no longer speak. These lines are of an absolutely brilliant poetic density and they are unauthored, they do not stem from a drive to write" (Cixous, 5).

Cixous has noted that it is fairly rare in a life devoted to literature that one suddenly discovers "an America." Yet with her fortuitous introduction to the works of the Brazilian writer Clarice Lispector, this is indeed what happened. For Cixous, such a discovery was all the more extraordinary given that it came at a time in her life "in literature" when she was feeling in "somewhat of a desert."

Through working on texts as a teacher, Cixous had come to sense the lack of something: "I was in the world of men almost exclusively. I worked on Shakespeare, Joyce, Kafka, on an amazing number of texts. But women? I did work on Virginia Woolf; in a sense I taught everyone, Marguerite Duras, Virginia Woolf, all the great writers. But Virginia Woolf, who is a great writer, isn't someone who satisfies me because she is slanted toward pain, which I understand very well, but I love life too much to content myself with such a morbid rapport to a form of death in women or death inflicted on women" (Cixous, 6–7).

Cixous describes herself at this stage of her life as restless, and then came "a very complex stroke of luck" that caused her introduction to the texts of Clarice Lispector:

> First, Editions des femmes was editing a text of hers, *The Passion According to G.H.,* and Antoinette Fouque showed me some passages from it. At the same time a student from Brazil had asked me to direct a thesis on Clarice Lispector. Here was a combination of elements that drew my attention to someone I knew nothing about. I read a page, I found the page I read very admirable and I assumed it was just chance, a writing coincidence. I waited for the publication of *The Passion According to G.H.,* and I experienced one of the great emotions of my existence. I read it and I changed worlds. I had this sudden meeting. Kafka, I had never encountered, I was so young when I read him and I read him in a sort of general

> collection. It was as if suddenly, at age 38 or 40, I stumbled on Kafka, without once having heard of him. The name Kafka circulates in the air. Clarice Lispector, never. So I discover another Kafka, and it is a woman. These are the texts of a woman. These are texts of extraordinary power and at the same time they see the world through the experience of a woman, in a woman's body, with the relationships of a mother, etc., and that saved something in me. (Cixous, 7)

The discovery of Clarice Lispector gave "great joy" to Cixous at a crucial moment in her writing career. Lispector has brought her "something immense, an entire country" as well as "a lesson in hope" (Cixous, 8). Many of Cixous's comments about the work of Clarice Lispector point us in the direction of other influential and decisive readings—among them the works of Russian poets Osip Mandelstam, Marina Tsvetaeva, and Anna Akhmatova and, more recently, the work of Austrian writer Thomas Bernhard.

Thematic Preoccupations and Stylistic Markers

One approaches the very idea of compartmentalizing the works of Hélène Cixous under such headings as "themes" or "style" with great trepidation, yet it is useful to note that there are thematic concerns that are omnipresent in all her writing in both theoretical texts and those texts that relate more to the "creative." The Cixousian style is as well deeply implcated in her thematics. Thematic clusters in her works most often center on the writer's relationship to language itself, to the questions of textual origins and "authorship," to the search for beginnings, births, and origins. In some texts there is a complementary obsession with death and the sense of ending, yet Cixous's texts in the final analysis are all intimately concerned with a thematics of life-affirming love. The questions of who loves, who gives, and who celebrates life are constantly posed, never answered; love, passion, and a deep sense of seeking a connection between "life" and "art" haunt all Cixousian texts.

Thematic material in Cixous is drawn from many sources: the grandmother texts; theoretical texts in psychoanalysis, philosophy, or anthropology; and the material of legend and myth. All these sources provide a certain fund of "inspiration" and produce dreamlike texts that combine the fantastic and the quotidian, where strange and bizarre narrational situations are commonplace. Flowers, women's bodies, small objects (a feather), or animals (a squirrel) form imagistic webs and intertextual echos from the earliest short stories to the latest writings for the stage. The chief stylistic marker is Cixous's constantly playful use of language in a deeply sensuous and evocative way. Her insistent use of metaphor to question and, indeed, to subvert the literary trope and her densely ambiguous syntax are also characteristic of her style. Adjectives such as *poetic, elegaic, lyric, exuberant,* and *passionate* are often used to describe her style. Many, if not all, Cixous texts are in some way autobiographical and thus allow the reader provisional entry at times into the most intimate areas of the writer's psyche. Yet there is always the veiled, hidden element in Cixous, the unspeakable lurking somewhere behind, or better still, between the words printed on the page.

The literary and imaginary fictional world created by Hélène Cixous is unceasingly fascinating. It both entices readers and puzzles them. For every question asked, there are either no answers at all or many possible answers, each of which leads to another set of questions. Each answer itself can perhaps be yet another textual pre-text. Hélène Cixous's *écriture féminine,* in form and in content, involves an intimate connection between writing and life.

Chapter Two
Écriture Féminine: Writing and Theory

What I most try to avoid is the turning of theory into an idol. We are not idolaters though neither are we ignorant. We have all undergone our programme of systematic theoretical initiation, but we have done this not to be confined by theory, but for theory to appear as what it is, useful and traversable.

Hélène Cixous

Critical Contexts: The Nature of Theory in a Post-Freudian, Derridean World

Although Cixous has stated on more than one occasion that theory has no importance isolated from texts, it is nevertheless true that all her writing, whether identified by the generic marker of essay or play or novel, "works" in a theoretical way, that it is informed and structured by the theoretical discussions that have been ongoing in France since the mid-1960s. This critical context has a dual lineage: from the discussions surrounding psychoanalysis (Freudian and Lacanian) and the philosophical poststructuralist work in philosophy of Jacques Derrida.

What Cixous means when she resists the label of theoretician is the demarcation of theory as distinct from practice. She says of her seminar at Paris VIII, "We are not outside theory in the seminar though I hope we are above it. We use theoretical instruments, but we use them as aids, as a means of advancing further. This is not a way of repressing or obliterating theory but of giving it a place which is not an end in itself."[1] Although we can be sympathetic with this reluctance to draw boundary lines where none are neccessarily required, it must be admitted that Hélène Cixous is primarily known to an Anglo-American reading audience as a "theorist" of écriture féminine. And the concept of *écriture féminine,* in its initial delineations and in its refinement over the years, remains clearly lodged in the realm of "theory." Thus it is both interesting and useful to read Cixous's more purely theoretical writing at least in part separated from what might loosely be termed her more "creative" texts. (Which is certainly not to deny creativity to Cixous's "theory"!) The critical texts to be discussed here span the time period of 1968 to 1989, from the period of Cixous's work on Joyce to a recent book devoted to readings of Clarice Lispector.

As we have seen, the events of Hélène Cixous's life led her not only to writing but also to a career in the French university system. Her writing production thus includes a corpus of what might be termed "academic writing." This academic writing includes her massive doctoral thesis on James Joyce as well as numerous essays on other writers she did research on in the late 1960s and early 1970s. Many of these essays appeared in learned journals in various forms and were then collected into a single volume in 1974 (*Prénoms de personne*). Within her academic writing there is clearly the mark of first structuralist, then poststructuralist theory. The readings of various texts—August Heinrich Hoffmann's *The Sandman,* Edgar Allan Poe's "Morella" and *The Murders in the Rue Morgue,* Heinrich Kleist's *Marionettes*—demonstrate a technical brilliance and a linguistic facility and opens the world of English, American, and German literature to deconstructive analysis and interpretation.

Within academic writing, however, this same deconstructive tendency seems to spill over into a different world with the publication in the mid-1970s of what could be termed Cixous's woman-centered theoretical writings (and these are the texts that brought her to the attention of a wider reading public, most especially the world of Anglo-American feminist and postmodernist critics); the seminal essay "The Laugh of the Medusa" (written in 1975), then *The Newly Born Woman* (written in collaboration with Catherine Clément in 1975), and the essay "Coming to Writing" (1977), which was her contribution to a collaborative work with Annie Leclerc and Madeleine Gagnon. Although there is certainly no repudiation of Derridean thought nor does psychoanalysis cease to be an integral focus for her thought, Cixous, during this second phase of critical writing, seems to leave behind a hard-edged critical "machine" and turn her energy toward the new—that is, toward her conception of a new way of talking about difference, *écriture féminine.*

In the 15 years that passed between the publication of the first works on *écriture féminine,* Cixous has the experience of "meeting" the writing of Clarice Lispector. The encounter with Lispector's texts is arguably another crucial turning point in any discussion of Cixous's "theoretical" writing. From academic writing to woman-centered writing to what we could call "approach-oriented" critical writing, Cixous is today not only more accessible in her critical style but also less concerned with the large questions within the world of critical discussion.

Critical Cixousian texts span virtually the entire time period of the author's writing career, from the 1967 doctoral disseration on James Joyce to a recent book devoted to Clarice Lispector. In the space of two decades, she has raised many important critical issues but remains most widely known for her writing on *écriture féminine* (which is commonly called "writing said to be feminine"). I do not mean to suggest that the progress of her critical thought has been necessarily linear or that it can be reduced to any kind of method by which we read or analyze literary texts. It is fair to say, however, that the writing of Hélène Cixous that we term "theoretical" has a weblike consistency that has spun itself into complicated patterns over the past two decades. To encounter her work is to encounter the thought, vocabulary, and general discussions of Western culture's philosophy, psychoanalysis, and linguistics in the France of the late 1960s and 1970s. For Cixous, psychoanalysis and Derridean deconstruction in particular are of prime importance.

No matter what one's theoretical, philosophical, or emotional position is regarding Sigmund Freud and psychoanalysis, it is virtually impossible to ignore the man's work in any discussion of French feminisms. Hélène Cixous is no exception to this rule. Freud's basic theories regarding infantile sexuality; the development of the human being through the stages of id, ego, and superego; the conflict between eros and thanatos; discussions of the pleasure principle and polymorphous perversity; and, most imporant, the use of dreams to explore the workings of the unconscious, as well as his focus on the artist and on the artist's unconscious relationship with the world all stake a claim to Cixous's critical and theoretical attention.

Not long ago, she writes, "Freud was prohibited in feminist circles, on the pretext that he was a misogynist. At the time I wondered how these feminists could possibly hope to get through life because everything had been invented by men. It was like saying, 'we can't go by plane because a woman didn't invent it.' Freud focused attention on the unconscious in an extraordinary series of discoveries. Do we behave as if the unconscious doesn't exist? We live in a post-Freudian, Derridean age of electricity and the aeroplane. So let's do as modern people do, let's use the contemporary means of transport. We owe Freud the exploration of the unconscious" (*Seminar,* 144–45).

Working with Freud's texts in relation to the works of other writers has been a constant source of theoretical musing for Cixous. To study the work of poets using a psychoanalytical framework provides a way in for Cixous, although she readily admits that "in their creation, they are poetically beyond psychoanalysis" (*Seminar,* 145). For Cixous, it is the "poetically beyond" that is important. "In the early stages of reading," she says, "we go much faster if we are in the analytic automobile, if we take Freud's plane. And we need to go quickly. We need to go quicker to begin with in order to go more slowly later on, to be able to take the time to meditate on the 'poetically beyond' which psychoanaysis can't deal with, philosophy can't deal with, because it escapes them, is stronger, more difficult, more complex, more alive" (*Seminar,* 145). For Cixous, then, it is not possible to reject Freud outright merely because of his misogynism; for Cixous, it is vital to have read Freud and then to have reread or rethought him in relation to other, different ways of conceptualizing the world.

Psychoanalysis in the post-Freudian world of French thought has been greatly influenced, of course, by the work of Jacques Lacan. Although at first glance it might appear that much of Lacanian theory regarding the structures of the unconscious and their analogous positions to the development of language would be important in a consideration of the writing of Cixous, Lacan's work, even his versions of the imaginary and symbolic orders, brings much less to her work than her own rereadings of Freud. While it is not true that Lacan is totally absent from Cixous's theorizing, it is certainly fair to say that there is much less Lacan than there is Freud. It is also within the world of philosophical discourse where we find much of Cixous's contextual theoretical interest, most especially within the world of Jacques Derrida. Like Freud, Derrida has been roundly criticized by feminists who consider his ideas to be entirely complicit in a patriarchal, phallocentric, and logocentric world, but for Cixous much of Derrida still serves as a kind of springboard or point of entry into a text—or, indeed, into the act of writing itself. Two basics of Derrida's are important in any discussion of Hélène Cixous: first, his concept of *différance* as it relates to a critique of Western philosophy's systematic use of binary logic; and, second, a basic understanding of the proper and the gift. Much of Cixous's theorizing about *écriture féminine* owes much to Derrida—and by extension to Heidegger.

One final word about Cixous and writing theory. As a professor of literature, she has said that the theoretical trend in France since the 1960s has been a negative criticism of meaning and representation. But she argues that "a text is neither representation nor expression. A text is beyond both representation—the exact reproduction of reality—and expression: it always says something other than it intends to say" (*Seminar,* 144). As a result of fashionable theoretical practices, all this has been repressed. "We have been," says Cixous, "in the phase of non-meaning, in the suspension, the exclusion of the message. This has had serious implication for reading in France. We began to read texts on a purely formal level. University practice is still very largely formal" (*Seminar,* 144). Let us turn now to the "university practice" that saw the first theoretical writing of Cixous in 1967.

Academic Writing

***The Exile of James Joyce or the Art of Replacement* (1968).** Hélène Cixous's first full-length published theoretical work was, not surprisingly given her career as a professor English literature, her mammoth (some 800 pages in length) doctoral disseration on the works of the Irish writer James Joyce.[2] Under her married name of Hélène Berger, several portions of the thesis had already been published separately in the early 1960s.[3] The thesis appears to belong to a genre of French academic criticism that is biographical in nature, although there is no chronological order imposed within the study nor does it attempt an exegesis of Joyce's individual works. Instead the thesis proceeds by examining selected themes from the Joyce oeuvre using a method that Cixous claims in her introduction to have been borrowed from the author himself. (Joyce has Stephen analyze Shakespeare's life by using his writings.) For Cixous, the life and work of James Joyce are consubstantial, his work being merely a copy of his life and his life a repetition of his writing. In this, says one Joyce critic, Cixous seems to belong to two traditions at the same time, "that of the French doctorat (and the Sorbonne thesis with its emphasis on 'the man and the work' in particular) and that of the Sartrean biography" (Lernout, 42). From the Sorbonne tradition we see the weightiness of footnotes and bibliography and from Sartre's existentialist brand of biography we see the emphasis placed on the subject's childhood, on his family, and on the culture into which the subject was born and spends his formative years. In Geert Lernout's opinion, the book suffers from the same weaknesses as Sartre's biographies on Flaubert, Baudelaire, or Genet: "Although it is based on extensive research, it tends to be more a reflection of the author's preoccupations than of those of his subject" (Lernout, 42).

The book is divided into four major sections with thematic interests centered on what Cixous calls the "family cell," the concepts of private and public heroism, the choice of heresy, the concept of exile as recovery, and Joyce's poetics. In part 1, on the family cell, Cixous discusses variously the family and its portrayal (as a Dublin family and the role the family takes within the works of Joyce); the importance for James Joyce of "the father's side" and the network of interdependence between real and fictional fathers in Joyce; the fear of marriage and the dream of freedom (discussing Joyce's marriage to Nora, analyzing "The Boarding House" as "marriage as epiphany," discussing Stephen's obsessive view of marriage and Bloom's "comic captivation"—a view of marriage as archetype); dreams of freedom; and variations on the theme of transsubstantiation—the artist as the proud beggar and the artist as cannibal, discussing the ambiguity of Joyce's relationship with his brother and the brother's contribution to Joyce's work.

Part 2, which concerns private and public heroism, involves a discussion and analysis of opposing ideologies (a consideration of the artist's formative years as history and a discussion of his first poem).The theme of politics as temptation includes a discussion of the myth of Parnell and Joyce's socialist creed (which Cixous describes as his "socialist pose"). Consideration of the 1904 *Portrait of the Artist* and *Stephen Hero* is followed by a chapter titled "Heroism as Ridiculous," which contains discussions of sport as mimic warfare and of *Ulysses* as a parody of the heroic age or the parody epic of a nation. A final chapter on the abolition of words discusses the Parnell affair as an excuse for political disengagement, the political ignominy of "Ivy Day," and Dublin citizens as "beingless beings."

In part 3 Cixous argues that Joyce makes "the choice of heresy" and focuses on the concept of *non serviam,* the recurring accusation felt by the child, heresy as a kind of heroism, heresy as acting a part. A second chapter considers the movement from hell to hell: the delight and disgust of the inner hell, the style of the troubled conscience, the illusion of beginning a new life, three antidotes to the claims of an ordered existence, Dublin as hell, from personal hell to new world, and reply to hell. Cixous also analyzes Joyce's discovery of language, his fascination with the mystery of words, the magic he derives from signal and silence, the model of the master who initiates into fearful mysteries, the shaping of the young artist's consciousness, the imagination inspired by strange words, the contribution of the Church, the priest of the imagination.

In part 4 Cixous turns to a discussion of the idea that exile can be a form of recovery and speaks of the choice of exile (the metaphor of exile, the models and functions of the Judas figures in Joyce), the exile of the soul (the fall treated as a game, love as play, Joyce as decadent poet), the notion of exile within (the simple woman, the artist's wife as mother church: Nora as epitome of exile), to leave without leaving (Nora as Erin, eroticism as perversion of Catholic worship). A final chapter on Joyce's play *Exiles* (the discovery of creative doubt) involves a treatment of the fruits of doubt and its pleasures and a lengthy analysis of the two couples in the play. A final chapter on the artist and his double discusses Joyce's dissimulating style, the Joyce Cixous sees behind Shakespeare, the ghosts, the inevitable self.

In the book's concluding section, which centers on Joyce's poetics, Cixous discusses the concept of reality in Joyce—approaching reality, going beyond reality, and the language of reality. In approaching reality, language is seen as the meeting place of subject and object. Cixous discusses the doctrine of the epiphany and its context as well as the evolution of the notion of epiphany, "applied Aquinas," and irony. In going beyond reality, Cixous concentrates on symbolism, most especially the use of Catholic symbolism in *Portrait* and Joyce's establishment of a personal symbolism and the illusion of surpassing reality by language. In her chapter on the language of reality, Cixous turns to Joyce's policy of recovery of the possibles, form as immediate message, and the co-ordinates of Joyce's personality and the pardoxes of art. In a brief conclusion entitled "Joyce's Dream," Cixous treats the metaphor of a crisis of awareness, her view that in Joyce language replaces reality. She discusses the form and function of language in "Ithaca," the article "the" as the article of death. Perhaps the most intriguing elements of this learned, traditional, and formalized approach to literary criticism of the Joycean oeuvre are contained within the appendix to the volume ("Thoth and the Written Word") and in the later addition of several long footnotes and the section on the disappearance of names, all of which were added later.

The rather severe criticism Cixous's book has received from Joyce scholars outside France can be traced in part to her "existentialist biography" approach in general but also to her use of sources in general. Joyce critics claim that Cixous "reads the author's life as a novel" (Lernout, 43) and that she relies too exclusively on two books by Joyce's brother Stanislaus and on Richard Ellmann's biography, resulting in "very schematic and doubtful judgments about people that would be perfectly acceptable if she had been dealing with mere characters in a novel" (Lernout, 43).

The later additions to Cixoux's text would appear to be her attempts to add on some Derridean insights into her study of the Joycean oeuvre.

In "Thoth and the Written Word" she first describes the relationship of the god Thoth and Egyptian religion and points out that Thoth is at the very hub of ideas founded on the "fundamental and corresponding oppositions between life and death, father and son, written and spoken word, good and evil, day and night, sun and moon."[4] Cixous continues with a discussion of Thoth as Shem or Shaun, the relationship between Joyce and Plato, and she seeks to address the question posed by Plato in the *Phaedrus*—of whether writing is a good or bad thing, arguing that Joyce attempts to answer it throughout his work "in terms analogous to those Socrates uses in his arguments" but with a different conclusion (*Exile,* 741). Socrates condemns writing as a poison while Joyce, for the same reasons, defends it as a good thing. Both make use of the myth of Thoth, and the entire discussion of writing as poison or cure will find its echo in later writing by Cixous herself.

Another interesting moment in *The Exile of James Joyce* occurs in the introduction when Cixous states that "the general, exterior form of the artist's life as seen by Joyce has . . . a rhythm of out-going and return" (*Exile,* xiv). "Joyce selects a series of 'moments of contact' around which crystallise whole networks of emotions (in the realm of life) or of symbols (in art). These moments can be easily identified by their recurrence in the work: that which is accidental when it first appears becomes coincidental the second time and determines a whole mechanism of repetition so that any gesture, act, or word connected with the first event will, if evoked or repeated, set off the complete mechanism" (*Exile,* xv). Joyce, according to Cixous, "imagined the work of art simultaneously as a spatio-temporal journey towards the point where the artist would know himself as such, and as the recording of this journey in the memory. Present, past, and future collaborate in constituting the person of the man of genius, a process both active and passive in which . . . he acts and is acted upon, he meets others and meets himself" (*Exile,* xv).

While it is not necessarily true that what Cixous has said about Joyce can be used to describe her own fictional world, the affiliation is clearly there. Both Joyce and Cixous express in their writing the sense of exile or marginalization—Joyce for a set of motives admittedly quite different from those expressed by Cixous. Both Cixous and Joyce are deeply involved in the creation of a fictional "reality" through the most radical and experimental use of language itself. What Cixous says about Joyce is often, at least tangentially, appropriately applicable to her own work: "Reality and its interpretation, object and subject, destiny and choice, are connected, sometimes to the point of confusion, in this work whose originality can be summed up thus: Joyce not only feeds the work of art on his life (a property common to all work), but also fashions his life so that its reality may already be the image of what is to be written in its image" (*Exile,* xiv).

Just as James Joyce devoted an entire writing career to making a connection between life and art, so do the works of Hélène Cixous, in a quite different set of cultural constructs, reach toward this same goal. *The Exile of James Joyce* is not a typical Cixousian text. It is an academic book, a required piece of academic writing that was produced at least in part to fulfill professional obligations. Yet in her choice of subject as well as her sometimes eccentric treatment of the particularities of the Joycean oeuvre, Cixous gives us a kind of preview of the critical-theoretical approach she would take in her own more creative writing. The deconstructive bits and pieces added on to *The Exile of James Joyce* will later become fully deconstructive in the essay "Joyce, la ruse de l'écriture," included in the collection of critical essays Cixous published in 1974 under the title *Prénoms de personne.*

***Prénoms de personne* (1974).** *Prénoms de personne* (a volume whose title echos the title of Cixous's first published volume of "fiction," *Le Prénom de Dieu*) can be loosely translated as "First Names of No One" or "First Names of Someone." A collection of critical essays published by Seuil in the Poétique collection in 1974, it contains 12 major essays, grouped into three divisions. The first section, titled "Du côté de l'autre," centers on studies of German literature and includes five essays—one on Freud's "Der Unheimliche" ("The Uncanny"), one on Hoffmann's *The Sandman,* one on Jentsch's proposition, one on *The Tales* of Hoffmann, and one on Kleist's *Marionettes.* The book's second section contains three essays on the writing of Edgar Allan Poe. The first essay, "A Poetics of Return," treats a group of Poe stories—"The Imp of the Perverse," "Morella," "Ligeia," "Berenice," "The Oval Portrait," "Leonore," and "William Wilson"—using Derrida, Lacan, and Freud. The second essay, "The "Paradox of Nevermore," presents a detailed reading of Poe's "Morella" and is a very dense text: the reader is aware that this is Cixous reading Derrida reading Bataille reading Hegel. The third major essay on Poe, "The Other Analyst," is Cixous's reading of *The Murders in the Rue Morgue,* again with a full panoply of deconstructive and psychoanalytical critical tools at her disposition. The final section of *Prénoms de personne* is a group of essays devoted to the work of Joyce; however, in contradistinction to the readings presented in *The*

Exile of James Joyce, the essays here are much more densely textured and deeply informed by readings of Freud, Lacan, Derrida, and Georges Bataille. The first essay, "Texte du hors," provides a short introduction to the essays that complete the section, praising Joyce's originality and his work's resistance to interpretation or translation. The second essay, "Les Hérésistances du sujet," is a very detailed analysis of the concept of "subjectivity" in Joyce's *Dubliners* and *Ulysses.* A third essay, "La Crucifixion," is a discussion of Joyce's "comedy of castration," which, according to Cixous, questions the very idea of logocentric mastery and phallocentric concepts of "possession" or property and economic exchange. The final essay of the volume, "Trait—Portrait de l'artiste," is a reading of a small fragment from *Finnegans Wake.*

The essays in *Prénoms de personne* show Cixous at the height of her deconstructive analytical period. In this period she is much more interested in textual analysis using the works of psychoanalysis and deconstructive philosophical theorizing than she is in larger questions of theory. All the essays deal with writings from the nineteenth or early twentieth century that, she argues, were subversive in that they opposed "conservative narcissism" or "the enslavement of the self." In virtually all these essays Cixous seeks to establish a parallel relationship between writing and "desire." She looks for texts that have their origin in true desire (a desire that is life-affirming and connected to "gift" and "movement" rather than a phallocentric desire that finds its power in "appropriation," "possession," "inertia," or "death"). One of the common features of all texts analyzed by Cixous in this volume is the fact that each "deconstructs" the very story it is in the process of building.

Only a few of the essays included in *Prénoms de personne* have been as yet translated into English. Those available in translation include "At Circe's or the Self-Opener," "Fictions and Its Phantoms: A Reading of Freud's 'Das Unheimliche,'" and "Joyce: The Ruse of Writing." The book remains, however, a fine example of Cixous's "academic" writing during the first period of her career.

Cixous is known as well for other "literary" critical essays on a wide variety of topics (from Lewis Carroll to Samuel Beckett and Julien Gracq to the performance artist Karine Saporta), but virtually none have been translated into English. One of her earlier essays, "The Character of 'Character,'" however, does point the way to one of her later preoccupations—the question of the status of the "subject." In "The Character of 'Character'" Cixous argues that the traditional function of "characterization" in writing has been to insert literature into culture by insisting on the unitary nature of an "I"—to insist that the subject is unified and whole. This, she says, does not take into account that the "the subject" is an "effect of the unconscious" and that the unconscious is not subject to analysis or to characterization. She then uses this "theoretical" positioning, or questioning, to read Hoffmann's *Kreisleriana,* an example of a text that brings the subject back to its "divisibility."

Écriture Féminine

Although it is impossible to put a specific date on Cixous's movement away from deconstructive academic writing, with its emphasis on past textual production and rereadings through the grill of psychoanalytical or philosophical texts, it is certainly clear that at some point her attention to the decentering of the subject, her insistence on the importance of "true desire" within the text, and her examinations of the logocentric and phallocentric phenomena within language leads her to a much larger and open-ended brand of "theorizing," toward what might be termed a woman-centered theoretical position that we call *écriture féminine.* Many key Cixousian texts are representative of her future-oriented theory toward a writing that is "said to be feminine"; however, the three texts now available in English that are crucial to an understanding of this centrist theoretical period in her writing career are undoubtedly her 1975 essay "The Laugh of the Medusa" ("Le Rire de la Méduse"); her 1976 essay "Castration or Decapitation?" ("Le Sexe ou la tête?"); her 1975 essay "Sorties," which forms the second half of *The Newly Born Woman (La Jeune Née),* co-authored with Catherine Clément; and her 1977 essay "Coming to Writing," which formed part of *La Venue à l'écriture,* to which France's Annie Leclerc and Quebec's Madeleine Gagnon also contributed.

A veritable explosion of theoretical writing within a short space of time, these texts are grounded, as were the more exegetical texts of *Prénoms de personne,* in Cixous's ongoing critical dialogue with Derrida, Freud, Lacan, Bataille, Mauss, Heidegger, and others. Their ideas have had a vast impact on feminist theoretical discussions the world over during the past decade and a half, and they continue to provide fertile ground for debate.

"The Laugh of the Medusa" (1975). "The Laugh of the Medusa" appeared in a special number of *L'Arc* devoted to Simone de Beauvoir. In this essay, which has been variously described by critics as political manifesto or prose poem or a hybrid of the two, Cixous sets out her ideas on the nature of "femininity" and on the ways in which difference is inscribed in writing. Using psychoanalytic theory but constantly subverting it, she points out the ways in which women have been repressed by the reign of the phallus and proposes that they free themselves of this repression through the act of writing. Writing from the body, Cixous asserts, will give power to women to transform the symbolic, to "bring about a mutation in human relations, in thought, in all praxis."[5] "I shall speak about women's writing: about *what it will do.* Woman must write her self: must write about women and bring women to writing, from which they have been driven away as violently as from their bodies—for the same reasons, by the same law, with the same fatal goal. Woman must put herself into the text—as into the world and into history—by her own movement" ("Medusa," 279). This clarion call to feminine writing, however, does not provide a definition. "It is impossible," says Cixous, "to *define* a feminine practice of writing, and this is an impossibility that will remain, for this practice can never be theorized, enclosed, coded—which doesn't mean that it doesn't exist. But it will alway surpass the discourse that regulates the phallocentric system; it does and will take place in areas other than those subordinated to philosophico-theoretical domination" ("Medusa," 287).

If woman has always functioned "'within' the discourse of man, a signifier that has always referred back to the opposite signifier which annihilates its specific energy and diminishes or stifles its very different sounds, it is time for her to dislocate this 'within,' to explode it, turn it around, and seize it: to make it hers, contain it, taking it in her own mouth, biting that tongue with her very own teeth to invent for herself a language to get inside of" ("Medusa," 291). For Cixous, women must recognize the nature of their own sexuality—"dispersible, prodigious, stunning, desirous and capable of other, of the other woman that she will be, of the other woman she isn't , of him, of you" ("Medusa," 291).

Cixous plays with woman's relationship to language itself by the double use of the French verb *voler* ("to fly" as well as "to steal"): "Flying is woman's gesture—flying in language and making it fly. We have all learned the art of flying and its numerous techniques; for centuries we've been able to possess anything only by flying; we've lived in flight, stealing away, finding, when desired, narrow passageways, hidden crossovers. It's no accident that *voler* has a double meaning, that it plays on each of them and thus throws off the agents of sense. It's no accident; women take after birds and robbers just as robbers take after women and birds" ("Medusa," 291).

***The Newly Born Woman* (1975).** In her introduction to the 1985 English translation of *La Jeune Née,* the American feminist critic Sandra Gilbert writes that for her, reading this text by Hélène Cixous was "like going to sleep in one world and waking in another—going to sleep in a world of facts, which one must labor to theorize, and waking in a domain of theory, which one must strive to (f)actualize."[6] For Gilbert, everything about the newly born woman described in the text is "intense, indeed hyperbolic. She is born of Flaubert and Baudelaire, of Rimbaud and Apollinaire, as well as . . . *The Malleus Maleficarum,* Freud, Genet, Kleist, Hoffmann, Shakespeare, and Aeschylus" (*Newly Born Woman,* x).

Originally published in 1975 and co-authored with Catherine Clément, *The Newly Born Woman* is divided into three interrelated yet severable parts. In part 1 Clément provides an analysis of two traditional female figures, the sorceress and the hysteric, with an underlying emphasis on these figures as they were appropriated by psychoanalysis. Clément writes at length as well about the notion of the family romance developed by Freud in his theory of infantile sexuality. As contemporary critics of Freud now admit, Freud initially believed his "hysterical" patients who told stories of what we would today term as parental sexual abuse but he later retreated from this position only to accuse the daughter reporting seduction by the father to be herself the seducer: "The plot of seduction and betrayal is further displaced as the history of the nuclear family, enmeshed in cultural codes, turns into a romance of accusation and counteraccusation on which guilt finally settles on the silenced figure who unites sorceress and hysteric in one body—the witchy, bitchy mother" (*Newly Born Woman,* xiv).

Clément attempts to map an escape route from the cultural trap women find themselves in. She suggests a kind of acultural nowhere/nonspace where a kind of radical bisexuality would refuse the rigidity of women's destiny and desire. This bisexuality, emblematic of a *jeune naissance,* a new young birth, would allow woman to transcend the heresies of history and the history of hysteria itself, flying and fleeing into a new heaven and a new earth of her own invention. Clément's contribution to this text, unlike Cixous's, which continues the highly lyrical tone of "The Laugh of the Medusa," is traditonally organized. Her general title "The Guilty One" contains two subsections, "Sorceress and Hysteric" and "Seduction and Guilt." The further subdivisions of these main topics allow us to follow the lines of argument developed within. The analysis of the dual image of woman—as sorceress and as hysteric—involves discussion of culture and its repressive structures; the "signs and marks" of hysteria or sorcery as they appear in "theatre of the body"; the thematic foci of attack, expulsion, celebration, and madness; images of the child and the savage; and crossing over and contagion. In her analysis of seduction and guilt, Clément organizes her text along theatrical lines. For instance, in the History of Seduction you have as the first scene "The Perverse Fathers"; as the second, "The Lying Daughters"; as the third, "The Guilty Mother"; and as the epilogue, "A Family Affair."

Cixous, too, deals with the necessity to break free, to transgress, to cross or traverse old lines; unlike Clément, however, she does not present her argument in an orderly or linear style. Titled "Sorties: Out and Out: Attacks/Ways Out/Forays," Cixous's section begins with the following oft-quoted passage:

Where is she?
Activity/Passivity
Sun/Moon
Culture/Nature
Day/Night
Father/Mother
Head/Heart
Intelligible/Palpable
Logos/Pathos
Form, Convex, Step, Advance, Semen, Progress.
Matter, Concave, Ground—Where Steps are Taken,
Holding-and-Dumping Ground.
Man
Woman (*Newly Born Woman,* 63)

This ever-present, overarching metaphor has permeated all our thought and speech in whatever domain—"throughout literature, philosophy, criticism, centuries of representation and reflection" (*Newly Born Woman,* 63). Thought has always proceeded through dual, hierarchical opposition—and logocentrism has reduced everything to a binary system that is in turn intimately and forever linked to the primordial couple man/woman. "Organization by hierarchy makes all conceptual organization subject to man. Male privilege, shown in the opposition between activity and passivity, which he uses to sustain himself. Traditionally, the question of sexual difference is treated by coupling it with the opposition: activity/passivity" (*Newly Born Woman,* 64).

Theories of culture, of society, symbolic systems in general—be they art, relgion, the family, or linguistics—all develop through conceptualization via binary opposition, then of necessity privileging one of the pair and condemning the other to inferior status. In philosophy, in literary history, the story is the same: woman is in the passive position: "Either woman is passive or she does not exist. What is left of her is unthinkable, unthought. Which certainly means that she is not thought, that she does not enter into the oppositions, that she does not make a couple with the father (who makes a couple with the son)" (*Newly Born Woman,* 64). Woman, then, for man does not exist: "She can not-be" (*Newly Born Woman,* 65). Philosophy itself is constructed, says Cixous, on the premise of woman's abasement and subordination of the feminine to the masculine order, "which gives the appearance of being the condition for the machinery's functioning" (*Newly Born Woman,* 65).

Now, says Cixous, it is high time we began to question this apparent unity between logocentrism and phallocentrism. It is time to threaten the stability of a masculine structure that has up to now passed itself off as both natural and eternal. "If some fine day," says Cixous, "it suddenly came out that the logocentric plan had always, inadmissibly, been to create a foundation for (to found and fund) phallocentrism, to guarantee the masculine order a rationale equal to history itself, . . . what would happen?" (*Newly Born Woman,* 65). What would happen to logocentrism, to the great philosophical systems, to the order of the world in general if the foundation for such thought were to be disturbed? Arguably all stories would have to be rewritten: "We are living in an age where the conceptual foundation of an ancient culture is in the process of being undermined" (*Newly Born Woman,* 65).

Cixous then proceeds to illustrate her position through women's narratives—the Sleeping Beauty of fairy tales; woman's trajectory traced through the Joycean "bridebed, childbed, bed of death"; and the male dream—to love the woman who is absent, hence desirable, "because she isn't there where she is" (*Newly Born Woman,* 67). Each story says to woman that her desire, as opposed to his desire, has no place in a phallocentric world. Love is a threshold affair. Male desire is kept alive through lack and is maintained by absence: "Night to his day—that has forever been the fantasy. Black to his white. Shut out of his system's space, she is the repressed that ensures the system's functioning" (*Newly Born Woman,* 67).

Cixous speaks of the "dark continent" trick that has been played on women—"She has been kept at a distance from herself, she has been made to see ("not-see") woman on the basis of what man wants to see of her, which is to say, almost nothing" (*Newly Born Woman,* 68). Women's bodies, women's desire have remained forbidden territory for self-exploration: "They have committed the greatest crime against women: insidiously and violently, they have led them to hate women, to be their own enemies, to mobilize their immense power against themselves, to do the male's dirty work" (*Newly Born Woman,* 68). Cixous points out that women have been caught between two equally terrifying myths—between the myth of the Medusa and the myth of the abyss. Yet, says Cixous, why not admit that not being castrated is not the worst thing imaginable, admit that women are not men, admit that mothers have no penis: "They say there are two that cannot be represented: death and the female sex" (*Newly Born Woman,* 68), yet the repression of the female by society must end and end, it will, says Cixous, though the act of writing.

Cixous then proceeds to a poeticized autobiographical account of coming to writing and of the problems inherent in marking out a speaking space for the marginalized:

> But I was born in Algeria, and my ancestors lived in Spain, Morocco, Austria, Hungary, Czechoslovakia, Germany: my brothers by birth are Arab. So where are we in history? I side with those who are injured, trespassed upon, colonized. I am (not) Arab. Who am I? I am "doing" French history. I am a Jewish woman. In which ghetto was I penned up during your wars and your revolutions? I want to fight. What is my name? I want to change life. Who is this "I"? Where is my place? I am looking. I search everywhere. I read, I ask. I begin to speak. Which language is mine? French? German? Arabic? Who spoke for me through the generations? It's my luck. What an account! Being born in Algeria, not in France, not in Germany; a little earlier and, like some members of my family, I would not be writing today. I would anonymiserate eternally from Auschwitz. (*Newly Born Woman,* 71)

Cixous's personal rebellion involves the search for a "somewhere else" which she as a child attempted to locate in books, choosing texts "where there was struggle" and paying particular attention to "masters" and "heroes." She identifies with the Achilles of Homer, loves Patroclus, but is afraid of being Ulysses. Yet as she approaches puberty she can no longer identify so readily with her heroes. The Algerian War comes, "and I quit being a child who is neuter, an angry bundle of nerves, a me seething with violent dreams, meditating widespread revenge, the overthrow of idols, the triumph of the oppressed" (*Newly Born Woman,* 74).

In a section titled "The Empire of the Self-Same," Cixous turns to ideas about physical property first presented by Hegel in *The Phenomenology of the Mind.* This account describes society's smooth and seamless functioning in a movement that sees the individual pass in three stages from family to the state. The entire Hegelian dialectical system is based on the empire of the self-same (self-same is the term the translator has chosen for *le propre*—oneself). The story of history is the story of phallocentrism endlessly repeated. In Cixous's words, "History of an identity: that of man's becoming recognized by the other (son or woman), reminding him that, as Hegel says, death is his mother" (*Newly Born Woman,* 79).

Recognition, however, must come through conflict, and desire for recognition is actually a desire for appropriation, a logic that proceeds in two stages. In stage 1 desire comes from "a mixture of difference and *inequality*" (*Newly Born Woman,* 79). Without a difference in force, there can be no movement. Yet with, in Cixous's terms, "a little surreptitious slippage," sexual difference with an equality of force does not produce the movement of desire. It is inequality that triggers desire—and that desire is desire for appropriation. Without inequality, without struggle, there is inertia—death" (*Newly Born Woman,* 79).

It is here, for Cixous, where we see the "great masculine imposture" at work. Why is it not possible, she asks, to imagine that difference or inequality (meaning noncoincidence, asymmetry) could lead to desire without negativity? "We would recognize each other in a type of exchange in which each one would keep the *other* alive and different" (*Newly Born Woman,* 79). But in the Hegelian schema, there is no place for the equal other, no place "for a whole and living woman" (*Newly Born Woman,* 79). She must recognize (and "recuntize") the male, then disappear—so that he wins, profits from the exchange. She must resist, then succumb, then go away, in order for the gesture to be repeated.

In Cixous's terms, "the unconscious ? strategem and violence of masculine economy consists in making sexual difference hierarchical by valorizing one of the terms of the relationship, by reaffirming what Freud calls phallic primacy. And the 'difference' is always perceived and carried out as an opposition. Masculinity/femininity are opposed in such a way that it is male privilege that is affirmed in a movement of conflict played out in advance" (*Newly Born Woman,* 80). Gradually one becomes aware that the empire of the self-same is indeed based on a fear of expropriation, of loss, of "losing the attribute"—in short, the fear of castration. In Cixous's words, "The (political) economy of the masculine and feminine is reoganized by different demands and constraints, which, as they become socialized and metaphorized, produce signs, relations of power, relationships of production and reproduction, a whole system of cultural inscription that is legible as masculine or feminine" (*Newly Born Woman,* 80–81).

Cixous makes a point of using qualifiers of sexual difference in order to avoid the confusion of man/masculine, woman/feminine: "For there are some men who do not repress their femininity, some women who, more or less strongly, inscribe their masculinity. Difference is not distributed, of course, on the basis of socially determined 'sexes'" (*Newly Born Woman,* 81). When Cixous speaks of political and libidinal economies, however, she does not do so in order to discuss the question of origins. Indeed, she criticizes both Freud and Ernest Jones for their thesis of a "natural," anatomical determination of sexual difference/opposition. She admits, however, that it is undeniable that there are psychic consequences of the difference between the sexes but argues that they cannot be reduced to the ones recognized by Freud (as, for example, in his discussion of the Oedipus complex, the difference between having/not having "the phallus"). Sexual difference for Cixous is located at the level of *jouissance,* "inasmuch as a woman's instinctual economy cannot be identified by man or referred to in the masculine economy" (*Newly Born Woman,* 82). "For me the question asked of 'what does she want?' is a question that woman asks herself, in fact, because she is asked it. It is precisely because there is so little room for her desire in society that, because of not knowing what to do with it, she ends up not knowing where to put it or if she even has it. This queston conceals the most immediate and urgent question: 'How do I pleasure?' What is it—feminine *jouissance*—where does it happen, how does it inscribe itself—on the level of her body or of her unconscious? And then, how does it write itself?" (*Newly Born Woman,* 82).

Although supportive of other ways of differently thinking the world, Cixous concludes that despite everything, phallocentrism simply *is*: "There is phallocentrism. History has never produced or recorded anything else—which does not mean that this form is destinal or natural. Phallocentrism is the enemy. Of everyone. Men's loss in phallocentrism is different from but as serious as women's and it is time to change. To invent the other history" (*Newly Born Woman,* 83).

For Cixous, there is no destiny, no nature, no essence. Rather, she sees "living structures" so caught and sometimes rigidly set within historicocultural limits "that for a long time it has been impossible (and it is still very difficult) to think or even imagine an 'elsewhere'" (*Newly Born Woman,* 83). Yet this historical period is a transitional one, says Cixous. Women and men remain trapped within a "web of age-old cultural determinations that are almost unanalyzable in their complexity. We are each of us trapped within an ideological theatre even speaking of 'woman' or 'man.'" Yet Cixous remains optimistic that change is possible:

> Let us simultaneously imagine a general change in all the structures of training, education, supervision—hence in the structures of reproduction of ideological results. And let us imagine a real liberation of sexuality, that is to say, a transformation of each one's relationship to his or her body (and to the other body), an approximation to the vast, material, organic, sensuous universe that we are. This cannot be accomplished, of course, without political transformations that are equally radical. (Imagine!) Then "femininity" and "masculinity" would inscribe quite differently their effects of difference, their economy, their relationship to expenditure, to lack,. to the gift. What today appears to be "feminine" or "masculine" would no longer amount to the same thing. No longer would the common logic of difference be organized with the opposition that remains dominant. Difference would be a bunch of new differences. (*Newly Born Woman,* 83)

Of course, Cixous points out, there have always been exceptions—men or women—"beings who are complex, mobile, open" (*Newly Born Woman,* 84). Accepting the other sex as a component makes these exceptional people "much richer, more various, stronger and—to the extent they are mobile—very fragile" (*Newly Born Woman,* 84). Creativity of all sorts is intimately connected to a kind of homosexuality. This does not mean, says Cixous, that one must be homosexual in order to be creative, but it does mean that "there is no invention possible, whether it be philosophical or poetic, without there being in the inventing subject an abundance of the other, of variety: separate people, thought-people, whole populations issuing from the unconscious . . . that there is no invention of any other I, no poetry, no fiction without a certain homosexuality (the I/play of bisexuality) acting as a crystallization of my ultrasubjectivities" (*Newly Born Woman,* 84).

What Cixous proposes is a reconsideration of bisexuality, making a distinction between two differnt types. In the first type, bisexuality is a fantasy of a complete being, a fantasy of unity that would replace the fear of castration by covering up sexual difference, melting together; in the second type, which Cixous calls the "other" bisexuality, "the one with which every subject, who is not shut up inside the spurious phallocentric performing theatre, set up as his or her erotic universe. Bisexuality—that is to say the location within oneself of the presence of both sexes, evident and insistent in different ways according to the individual, the nonexclusion of difference or of a sex, and starting with this 'permission' one gives oneself, the multiplication of the effects of desire's inscription on every part of the body and the other body" (*Newly Born Woman,* 84–85).

For Cixous, saying that woman is somehow bisexual is "an apparently paradoxical way of displacing and reviving the question of difference. And therefore of writing as 'feminine' or 'masculine'" (*Newly Born Woman,* 85). For Cixous, femininity and bisexuality go together, and writing is the way in which the woman can let the other come through her, traverse her. "Writing," says Cixous, "is working; being worked; questions (in) the between (letting oneself be questioned) of same and of other without which nothing lives; undoing death's work by willing the togetherness of one another, infinitely charged with a secret exchange of one with another not knowing one another and beginning again only from what is most distant, from self, from other, from the other within" (*Newly Born Woman,* 85).

But, asks Cixous, where does difference come through in writing? Usually in the manner or way in which a return or revenue is expected. Can women escape this? (We have already seen that man is the engrossing party in the development of desire, of exchange.) Really, says Cixous, there is no "free" gift: "In the values that the gesture of giving affirms, causes to circulate; in the type of profit the giver draws from the gift and the use to which he or she puts it" (*Newly Born Woman,* 87). What men want in return for the gift is a gain in masculine value—the "plus-value of virility, authority, power, money, or pleasure" (*Newly Born Woman,* 87). Society is structured this way: masculine profit "is almost always mixed up with success which is socially defined" (*Newly Born Woman,* 87).

But how does a woman give? She, as well, gives in order to receive—"pleasure, happiness, increased value, enhanced self-image" (*Newly Born Woman,* 87). Unlike the man, however, the woman is not concerned with recovering her expenses. "She is able not to return to herself, never settling down, p——ing out, going everywhere to the other" (*Newly Born Woman,* 87). "If there is a self proper to woman, paradoxically it is her capacity to depropriate herself without self-interest: endless body, without 'end,' without principal 'parts,' she is a whole, it is a whole made up of parts that are wholes, not simple, partial objects but varied entirety, moving and boundless change, a cosmos where eros never stops traveling, vast astral space" (*Newly Born Woman,* 87).

Woman's sexuality is not centered on the penis, thus her libido is "cosmic," just as her unconscious is "worldwide" (*Newly Born Woman,* 88). "Her writing also can only go on and on, without ever inscribing or distinguishing contours, daring these dizzying passages in other, fleeting, passionate dwellings within him, within the hims and hers whom she inhabits just long enough to watch them, as close as possible to the unconscious from the moment they arise: to love them, as close as possible to instinctual drives, and then, further, all filled with these brief identifying hugs and kisses, she goes and goes on infinitely" (*Newly Born Woman,* 88). For only the woman writing "wants to know from within where she, the one excluded, has never ceased to hear what comes before language reverberating" (*Newly Born Woman,* 88).

Cixous describes the "beginning" thus: "There is a ground, it is her ground—childhood flesh, shining blood—or background, depth. A white depth, a core, unforgettable, forgotten, and this ground, covered by an infinite number of strata, layers, sheets of paper—is her sun (sol. . . soleil). And nothing can put it out. Feminine light doesn't come" (*Newly Born Woman,* 88). Cixous calls for a rethinking of the maternal, charging both men and women to "make the old relationship and all its consequences out of date; to think the launching of a new subject, into life, with defamiliarizaiton" (*Newly Born Woman,* 89).

There is a bond, says Cixous, between women's libidinal economy—her *jouissance,* the feminine imaginary and her "way of self-constituting a subjectivity that splits apart without regret, and without this regretlessness being the equivalent of dying" (*Newly Born Woman,* 90). In a poetic hyperbolic passage, Cixous describes feminine creative energy: "Unleashed and raging, she belongs to the race of waves. She arises, she approaches, she lifts up, she reaches, she covers over, washes ashore, flows embracing the cliff's least undulation, already she is another, arising again throwing the fringed vastness of her body up high, follows herself, and covers over, uncovers, polishes, makes the stone body shine with the gentle undeserting ebbs, which return to the shoreless non-origin, as if she recalled herself in order to come again as never before" (*Newly Born Woman,* 90–91). "She has never 'held still'; explosion, diffusion, efforvescence, abundance, she takes pleasure in being boundless, outside, self, outside same, far from a 'center,' from any capital of her 'dark continent' very far from the 'hearth' to which man brings her so that she will tend his fire, which always threatens to go out" (*Newly Born Woman,* 91). Whereas masculine energy has but limited reserves, feminine energy, in Cixous's terms, has vast resources—a fact that is not without consequences for "exchange in general, for love-life, and for the fate created for woman's desire" (*Newly Born Woman,* 91).

Cixous locates a linkage between writing, femininity, and transformation, "between the economy of feminity—the open, extravagant subjectivity, that relationship to the other in which the gift doesn't calculate its influence—and the possibiltiy of love; and a link today between this 'libido of the other' and writing" (*Newly Born Woman,* 91–92). As in "The Laugh of the Medusa," she asserts that defining a feminine practice of writing is an impossibility but that simply because the practice cannot be theorized or encoded does not mean it is nonexistent. Even if it is impossible to speak of a theory of feminine writing, however, it is possible to underline "some effects, some elements of unconscious drives, some relations of the feminine Imaginary to the Real, to writing" (*Newly Born Woman,* 92).

Cixous locates femininty in writing primarily as a privilege of voice: "*writing and voice* are entwined and interwoven and writing's continuity/voice's rhythm take each other's breath away through interchanging, make the text gasp or form it out of suspenses and silences, make it lose its voice or rend it with cries" (*Newly Born Woman,* 92). Feminine writing "never stops reverberating from the wrench that the acquisition of speech, speaking out loud, is for her" (*Newly Born Woman,* 92). Women's discourse, even when theoretical or political, is "never simple or linear or 'objectivized,' universalized; she involves her story in history" (*Newly Born Woman,* 92). Cixous notes that in feminine speech, as in writing, "there never stops reverberating something that, once having passed through us, having imperceptibly and deeply touched us, still has the power to affect us—song, the first music of the voice of love, which every woman keeps alive" (*Newly Born Woman,* 93). "The Voice sings from a time before law, before the Symbolic took one's breath away and reappropriated it into language under its authority of separation" (*Newly Born Woman,* 93).

Within woman there is always something of the mother; the relationship to her childhood remains as well:

> Text, my body: traversed by lilting flows; listen to me, it is not a captivating, clinging "mother"; it is the equivoice that, touching you, affects you, pushes you away from your breast to come to language, that summons *your* strength; it is the rhyth-me that laughs you; the one intimately addressed who makes all metaphors, all body possible and desirable, who is no more describable than god, soul, of the Other; the part of you

> that puts space bewteen yourself and pushes you to inscribe your woman's style in language. Voice: milk that could go on forever. The lost mother/bitter-lost. Eternity: is voice mixed with milk. (*Newly Born Woman,* 93)

Whereas a man journeys back to the point of origin, in order to appropriate it for himself and there die, the woman's journey is to the unknown, "to invent" (*Newly Born Woman,* 93).

Why does the woman possess this privileged relationship to voice? asks Cixous. Perhaps because she remains constantly linked to the maternal "as no-name and source of goods." The woman writes metaphorically with white ink (*Newly Born Woman,* 94).

The maternal voice will allow women to write the body, for, as Cixous reminds us:

> Women have almost everything to write about feminity: about their sexuality, that is to say, about the infinite and mobile complexity of their becoming erotic, about the lightning ignitions of such a minuscule-vast region of their body, not about destiny but about the adventure of such an urge, the voyages, crossings, advances, sudden and slow awakenings, discoveries of a formerly tamed region that is just now springing up. Woman's body with a thousand and one fiery hearths, when—shattering censorships and yokes—she lets it articulate the proliferation of meanings that runs through it in every direction. It is going to take much more than language for him to make the ancient maternal tongue sound in only one groove. (*Newly Born Woman,* 94)

Women have turned away from their bodies—taught to remain ignorant of them, taught to love the opposite sex—yet Cixous urges women to write the body: "Now, I-woman am going to blow up the law: a possible and inescapable explosion from now on; let it happen, right now, in language" (*Newly Born Woman,* 94). It is not, however, a question of a simple reversal of positions of power, of appropriation of male discourse, of wishing to be "in their position of mastery" (*Newly Born Woman,* 96). Cixous is concerned, on the contrary, to depropriation and depersonalization as she "exasperating, immoderate and contradictory, destroys laws, the 'natural' order" (*Newly Born Woman,* 96).

As in "The Laugh of the Medusa," Cixous then plays with the double meaning of the French verb *voler* ("to fly," "to steal") as she describes the woman's gesture as she moves into writing:

> To fly/steal is woman's gesture, to steal into language to make it fly. We have all learned flight/theft, the art with many techniques, for all the centuries we have only had access to having by stealing/flying; we have lived in a flight/theft, stealing/flying, finding the close, concealed ways-through of desire. It's not just luck if the word "voler" volleys between the "vol" of theft and "vol" of flight, pleasuring in each and routing the sense police. It is not just luck: woman partakes of bird and burglar just as the burglar partakes of woman and bird: hesheits pass, hesheits fly by, hesheits pleasure in scrambling spatial order, disorienting it, moving furniture, things, and values around, breaking in, emptying structures, turning the self-same, the proper upside down. (*Newly Born Woman,* 96)

A feminine text must of necessity be subversive: "If it writes itself it is in volcanic heaving of the old "real property crust" (*Newly Born Woman,* 97). Writing is "the act that will 'realize' the un-censored relationship of woman to her sexuality, to her woman-being, giving her back access to her own forces" (*Newly Born Woman,* 97). The clarion call of *écriture féminine* rings out: "Write yourself: your body must make itself heard. Then the huge resources of the unconscious will burst out. Finally the inexhaustible feminine Imaginary is going to be deployed. Without gold or black dollars, our naphtha will spread values over the world, un-quoted values that will change the rules of the old game" (*Newly Born Woman,* 97).

Woman writing is constantly moving toward something "that only exists in an elsewhere" (*Newly Born Woman,* 97), and Cixous speaks of a writing that "deals with the no-deal, relates to what gives no return" (*Newly Born Woman,* 97). Hence, "a 'place' of intransigence and passion," "a place of lucidity where no one takes what is a pretense of existence for life" (*Newly Born Woman,* 97). Cixous speaks of the possible "elsewhere" that is available because opened up by men who are capable of becoming women—"poets who let something different from tradition get through at any price—men able to love love; therefore, to love others, to want them; men able to think the woman who would resist destruction and constitute herself as a superb, equal, 'impossible,' subject, hence intolerable in the real social order" (*Newly Born Woman,* 98).

Cixous identifies herself with Kleist's Penthesileia, not with Achilles, describes herself as being Antony for Cleopatra and she for him, Shakespeare's Juliet ("because with Romeo I went beyond the father cult"), and Saint Teresa of Avila ("that madwoman who knew a lot more than all the men"). Identifying with the hysterics as her sisters, she claims to be "what [Freud's case study] Dora would have been if woman's history had begun" (*Newly Born Woman,* 99). "Other-Love" is, for Cixous, writing's first name: "The new love dares the other, wants it, seems in flight, be-leaves, does some stealing between knowing and making up. She, the one coming from forever, doesn't stand still, she goes all over, she exchanges, she is desired-that-gives. Not shut up inside the paradox of the gift-that-takes or in the illusion on onely uniting" (*Newly Born Woman,* 99). The woman writing does not measure what she is giving, "but she gives neither false leads nor what she doesn't have"; she gives "cause to live, to think, to transform" (*Newly Born Woman,* 100). "That 'economy' can no longer be expressed as an economic term. Wherever she loves, all the ideas of the old management are surpassed. I am for you what you want me to be at the moment in which you look at me as if you have never before seen me so: every moment. When I write, all those that we don't know we can be write themselves from me, without exclusion, without prediction, and everything that we will be calls us to the tireless, intoxicating, tender-costly-search for love. We will never lack ourselves" (*Newly Born Woman,* 100).

In the section of *The Newly Born Woman* titled "The Dawn of Phallocentrism," Cixous reviews the development of the phallocentric narrative in Western culture and civilization, briefly discussing, in turn, Freud, Joyce (fatherhood as a legal fiction), and Kafka's "Before the Law," then turning to Aeschylus's tragedy of Orestes, Electra, Agamemnon, and Clytemnestra as the paradigmatic narrative that tells us our story, our history.

The concluding section of "Sorties" is a reading of Kleist's *Penthesileia.* Cixous's debt to Kleist is expressed in extreme terms: "I said I owed my life to Kleist. For a long time I lived on the knowledge that he had existed. I owed him not only the will to live but the will to live several lives. To be more than one feminine one or masculine one, to catch fire and burn, to die of life because he caught fire, took on body, pain, and death for me" (*Newly Born Woman,* 112).

Chapter Three

From *God's First Name* to *Angst:* A Question of Self and Subject

To find what keeps on disappearing, forcing you to go on searching for it; what is hidden yet not lost. To find what affectionate human beings are forbidden to re-call by a name, a face or the gradual fading of a pain—but seers may.

Hélène Cixous, *Angst*

Hélène Cixous's life in Paris, her work as a professor of literature at Paris VIII and the Centre en études féminines, and her theoretical writing have all been shaped in complementary ways by her parallel career as a writer of fictions and plays. Since 1967 she has produced at least one volume of "creative" writing on an almost annual basis. Prolific and stylistically brilliant, she is an exemplar of *écriture féminine* in contemporary France. Yet her creative writing career, like her theoretical writing career, is not easily categorized, nor does it coincide with any traditional typologies of genre. Her style as well has shown remarkable change over the course of the past 25 years. Indeed, her creative writing, like her theoretical writing, has undergone a certain evolutionary process, a *chéminement,* which has seen the work move from what might be described as a narcissistic, inner-directed fiction to a much more other-directed kind of writing (mostly for the theater)—writing that encompasses the great human questions of history.

We can identify three periods that serve as boundary markers in Cixous's work. In the first period texts seem to be essentially self-referential and caught in a web of Freudian dream analysis. During this period autobiographical elements figure prominently (most especially the effect of the loss of the father on the female narrative voice). A second period produces texts that are basically focused on "the other," while the third and most recent period involves texts in which the creative writing itself is split effectively between writing for the theater (basically outer-directed writing) and the writing of "fictions" that are of a hybrid narrational style (most obvious in texts such as *Manne, Jours de l'an,* or *Déluge*) and in which the "real world" of historical persons and events weaves narrational patterns among the autobiographical lines of the author herself—her own readings, her own recurring obsessions with texts from her past.

Although any kind of chronological dating remains arbitrary to a large extent, it is possible to place the beginning of the first moment of Cixousian creative writing in 1967 with *Le Prénom de Dieu* and its ending in 1977, with the novel *Angst*. Embedded within this phase, however, we also find quite clear indications of the potential power of *écriture féminine* to come to the aid of the writer who is struggling with problems of subject and voice. In the second phase of Hélène Cixous's creative writing trajectory, we observe a gradual movement away from the narcissistic concentration on the writing self trapped within various Freudian psychosocial situations toward a textual production that is much more overtly centered on questions of sexual difference and theory, thereby directly connected to Cixous's theoretical writings on *écriture féminine* of the same time period as well as to her discovery of Clarice Lispector. Texts of this period demonstrate the effects both of "woman-centered" and "other-approach" critical strategies by Cixous. Again, somewhat arbitrarily, we can fix their beginnings with *Préparatifs de noces au-delà de l'abîme* in 1978 and include her more recent work *Déluge* (1992).

A third phase of Cixous's creative writing path is one that runs along parallel tracks to the second and sees her move quite deliberately "from the scene of the unconscious to the scene of history" in her writing for the theater. Indeed, this dramatic production, both in its collaborative nature (Cixous has worked closely for the past decade with Ariane Mnouchkine of Paris's Théâtre du Soleil) and in its demands on the reader/spectator shows yet another facet of Cixous's writerly talent. Although the same questions are constantly posed (Who are we in relation to the other? Who is the other within? How do we understand the paradoxical couplings of love and hate, life and death, movement and stasis?), the audience is different, and the presentation of voice through the dialogue of actors demands continual stylistic adjustments.

Le Prénom de Dieu (1967)

Although the 10 short stories of *Le Prénom de Dieu* are not particularly well known within the Cixousian oeuvre, we discover in them the preliminary outlines of much of the creative fictional work she produced over the next decade. Only one of the stories, "The Step" ("La Marche"), has been translated; the others are "L'Outre vide" ("Beyond the Void"),

"Le Successeur" ("The Successor"), "La Lyre" ("The Lyre"), "Le Sphinx" ("The Sphinx"), "La Ville" ("The City"), "Le Veau de plâtre" ("The Plaster Calf"), "Le Lac" ("The Lake"), "La Baleine de Jonas" ("Jonas's Whale"), and "Anagramme" ("Anagram"). The collection's title, which translates as *The First Name of God,* points to one of Cixous's enduring preoccupations—the act of "naming" itself. In the formal organization of these short texts and in their insistent use of baroque images as well as in their style—at once picaresque, fantastic, Joycean, and Kafkaesque—we see the operation of what could be called a negative theology.

In general, the reader of *Le Prénom de Dieu* is struck by the peculiarly Cixousian narrative "voice." Despite the fact that through the normal reading process this voice is understood as male (given the various grammatical indices at the reader's disposal—gendered endings of adjectives and past participles, for example), one can just as easily "hear" the feminine voice in the text. One of the stories, "Le Lac," actually does have a female protagonist; the others, however, have male "characters" (using the term in its broadest sense) with sometimes a "wifely" vocal counterpart. The wives (or mothers) in the stories are usually described in terms of silence and passivity, yet they also constitute the means whereby "knowledge" is acquired. Cixous has inserted the gendered sexuality of her characters within the temporality of the text even though there is neither "story" nor historicity as such. This points to something familiar to readers of Cixous: the primacy of place given to an ontological inquiry on the very nature of sexual difference.

"L'Outre vide," the first story in the collection, is the story of a man's reliving the stages of dissociation from his mother. Reminiscent of the various stages described in developmental psychology by D. W. Winnicott and others, this liberation from the mother is dramatized through dialogues, one of which involves her symbolic murder. An interplay of the voice of suppressed desire (on the part of the male child) and the voice of the mother constantly telling him to *act* sets the stage for the death of the mother and the protagonist's subsequent discovery of an identity based on autonomy. The movement is from *"Je suis seul"* and the solitude associated with the self of childhood to *"Je suis lui,"* or the integration of self in adulthood.

"La Marche" is narrated by a man who is both a father and a husband. As head of the family, his primary role is that of father. Married to a woman whose sensual desire seems to have disappeared, the narrator relives a recurring dream that has taken place 60 times and that features steps (symbolically degrees of anxiety and shame) and a ritual strangulation. The nightmare takes the same inevitable form each time, with a child's hand grabbing the narrator by the throat and a then a fall. The nightmares bring about a gradual change in the awareness he has of his family: he becomes more sensitive to his wife's sexuality, and there is a new relationship with his son. A luminous circle appears around his son's head, and the ritual embrace that bound them in the past occurs one final time. Father and son fall, and the feeling moves from joy to death. This symbolic struggle marks both a coming of age for the son and a symbolic death for the father.

"The Successor" is a tale narrated with a tone of biblical authority focusing on the imaginary world prior to the psychic shift to the symbolic world. The story of a king who has succeeded his father following a parricide, this triangular situation is a fictionalized reworking of Freud's Oedipal material in a narrative exploration of the journey toward an integrated identity. It is a tale that demonstrates the necessity to move away from the birthgiver and the love and comfort located in parental love toward an autonomous self. The structure of the son's emotional development is described through the themes of the leaving of the house of childhood and the reversible chain of generation-life-degeneration-death.

"La Lyre" is a philosophical tale, again with biblical overtones, narrated by an Elder. It is the story of an inverted messianic figure who embodies hatred, shame, and hope and who relinquishes his humanity for God and represents "the other." Yet in his relationship with God and the world he is confronted with his own narcissism rather than his divinity—a discovery that causes him great anguish. His future death is symbolized by a female (the angel of death) whom he wants to entertain with his lyre. When he discovers that the lyre has been destroyed, the man seeks counsel from the Elder, who tells him the parable of the rich master and his servant. The Elder despises the little man, sending him away with the advice to forget his lyre and to drink his blood and tears instead. As in many Cixousian texts, the status of the dream narrative remains ambiguous.

"La Ville" is a variation of the typical French *conte philosophique.* In it Cixous questions traditional notions of past and present time, history, memory, and other "absolutes"—truth, wisdom, and the eternal quest for happiness. These mental categories are embodied by the elderly members of society, by societal structures (especially the language and methodology of mass media), and by history itself. "The City" presents a vibrant parody of the socialization of people totally programmed by institutionalized thinking in their relationship to temporality and to various modes of thinking. Institutionalized thinking and the subversion of language within the city bear responsibility for the deformation of mental constructs. Cixous's "city" presents a satiric and subversive view of Utopia, subversion providing both "content" and "form."

The title of "Le Veau de plâtre" obviously recalls the biblical imagery of the golden calf of pagan idolatry. This text features a dream that simulates the passage from consciousness to semi-consciousness—a movement from the conscious self to death narrated by a male voice. The narrator experiences this nightmarish passage from life to death. His arms and legs are made of plaster, which he experiences as a "false body." The tone of his ontological quest suggests both self-discovery and an investigation into the perception of self in relation to others and to the world. Recurring themes and images—light, tunnel, cage, walls, and cave—suggest the possibility of rebirth. This rebirth is echoed by a narration of sexual coupling, with both symbolic and "real" implications, at the story's beginning and ending. The first-person narrator uses his wife as a tool of consciousness, as an aid to help him move from one level of perception to another. On a superficial level, she brings him happiness, but she also brings him death. At the same time she enjoys his plaster "cast" and feels more tenderness toward it than she feels for the man himself.

The dream recounted in "The Plaster Calf" involves, in similar fashion to other Cixousian dream narratives, a reassessment of the concepts of permanence, reality, and illusion. Life is a passage, a dream that has the potential of becoming death, nightmare, or understanding. There is an unspoken dialectic between the narrator, whose ontological quest turns out to be a vain one, and the narrator's brother, who invites him to celebrate life. The text's highly poetic style, in typically Cixousian fashion, conveys both a state of textual weightlessness and a state of abnormal weightiness.

In "Le Lac" the third-person narrative voice is female. Again images of caves, tunnels, cages, walls, and light suggest a narrative of self-discovery—this time, however, in the feminine. The text negotiates a successful slippage between levels of consciousness and the dream state, between "reality" and a kind of semi-consciousness. It deals with the emergence of a conscious "self" as distinct from externally imposed identities within a family, where the mother is nonexistent and where all the psychic incestuous links between the father and the daughter-narrator and two sons are played out. "Le Lac" is the story of a young woman's search for her identity and for that privileged space where she will find both knowledge and freedom.

After the death of her parents, the narrator attempts to free herself from the restrictive identities imposed upon her by the structure of the family: as her father's daughter, her brothers' sister. She wants to shatter these images of herself, desirable within her mother's consciousness, particularly those connected to submission to men and conformity to the patriarchal order. In this respect, "Le Lac" is the most openly feminist story in the collection. The protagonist's inner journey toward self-discovery takes the form of a search for a secret (and secretive) space where she will again find "wholeness." In order to retrieve such space, however, she must do battle with societal taboos as well as with preexisting ideas about race, language, and religion. This ontological struggle leads her to find her father—in the form of a tree. She fights against becoming entangled within the root system (yet another mystical coupling) in order to extricate herself from his embrace. The textual floating between semi-consciousness and dream state allows for both equivocation (is this a real or symbolic coupling?) and a space for questions.

In this text the self actually merges with the elements through the image of the lake. The lake, however, proposes yet another perspective on the theme of self-discovery as the female narrator becomes the initiator in a mystical embrace with her younger brother. The younger brother then "melts" into an image of the father, and together they flow into the past, forming a bizarre but interesting circle, given the woman's active rather than passive role in its movement. Although "Le Lac" initially describes fathers as inscribers of meaning and creators of consciousness, the story's ending, which includes a letter written by the narrator's father (but only read posthumously), suggests a reversal, as the father leaves his children this legacy: "Your sense of reality is yours to be dreamt."[1]

In "La Baleine de Jonas" Jonas is one of a hundred Jonases—all with the same Master. This "biblical" tale begins with a description of a patriarchal clan where the women give their names to their sons. The women of this society live segregated from their men and are uneducated, although they are wise. It is the women who are able to be ironic at the expense of the Master, whose very identity is being questioned. Jonas would rather have been George (of Saint George and the Dragon) or Samuel (the wise man), but unfortunately he has been elected, "fished," and caught by the Master, who is the object of the narrative's philosophical inquiry. In Cixous's version of the story of Jonah and the whale, Jonas plays the role of Saint George awaiting the momentous meeting with his adversary. Then we see Jonas inside the whale, divided between two levels of emptiness and fullness. Although Jonas identifies with God, God appears to be both primitive and uncaring. This philosophical but biblically grounded inquiry deals then with God's essence, with the relation of man/woman to the absolute as well as with humanity's need to create an absolute in the first place. It introduces the reader to the issues of women and spirituality, women and the absolute, sexual difference and the absolute.

In "Anagramme" Cixous presents the reader with a vibrant interior monologue. With its antirationalist approach (reminding the reader, paradoxically, of a prayer) "Anagramme" focuses on understanding the inherent philosophical and spiritual relationship between life and death. This relationship is echoed by the story's title as the text clearly attempts to redefine the two concepts of life and death and, playing with their ordering, reverse them. A disembodied, desexed male voice confronts, within a dream state, the implications of life and death. Understanding death is understanding life, and the narrator wishes to control his impending death by accepting it, wishing it, desiring it, and comprehending it in physical as well as mental terms.

Solitude and destruction permeate all human relationships, and one experiences an acute form of solitude in the face of death. Because death permeates all human relationships, the sole "remedies" available are generosity, loving, contemplation, and self-denial. Yet at the same time it is only consciousness and knowledge that give death its meaning: "I could only be my own death" (*Le Prénom de Dieu,* 194). Reversal of the absolute is the key here, which is clearly to be understood in spiritual terms, given the text's religious symbolism. "Anagramme" allows the reader access to the human voice as it attempts to understand and comprehend absolutes. The text concentrates as well on the desire to participate in one's own destiny through conscious and active perception and inquiry. Dealing with the dual concepts of "consciousness" and "knowledge," the last sentence of the text suggests, as always with Cixous echoing Derrida, an emphasis on the eternal, the cyclical: "And for a long time everything had always already been said" (*Le Prénom de Dieu,* 205).

Although the stories collected in *Le Prénom de Dieu* are interesting examples of Cixous's earliest creative writing efforts, they belong more to a New New Novel approach to writing than to more radical experimental efforts that came in texts such as *Les Commencements* or *Le Troisième Corps.* In matters of thematic concern, however, the stories in this collection point to what are constant preoccupations with Hélène Cixous: the virtual interchangeability and reversibility of real and not-real, the lack of stability in absolute concepts such as truth or presence or history, and the permeable membrane separating life and death.

Dedans (1969)

Winner of France's prestigious Prix Médicis in 1969, Cixous's novel *Dedans (Inside)* has no real plot, no characters in the traditional sense, and no adherence to linear chronology nor to any normal readerly expectations of motivation or cause and effect, even of the fictional variety. Instead, *Inside* presents, in stark contrast to what readers might ordinarily expect of a first-person narrative recounting the death of a daughter's beloved father, a highly dramatic and dramatized account of experiential initiation as the female narrator explores, in agonizing and often painfully graphic scenes, the passionate love (and hatred) she has experienced and continues to experience for her dead father.

The text is divided into two parts—the first devoted to one period in the narrator's life, and the second some 20 years later. The narrator begins her text with the following contradictory and enigmatic preface, which is almost an incantation: "The sun was setting in our beginnings and is rising as we end. I was born in the east I died in the west. The world is small and time is short. I am inside. It is said that love is as strong as death. But death is as strong as love and I am inside. And life is stronger than death, and I am inside. But God is stronger than life and death. It is said that words have power over life and death. In my garden of hell words are my fools. I sit upon a throne of fire and listen to my language. Truth has been."[2] The sun, in its contradictory rising at the ending and setting at the beginning, the twinned and inextricably bound images of love and death, life and death, and the evocation by the narrator of the power of language over both death and life all point to the central thematic concerns of the text. The themes of water (bathing and drowning) and the garden, as well as the narrator's use of the inside/outside, remember/forget, here/there, laugh/cry dichotomies are also focal points.

The narrator begins with a description of her house and tells us, in somewhat enigmatic terms, of her family. She has a brother and a mother, but her father is dead. This "problem" of dealing with the dead father—the love for the dead father and the anger at the father for having died and deserted her—indeed forms the substance of the novel. Each "chapter" or section of *Inside* begins with a sentence, phrase, or single word in capital letters, hence, "OUTSIDE: I SAY FATHER,

MOTHER, GOD, BUT WHAT IS IT? AND MY FATHER IS ROTTING" (*Inside,* 16). Each textual fragment has an internal logic based within the psychic reality of the narrator, either in a total state of dreaming or in a kind of half-way state between dreaming and waking.

This novel is about what is means to be a daughter within a family structure as described in psychosexual terms by the world of psychoanalysis, although this is also a text that attempts to decipher or uncover that same space by the stripping away of layers within a specific feminine psyche and in a nontraditional narrative fashion. Repressed images abound: of sexual relations with the father, of bodily fusion with the father, of hatred of the mother (for "stealing" the father from the daughter, for not protecting the memory of the father sufficiently after he is dead), and of incestuous coupling with the brother. There are also long lyrical reminiscences about the womanly linkages within the narrator's remembered (and disremembered) pasts. In many ways a personal or subjective novel, finding its deepest source most probably in Cixous's own traumatic loss of her father, *Inside* is at the same time a universal depiction of a feminine psyche in crisis.

The narrator measures time—the time of her life, from "yesterday" (before the death of the father), when she had been "fragile and all-powerful at the same time," and where she had "the right to rule in a world created for my pleasure" (*Inside,* 17). Following her "secret father," the narrator experiences in dreams what her psyche has constructed as the father-daughter relationship. "I forgot the limits, I forgot the beginning, I mixed up the end with the curve of his arms, thinking I was in the inalterable center" (*Inside,* 21). Yet death comes, taking the present father away: "To me had come down upon me with all the weight of its waters, which the sky could no longer contain" (*Inside,* 22). Memories return to haunt her—her father shaving, family outings to the zoo or to the museum. There is denial of the death as well as anger.

Incidents within "real life" following the father's death become textual triggers linking the daughter's body to the father's. The narrator's mother studies the diagram of the male body in a large reference book entitled *Man;* the turning of the mattress elicits a long imaginary reminiscence of sharing the father's bed, as well as the narrator's grandmother's recollections of being in bed with her young son. The narrator even "kills" her mother in her mind, thus allowing herself to recapture the father: "how young and beautiful we are, how strong and full we are, if the Hand of God closes upon us; I knew very well that he would return, I knew, he knew" (*Inside,* 49).

Like all human beings confronted with the "reality" of the death of a loved one, or, indeed, confronted with the certainty of their own mortality, the narrator of *Inside* feels denial, anger, sorrow, and confusion as she confronts the loss of the father. For the narrator, the father is psychically split into the dead father and the "live" or "secret" father; other splittings include the "real" corporeal father (who is now dead but remembered corporeally by the daughter, both in day and night dreaming) and the psychic father who is necessary in her mind. She states the problem thus: "Now, planted between my father and me, were death and God, arguing, and on death's side were also every habit and blind belief, then the other and the kinsmen, then the city, my ignorance and my father's fragile body; and on God's side, all the disbeliefs, the fear, the indifference of my kinsmen, and the hatred of the others, there was the forbidden, the accepted, my father's age and mine" (*Inside,* 53). But, she fantasizes, if she and her father could only become "one flesh," there would be no room for anything or anyone to come between them. Every night, the narrator tells us, she would go back to her father, "in our private silent space, within our worldless immortality" (*Inside,* 54). Scenes of visitation of graveyards in this text represent for the narrator the impossibility—which is at the same time the only possibility remaining for her—of communicating with her father. The father-within-the-daughter—the internalized father—still does speak to her, however.

Inside frames other narratives as well within the narrator's basic story of death, loss, and recuperation: the story of the marriage of the narrator's parents and the story of the marriage of the narrator's paternal grandparents are told and retold within the main narrative framework, yet these subtexts constantly avoid representation of anything tangible within the "real" autobiographical world of Cixous herself or, indeed, within the fictive "life" of the grandmother (whom the narrator calls the Beast). The grandmother's "killing" of her husband, her incestuous love for her son, her physical playing out in a hysterical way the grief of losing her child are simply permutations of the themes of love and loss.

The narrator gives herself over to the voices surrounding her consciousness. What she learns in the course of her psychic journey is summed up in five points. She has discovered something about the act of birth—just before or just after coming out of the womb. She has realized that it is important to personally participate in the event. She discovers that sex is determined independently of anatomical and physiological requirements, whence the conflicts or contradictions that often follow, after "being born" into the world. She believes that other worlds must have existed, coexisiting in time and space with her own world but inaccessible, and that "the only incontestable difference is not that of sex or age or strength, but that of the living and the dead: the former have all the power, which they don't always know how to use, the others have only knowledge without power" (*Inside,* 79).

The narrator tells her story in nonlinear fragmented blocks of text. At times there are comprehensible logical linkages between them—the memory of watching her father shaving at the mirror leads to memories of her father in the hospital; the sensual memory (scent of lemon, touch of hot sun on skin) leads to narrational recapitulations of a family event (a trip to the zoo or to the museum), yet one of the important structural principles upon which the novel is based is an apparent lack of structuring consistency.

The second section of *Inside* has, as an orientation point for the reader, a time gap of 20 years separating it from part 1. The narrator has now returned to her first home, the city where she was born and where her father died. This second section also combines the psychic pain of a father's death and the loss of the father's love, both in its emotional sense and in its fantasized sexual sense as well, with the loss of an adult lover. Intermingled with the visit to the cemetery, where her father's tomb is marked by a sprig of yellow jasmine, are the memories of other loves: "All the men who have not been him die in my last lover" (*Inside,* 104). Scenes that recall the loss of a lover (an argument in a restaurant, the giving of a hand, the taking away of a hand) combine with images of severed fingers, scenes of castration, and the internalized return of the father after his death as experienced by the daughter.

The narrator makes a final dream visit to the dead father, and when she is sure he has come back for the last time, she returns to the clothes closet of childhood memory, slipping on a blue dress ("like the sea where my body has grown, slept, aged" [*Inside,* 134]). She lies down on the bed, and the dress itself undergoes a metamorphosis, enlarges, turns green. When night comes, the narrator runs through the streets of the town ("a raving morning glory"), finally reaching the walls. The white door opens for her, and the blue door fades away: "through the white one goes my flesh on fire, my soul streams through the blue" (*Inside,* 135). "Someone" goes through the white door at the same time as the narrator, tearing off a piece of her blue dress. Through the space of the tear the narrator then sees "an old, white, misshapen thigh floating in skin too big for it." She recognizes herself:

> It is me tomorrow and I'm already thirty and could be sixty in my young girl's dress, and I sit down on the granite terrace of the last house. We

form the eternal couple, me in my blue dress from the old days, he in his granite suit. Now I'm sick and tired of standing at the shores of death and I'm sick of substitutes. And though I am the princess of anterior time and the daughter of a dead god, and the mistress of tombstone inscriptions, of books of stone, of seawater gowns, I am not happy. I want him to come, I deplore loneliness, boredom, deception, I, too, am betrayed, like his mother, I hate beauty, dust, patience, passion, the stubborn wish for death, silence, the nobility of the soul, the deprivation of the body, and I rejoice in my power to speak, in the fact that I am ten years old, thirty years old or sixty, and that I can say kiss off kiss off to death. (*Inside,* 135)

The last words of *Inside,* however, are given to the dead father to speak: "I shall see you beyond walls and time. If you will have me I will hold you in my arms and we shall create new tales. I shall ask your forgiveness. You will be up above and down below and I shall be inside. Outside, the mystery of things will dry up, under the sun the generations will wash up worlds over words, but inside we shall have stopped dying" (*Inside,* 136).

Les Commencements (1970) and *Le Troisième Corps* (1970)

Following the short stories of *Le Prénom de Dieu,* with their New New Novel techniques and the haunting variation of the Oedipal story of *Inside,* Hélène Cixous published two complementary texts in 1970: *Les Commencements (Beginnings)* and *Le Troisième Corps (The Third Body).* A short novella published in 1971, *Un vrai jardin* ("A True Garden"), as well as a third text published in 1972, *Neutre (Neuter),* seem to comment on each other and are perhaps best considered together.

In *Les Commencements* Cixous places at the center of her narrative Titian's painting of Saint George but allows the subject of the portrait, both as "angel" and "eagle" (*ange/aigle*), to step out from his position within the frame of the painting and literally represent the act of representation itself. Like many of Cixous's theoretical productions of this period, *Les Commencements* relies heavily on wordplay and on the ambiguous doubling of meanings. *Aile* and *plume* are prominent (as wings, but also as feather and pen) as well as *uccello* (bird) and *ocelle* (little eye). The text moves in totally nonlinear fashion, constantly undergoing splittings and fusions, even at the level of Saint George's name (*sein/gorge, sang, geint, singe*—breast, throat, blood, bemoan, monkey). As is common in

Cixous's writing, given her interest in philosophical and linguistic debates of the day, "The subject as effect of the signifier exists only in relation to other signifiers" (Conley 1984, 35).

The shifting text of *Les Commencements* is viewed internally by the eye of "Essor," an eye that is located on the narrator's foot. The narrator's intense desire for Saint George culminates in her "intersection" with him. The word used at this point in the text reads triply as *essor* ("jump"), *et sort* ("and leaves"), *des sorts* ("of destinies," "of fate"). Cixous's father's name (Georges) is coupled in *Les Commencements* with the name of her mother (Eve). With the arrival of Eve, indeed, the text turns toward a different kind of "beginning"—one associated with the mother's lineage rather than the father's. The feeling engendered by the mother—with numerous textual allusions to openness, openness especially to the sea/mother (*mer/mère*)—is one of "absolute vertigo that comes from the heart, not from intelligence with its machinations of possible and impossible" (Conley 1984, 36). This questioning of paternal authority indeed transforms a singular "beginning" or origin into a plurality of beginnings, and the question of the mother allows us to see that she is almost *without* beginning. She is, in fact, in the Derridean sense, "always already there."

In *Les Commencements* Cixous plays with the psychoanalytical concepts surrounding family structure (Georges the father and Eva the mother) in such a way as to question the origin of "self" and "being," to question the very concept of existence. Yet as in much of Cixous's writing of this period, the narration remains under the sign of the dream:

> I was in the dream and the dream was in my will. I was preoccupied by the locus where I was dreaming. There, I was for the first time of an innocence which did not know itself, which did not know me any longer and which could not be seen and which was this inconceivable and real margin where I could be in the dream while it was within me, where I was not bothered by having entrails for skin. This innocence had no common or proper noun. It is the only name which I had to qualify later on, in order to talk to Saint George, the condition of sovereign indifference which would read me there where everything is possible because succession has not been introduced yet.[3]

Le Troisième Corps should be considered as a companion volume to *Les Commencements.* Again written in nonsequential style, it is a complex associative text that weaves references to other works into its own narrative line, causing disruption at every turn. The female narrator of this text writes with her hollow "phallus"—a phallus that bears the highly unusual name of "T.t." (with multiple possible meanings from *Tod* ["death" in German] and *tôt* ["soon"] to Thoth [the Egyptian god of knowledge]). She inhabits, as does the narrator of *Les Commencements,* a dream world in which there is no stability of the first-person subject.

The "plot" of *Le Troisième Corps* revolves around the writing out or rewriting of the narrator's various dreams. These dream narratives, which find their origins in texts by Wilhelm Jensen, Freud, and Kleist, involve for the most part natural disasters—earthquakes, volcanic eruptions, and war. Just as the oneiric (dream-related) world constantly allows for multiple contradiction, ambiguity, and absence of logic, so the writing practice here visible in *Le Troisième Corps* grounds itself in endlessly swirling images without causal links.

A key work forming part of the ever-shifting textual ground in *Le Troisième Corps* is Jensen's "Gradiva," as commented upon by Freud. In this text the male protagonist, Hanold Norbert, falls in love with Zoë Bertgang yet represses his desire for her, transferring it instead to Gradiva, a female figure from a Roman bas-relief whom Norbert believes died and was buried during the volcanic eruption of Pompeii. During a trip to Pompeii, Norbert searches for his "love" but sees Gradiva flitting in and out between the columns like a lizard. Playing on the French *lizard* (lizard) and *lézarde* (fissure), Cixous produces a text that plays on the intersections of differences. Gradiva (the one who advances) and Zoë ("life" in Greek) *Bert*gang (*Bert* is German for walk or step) meet with Nor*bert,* demonstrating the dichotomous doublings of north and south, masculine and feminine.

In the actual bas-relief, Gradiva's foot is slightly lifted above the ground, a posture that gives her a kind of frozen verticality, one that resembles a dancing movement upward. She wears sandals—sandals that have a direct link within the text to the white sandals Cixous recalls from her own childhood. Just as Gradiva's step is never "grounded" but is always almost ready to escape, so the text's writing never becomes fixed or immobilized. Indeed, this text, in a slightly different manner from *Les Commencements,* attempts the representation of the act of representation or, indeed, of writing itself.

A second text that is crucial for an appreciation of Cixous's *Le Troisième Corps* is Kleist's *Earthquake in Chile.* This text presents the story of two lovers, Jeronimo and Josepha, who have been condemned by society and are about to be executed. At the last moment, however, the doomed lovers are rescued by a natural catastrophe—an earthquake that destroys their prison walls and allows them to escape. Their reprieve is short-lived, however, and they end up paying for their transgression with their lives. The final text woven by Cixous into the vertiginous text of *Le Troisième Corps* is another text by Kleist, *The Marquise von O,* in which Count F continually manipulates the strands of the text. The phonetic *f* points variously to fire, phallus, friction, fiction.

The general impression the reader receives after finishing *Les Commencements* and *Le Troisième Corps* is one of richly evocative dream narratives shot through with intertextual references to the visual arts and to other literary works, as well as, of course, to the original historical events upon which the previous fictions were based. Interestingly enough, even though these texts have never been translated, initially because they were considered too difficult, with the passage of 20 years they begin to shed more light on the Cixousian oeuvre.

Neutre (1971)

Neutre (the title could be translated simply as *Neuter*) carries with it in French, as it does in English, a multiplicity of signification—from the gender-based sense of neuter, having neither male nor female traits or, conversely, having no marked sexual position at all, to a more generalized sense of lacking in affective reaction to words or events. Like *Les Commencements* and *Le Troisième Corps,* it carries the generic identifying marker of *roman.* Marked even more boldly by the postmodern tendencies observed in the paired novels of the previous year, however, *Neutre* is a novel that is at once text, textual analysis, and dream—with dream analysis constantly woven into the novelistic fabric.

Three formally identified epigraphs and two other quotations mark the text's opening: Cixous first quotes the epigraph (from Sir Thomas Browne's *Urn-Burial*) used by Poe as his epigraph to *The Murders in the Rue Morgue,* then a passage from Poe's *Murders in the Rue Morgue,* then Ferdinand de Saussure's description of the chess game as analogous to language, followed by Herodotus's retelling of the phoenix myth, and, finally, a quotation from Freud's *Interpretation of Dreams.* As always in Cixous, this epigrammatic material is crucial to an understanding of the reading process necessary to decoding the text. Or, perhaps more modestly, some basic appreciation or contextualization of the epigraphs provides an initial road map for the reader to follow in the reading process.

The Browne quote points us to the songs the Sirens sang and the name Achilles assumed when he was among women, and the Poe excerpt, a description of the analytic ability of Poe's detective Dupin, features "the old philosophy of the Bi-Part Soul . . . —the creative and the resolvant."[4] Cixous's use of the Saussurean analogy between chess and language opens up the field of linguistic play of signifier and signified, while the Herodotus retelling of the phoenix myth (in which the body of the dead father is transported from Arabia to Helios in an egg by the son) is not only reminiscent of Saint George in *Le Troisième Corps* but reminds the reader as well that within the Phoenix there is beginning and ending, creation and destruction, masculine and feminine. Finally, of course, the quotation from Freud's *Interpretation of Dreams* gives us the clue as to the "how" of reading this text: just as dreams give their content to us in the form of what Freud refers to as "hieroglyphs," so does the Cixousian text present a kind of linguistic dream rebus to be solved. In dream analysis each "image" from the dream is replaced by a syllable or a word in order to discover the "meaning" of the dreamer's text.

Neutre is divided into seven sections of varying lengths with a dreamlike, nonlinear connective pattern among them. The first section is entitled "Actors, Plays, and Ghosts." Among these Cixous includes analyst, subject, *récit,* text, lonza, chance, the chain of signifiers son/thread/threads *(fils/fil/fils),* and various word associations with linguistic trees involving ground and words beginning with *s*. This list of "characters" and "plots" provides us with a set of playing pieces with which to work. The title itself appears prominently within the context of giving birth (or rather, giving birth to oneself)—the one is never without the other. The objective of the *récit* (as it can be seen to be a *récit* of the *récit)* is to put together as many parts of its own corpus (or corpse or body) as possible, to "marry" the different and the same. The text is about polysemy, which is marvelously illustrated by Cixous's autobiographical reference to her German grandmother's *Gefüllte Kuchen,* which in its layers of cream and pastry must be eaten and enjoyed, layer after layer, but all layers at once, just as the text is processed by the reader.

The second section of *Neutre* is entitled "Chance—the Motif of the Belly." The references in the section's title are, as always, multiple: *hasart* in French is spelled with a *t* rather than a *d,* thus giving (in English-French combination) "has art." Cixous will continue this wordplay in the next section, when she puns on the name of Mozart. The motif of the belly is, of course, a reference to the womb and childbirth, since for Cixous, birth and writing are always intimately connected, at least imagistically. The reader is given a long list of possibilities: this book

is—my mother, despite myself, however,
ne-uter (born from the uterus, neuter)
a series of impossible tête-à-têtes
passion of/for the text
accompanied by a huge concours of people, birds, circumstances
nightmares, and
things seen by the "mind"
an effacement (erasure) (*Neutre,* 33)

In the novel's third section, "And Why Mozart?" the "author" appears for the first time, intervening in the text like Poe's Dupin and metamorphosing into the ghost of Hamlet's father (Cixous habitually has many allusions to Shakespeare in her texts; here they are mostly to *Hamlet* and *Julius Caesar*). The play on the name of Mozart (*mots-arts*) is illustrative of the writer's incredible facility with language: *"Par les mots et les arts, et par le morceau qui recoupe (ha)zart et par anagrammes et condition humaine, par l'argent et la mort"* ("By words and arts and by the music which combines chance and human condition, by money and death"). The Freudian concept that everything that has been lost will be found again and will return again in dream is illustrated by the example of the dreamer/reader receiving images in succession, in alternating colors of red and yellow, of all that she/he has lost.

Cixous presents various images of the Earth (the planet as well as the substantive possibilities of *ground/dirt/basis*), outlines the eternal question of dualities, and then centers on the situation of the subject. Turning to an analogy between the family as system and the game of chess, she writes, "In reality the family system is a sentence without a subject but a sentence overrun by action/the verb" (*Neutre,* 50). The subject is "described" as having "two Eyes"—one for looking behind, one for looking ahead (two eyes/two "I"s); there are several substantial references to the activities of moles (*la taupe*) as animals who burrow beneath the ground, making various rooms in their burrows in order to protect themselves from enemy attack. The section concludes with a convoluted allusive passage that sends the reader to Poe's "William Wilson."

The fourth section, "The Child, Issue from the Loss of Such an S . . . ; Could He Be Named Light?" or "The *Daskind*/Child Motif," again combines the metaphor of childbirth and textual genesis and contains a highly provocative analysis of the role of male and female in procreation. Cixous, like many French women writers of this period, plays on the *mer/mère* dichotomy available to her in French (the sea/mother), using the example of birth to illustrate the problematic position of the subject within discourse, within the *récit.*

There is a lengthy reference to Freud's concept of the uncanny, a text that will traverse Cixous's writing again and again. Is the subject, then, nothing more than a "mother"? "Thus, carrying its art to the highest point of cruelty, from black sea [mer] to white mother [mère], our *Récit* places two Queens in opposition, one deprived of all property, driven to the edge of the imagination, almost invisible, the other threatened with abandonment by a son who wants only her" (*Neutre,* 97). If the die is already cast, continues the text, then *"cette histoire n'est qu'un conte"* ("this story is nothing more than a story"). If it is not, then this *conte* is but one of the monstrous facets of a dream. And if this is a dream, then anything goes: everything can return, even the dead, and certainly children (one's childhood) and names.

At this point a bizarre female character enters and speaks to the mother (who has just given birth). The newcomer has no breasts, appears grey and dried up, and seems to be angry with the mother. She asks that the child be handed over and insists that it is her right to hold the child and that the child should be given her name: Light. When the woman draws nearer, it is clear why she speaks so strangely: her own face is perfectly smooth, without a single eye. What are all these biological or semiological games for? Their purpose is to have names carried, transported without any particular regard for semantics. It works very hard in order to make appear, by the complicated play of each figure on all the other faces, to produce the eye—"capable of putting together day and night or worse, to cause to appear a kind of Eye-son ignorant and prescient at one and the same time" (*Neutre,* 100). There is also "Hysterical-Eye," the one resembling the lonza, a leopard whose number of spots varies (even or odd) according to whether its intention is to attract or to flee.

The first-person narrator feels a split between *I* as mother of the dead child and *I* as observer of the other woman, mother of the dead child. She returns to the bedside of the dying son; in the other room the unmoving child is cold and permanently attached to the mother. Seen by the "author," this object is simply the maternal breast; but for the subject, who still works through word associatons, the situation remains problematic. The *récit,* however, which is constantly moving and which expresses anguish and pain at any sign of stoppage, keeps the anxiety level high by noting the "lack" in this scene, the other breast. Indeed, the woman has but one breast, which to the first-person narrator is the equivalent of the "bad breast" in the child-psychoanalysis theories of Melanie Klein.

The book itself is a production of the text, which dates from time immemorial; thus it is a spirit, a ghost that haunts us and a descendant as well. The descent, which is described paradoxically as both horizontal and vertical, invisibly digs into the two axes of language. On the allegorical level it mimics in its path a double reading of history and is itself divided between diachrony and synchronicity, between fear and pleasure, disgust and desire. The feeling is virtually unspeakable; the analyst, for whom the return of the book is not earth shattering, knows but does not feel what the text feels but does not know. If the text could reread itself, the unspeakable would be evident: it would remember; it would speak. In the following section, "La 'F'onte des genes," textual transformation "melts" *(fondre)* everything down into the magical word *Sorbet*—playing on the duality between the melting of an ice-based dessert and the printing trade where letters are placed in a font. In turn, "La Re-fonte des Genes" shows the sorbet that resuscitates the dead subject.

What *Neutre* is about, then, is the production of the text and its reproduction through the process of reading and analysis. Just as the dream must be interpreted by the analyst in order to inject meaning into the patient's psychic process, the literary fiction, here called a "novel" but surely "novel" only in the most ironic sense of the term, can be interpreted by the reader in order to give "meaning" to the novelist's process of writing. And just as interpretations of dream hieroglyphs are neither unitary nor definitive, so the search for meaning for the literary text remains elusive and ever mobile. The *récit* and *sujet* are constantly in pursuit, one of the other, and the entire process of "interpretation" in this Cixousian text is very much one of Chinese boxes or Russian dolls or layers upon layers of pastry—one layer constantly leading to another and to another. Yet the point of all this is, in the final analysis, to make sense of things that at first seem totally illogical or nonsensical according to received knowledge.

Neutre is a fine example of what some call Cixous's brilliance and what others call her pretentiousness during the early stages of her creative writing. It seems clear that Cixous's readings of Freud, the German romantics, and Poe have left their mark. She is linguistically and thematically gifted and quite able to out-Freud Freud. The reader/analyst is placed in the somewhat difficult position of being required to be as conversant with Freud as Cixous is and to be at least passingly acquainted with Friedrich Hölderlin, Hoffmann, Poe, Hegel, and Shakespeare, as well as with specific texts—"William Wilson" and the other tales of Poe discussed in the essays in *Prénoms de personne,* Hoffmann's *Sandman,* Kleist's *Penthesileia.*

One of the techniques that helps to make reading Cixous during this stage of her literary development less arduous is to simply consider each text as a kind of puzzle for which there are many possible solutions—solutions that will change and metamorphose with each successive reading. It is also desirable to do as much reading outside the text as possible, as Cixous's own choice of readings and her "readings" of those texts may at first confuse or puzzle. The more Cixous texts the reader comes to know, however, the more readily connections can be made. Just as one could say of Joyce, reading "in" Cixous is important, but reading "through" Cixous is probably an impossibility. If, however, a ludic posture is taken in the reading process, that spirit of playfulness will make the reading and interpretive tasks easier. The site of criticism is only "difficult" if we are committed to finding The Answer, The Word, or "God"—possibilities that Cixous constantly denies us. Denying us that, however, she offers us something equally intriguing.

Un vrai jardin (1971)

Un vrai jardin ("A True Garden") is generically titled a "poetic novella" and is a short text of only some 20-odd pages. Nonetheless, it is profoundly marked by the presence of the Cixousian voice—one that links the world of the contemporary author to a world of the first music, the first vocal expression of love. *Un vrai jardin* presents a first-person narrator who, from all grammatical indications, is male, yet the sexual ambiguity of Cixous's writing is here, as elsewhere, maintained. As do many of the stories in *Le Prénom de Dieu,* the text presents a miniaturized Cixousian world in allegorical form.

The textual world of *Un vrai jardin* is again the world of dream—or, rather, that state favored by Hélène Cixous: one located somewhere between dream and consciousness and where the "reality" of the garden described by the narrator is placed in quotation marks in order to signal its ambiguous status. The title, too, is intriguing in a Cixousian way. Indeed, what is a "real" garden? A garden rooted in reality rather than in a dream? A genuine garden rather than a fake or false garden? A garden? A park? For riding ponies, jogging, or pushing babies in prams? The Garden of Eden? Not the Garden of Eden?

The narrator enters the garden, the park, noting its reality because of the existence of earth within it. Within the garden or park the narrator is enclosed in a world that is the "not outside." Outside, and in the distance, the narrator notes that people are at war. Bombs fall and rip the "tent roof" of the sky, whose smooth surface is thus distorted. The narrator has apparently lost his identity: "I had a name. The city had a name, everyone had one except for the park which was just called the park because there was only one. But since no one called me anything, my name ended up falling into disuse."[5]

The narrator struggles with solitude and silence, retreating into unconscious memory in an attempt to recover an original "being with." He notes that he "must have been with someone, perhaps even inside someone," since he has a navel in the middle of his belly. Yet even this piece of knowledge has become questionable to the narrator ever since one of the park's nursemaids, sticking the end of her umbrella into his navel as she spoke, had announced to the park wardens that they really ought not to allow such "garbage" to remain inside. This gesture, which had hurt the narrator "both physically and mentally," gave him as well an intolerable level of self-doubt, which finally affects his entire life and being. Because he can no longer remember ever being elsewhere, nor what there was outside nor what had been behind him when he'd entered, he begins to suspect the worst—that in a world where one could be treated the way the nursemaid had treated him, anything can happen. Even trying to remember his own name seems to be a dangerous undertaking, for what if, indeed, it really was a name like "garbage" or something worse, which would make him even more insignificant? The image of the phallic umbrella haunts the narrator, for it is by the umbrella (we hear the echos here of the French *ombrelle* and *nombril*) and its pointing gesture that the narrator has become certain that the nursemaid meant him. The nursemaid herself assumes enormous proportions in the eyes of the narrator. As he sees her in memory standing so that her white uniform completely fills the visual field, his eyes totally fill by her "milky opacity" (*Un vrai jardin,* 14).

The narrator describes his "selective myopia" that allows him to make out lines, perspectives, or objects as well as providing photographic vision of both plants and insects. But, in contrast, the narrator sees human beings with great difficulty, only being able to distinguish the difference between the nursemaids and the park wardens by the color of their respective uniforms (white for nursemaids, blue for wardens), and the crowd of children, who are smaller than the adults and brighter and more variegated in terms of color. Doubt sets in, and the narrator, now truly regretting the loss of his name, settles once more into his solitude and thinks about the bombs exploding outside, working through three "activities": desiring, believing, and praying. Since the narrator does not know any prayers, he is obliged to invent one, which he does, accompanying it with a child's offering of cricket feet, butterfly wings, laying them out in the shape of flowers.

A second incident then occurs that also threatens the narrator's already precarious sense of self. Two park wardens pass by, one saying to the other, "Get that thing (*ça*) out of here!" The narrator admits to feeling less pain at this remark than at the remark made by the nursemaid, but he is aware that a regression of sorts has occurred; whereas formerly he was still on the margins of the animal kingdom, he has now been relegated to the realm of the "indefinable" (*Un vrai jardin,* 18). Unable even to write a letter of protest (since he has no signature), the narrator discovers that rather than being an object of hatred for the two wardens, he is merely a pawn in their psychological games—a situation that leaves him at first terrified, then cold, then indifferent. To protect himself from any possible attack from the wardens, however, the narrator develops a plan whereby he will allow them to think that "someone" will soon be coming to pick him up. "I wouldn't have stayed around so long if I hadn't been waiting for my father" (*Un vrai jardin,* 20), he tells them. The wardens then shout, "There he is! There he is!"

The narrator hastens to explain that "father" had merely been intended as a metaphor but that the wardens had understood the word literally, and now "believed" that they had seen him. The narrator in turn believes it his duty to believe them. ("Your father's waiting for you, hurry up, hurry up," the wardens shout confidently.) The narrator begins to run, thinking that if his father were waiting for him, it was not because the narrator had said he was waiting but because by saying so the narrator had somehow intuited his father's arrival. The narrator, with his poor vision, runs and runs, encouraged by the nursemaids who urge him on toward the embankment where he arrives at last, flinging himself headlong onto the ochre-colored surface, then crawling forward. He has noticed the silence surrounding him, sees "blackness" very near. He leaps forward with all his might and embraces the plump black-stockinged legs of an unfamiliar nursemaid: "I've got him!" she cries, spreading her legs. The narrator falls in, and a great shout of laughter goes up. The narrator feels a sudden burst of shame, for between the nursemaid's legs there is nothing.

The narrator becomes convinced that he is intimately linked to the garden itself, that he and the garden are made of the same substance, and in his new relationship, almost Beckettian in its primitive sense of time and space, he grasps a handful of sand. Bombs fall in the garden;

the nursemaids and wardens rush by. Finally, the narrator is alone. A moment later a bomb drops precisely at the spot where the narrator had believed his navel to be. The narrator explodes. In the past he would have experienced fear, but now the explosion is a joyous one, of life in death, since now, in his words, "I knew that I was the garden. I was the garden, I was inside, I was made of unique diamonds, and I didn't have a name. Earth, Earth, I cried" (*Un vrai jardin,* 34).

The search for origins presented in this text is a common Cixousian topos—one that owes much of its significance to the discourse of psychoanalysis. Surface elements easily recognized include the nursemaid mother armed with the phallic umbrella, amnesia regarding the proper name, the sense of shame when "pointed to" by others, and selective myopia that does not allow the conscious mind access to those memories constantly repressed within the unconscious—the white bone, the phallus seen but "not seen" as the indicator of sexual identity, the confusion (in French) between *terre* and *père* (earth and father) as source of life. Biblical references and mythological ones (the Garden of Eden, the "laughter of the gods") are omnipresent. Everything must be read simultaneously in an effort to hold the text together—beginning and ending, question and answer, inside and outside—in a kind of wonderfully magical (because mentally vertiginous) oscillatory movement that produces textual energy.

Constant reversals of death and life—of death in life and life in death—of origins and beginnings, and of disappearances and endings, as well as possible gender reversals or transmutations of male and female, become the reader's guideposts. Where one reads *life* in Cixous, one reads, of necessity, *death* as well. This is not, however, to fall into the ever-enticing trap of dualistic thinking. And/or, both/and, neither/nor are abolished in Cixousian textual space in order to be reenclosed within a unified mental space that can then allow all difference its being.

Tombe (1973)

Tombe, which bears the generic marker of novel, is the story of a love triangle—the drama of a pair of lovers facing death, which in the text is often seen as the double of love itself. This ménage à trois is constantly pivoting, with Death at times becoming the other spouse, under the name of *l'Apparente.* Cixous describes the action of the plot as centered on several mythical places: in a garden in Peru, in a great high-poster bed, in a hotel room, or (shades of *The Arabian Nights*) in a "wandering bed" (*lit errant*). Because *Tombe* is set in Cixous's Peruvian city of Pergame (whose name is derived from the Latin parchment [*parchemin*], or writing paper), the writing of the text occurs through a sort of transmutation of sperm into ink. White bed sheets (*draps blancs*) become blank sheets of paper (*feuilles blanches*), and the bodies of the lovers themselves are seen as engraved monuments—monuments to love and to death.

In *Tombe* the final significant site is the place of a chain of signifiers that link myth to a new rewriting. Giving birth to themselves, like the phoenix, the signifiers of *Tombe* (from the French *tomber,* "to fall") incite the renaissance of many and varied intertexts: Adonis, Milton's *Lycidas,* Kleist's *Penthesileia.* Using, as usual, a veritable treasure trove of wordplay, Cixous transforms *lierre* (ivy) into *l'hier* (the past) and *lit/erre* ("wandering bed"); *Amante* (female lover), becomes *la menthe* (mint) and *lamentation* (lamentation), but also *testament* (will, testimony) or *textament* ("loving text," "text of love").

Gilles Deleuze, describing Cixous's style, terms it a new and original kind of writing, which he characterizes as "stroboscopic"—that is, where the *récit* itself becomes a living organism and where the different themes enter into connection, where words form variable figures, according to the associations provoked by the reading process.[6] It is possible that in *Tombe* we have, along with *Partie,* one of Cixous's best examples of Joycean writing.

In *Tombe* creation becomes destruction. The text inscribes dead love, and dead friendship as well. The relationship between Dioniris and Orphelin ("or-fait-lin" = gold turned to cloth, the cloth from which a shroud is made) is key; only desire will be powerful enough to overcome the obstacles that death continually puts in the way of life. The narrator protagonist is transported textually, constantly on the move in the impossible task of overcoming death. The ongoing struggle between Death and Orphelin is represented symbolically in the text by the image of Orphelin stitching away at a tapestry that the various masks of Death continually take apart. As the Fates spin and measure out the thread of life, it is cut again and again, only to be caught up once more and knotted into the fabric.

This "thread of life" serves in *Tombe* as the basis for many kinds of textual embroidery as it is closely connected to the act of writing as a kind of "tracing" on the page: "On the white sheets of the blouse danced thousands of white signs traced by the needle—many-hued, delicate, stamped with echoed traces."[7] Writing appears and then erases itself, only to reappear somewhere else. The embroidered blouse points in turn to the sails of a boat, and the cord that ties the blouse (and that fingers have difficulty unknotting) is the *fil de lin,* which is later transformed into a *fil d'or,* the bed sheet that becomes the shroud (love turned to death).

Claudine Fisher describes *Tombe* as primarily an olfactory text,[8] and indeed the perfumes and aromas of this text are omnipresent: cinnamon and heliotrope, "all the perfumes of Araby," incense, myrtle, and, most important of all, mint. Aromatic mint and wild mint (*la menthe* in French to link with *l'amante*) are connected to the story of Mintha, Hades, and Demeter. As well, mint is an aphrodisiac which, if used improperly, can actually cause sterility rather than fecundity. Although the constant struggle with death may seem to cast a shadow over the text, Cixous in *Tombe* demonstrates her belief that it is through the act of writing itself that she can best counteract the finality of death.

Portrait du soleil (1975)

Portrait du soleil is a deeply autobiographical Cixousian work, but it is not confined to the setting out of descriptive facts and analytical observations about the author's "life." As with Cixous's earlier title, *Le Prénom de Dieu,* the title of *Portrait* shows her continual ironic stance regarding the possibility of depicting something that would blind us if we could actually view it head on. The impossibility of painting the portrait of the sun becomes the pretext for another impossible project: writing a life. Again mixing genres and using a consistently lyrical tone, Cixous weaves her intertextual web through a combination of scenes taken both from dream and eroticized daydreaming.

The opening pages of the text concentrate on the image of the blood orange (*une sanguine*) and center on the phrase: *"L'oranje est mon fruit de naissance et ma fleur prophétique"* ("The orange-I is my birth fruit and my prophetic flower").[9] The first-person narrator tells the reader that seeing, dreaming, and feeling are all accomplished "orangely." On the other side of the orange is blood, the blood of the Mediterranean. We are then introduced to two "characters," Jeor (I/gold) and Dieubis (a double of God), to sand, secrets, and riddles, the most important question of all being: What is "le secret"?

In *Portrait du soleil* Cixous also makes use of material from Freud's famous case study on hysteria, the Dora case: references to throat problems ("It ought to have been possible to begin a sentence with 'I,' but the sentence came out headless, the subject would not come" [*Portrait du soleil,* 17]) and doors ("There is a door in Vienna which everyone can go through but me" [*Portrait du soleil,* 25]) and descriptions of Freud himself point to the difficulty of the female self to find its "voice." A second preoccupation of Cixous in *Portrait du soleil* is the work of Rembrandt. This reference to the famous painting *The Anatomy Lesson* is typical: "Rembrandt had put the entire body into a frame: the cadaver was twice dead, made for the eyes, to attract them and to repulse them and to deceive them with precision: . . . it was neither animal nor human, neither beautiful nor ugly, it was a lesson inscribed within a frame, a geometry of death, with contours, proportions, measurements. That I understood. It was right" (*Portrait du soleil,* 40, 42). Rembrandt's *Samson and Delilah* is described as a monochromatic bad dream, but the autobiographical project finds its energy therein.

In this text the author provides one of the more accessible descriptions of her own writing practice:

> I put things together in order to see the effect: a cosmic kitchen with raw stars, pans of painted beef, slices of orange color or carrot, secret books or lips, everything which is in God's territories; a series of adored furious objects; a field of beets; a series of swimmers in celluloid, unsure of their sex; an unknown woman; my letters . . . to establish the infinite system of possible relationships among the elements, things which go together, terms-objects, semantic contents, language-object, systems of, relations, possibilities, the betweens, the thes, inundate with sense the senses of sensations and see what floats, drench with essence/gasoline the sense of senses and see what flames; see what remains. Not much remains. (*Portrait du soleil,* 55)

There are humorous moments in this text: the narrator dreams that she is with Freud in a supermarket buying chicken, trying to find her coat (made of a smooth animal skin, orange in color), which she discovers hanging on a hook (*Portrait du soleil,* 79). She sees a black hearse coming out of the sky, her funeral hearse filled with flowers, and in dream language confusing the words *mur/mûre* and *pétrir/mûrir* (wall/ripe and "to knead"/"to ripen"), she sees girls coming through a wall (in Algeria) carrying large bowls of bread dough, waiting for it to rise (*Portrait du soleil,* 80, 87).

The narrator constantly returns to Freud's Dora case: in one scene everyone is seated in "the king's" office. He's not there, but you can "smell him," since everyone is smoking, Dora along with all the others. The narrator excuses herself, saying that she has work to do. The text then shifts its focus, moving to a mocking Dora who finds herself in the

"Asile du vrai" (the Asylum of the Truth) and sees the waiting room (all the patients wearing dresses made of matching material except for the narrator, who is the only one without a dress). Virgil then appears, holding Sophie (goddess of female wisdom) by the hand. The narrator begins looking for keys in her purse, which of course allows the text to return to the details of the Dora case—the well-known references to keys and purses and their sexual symbolism.

The activity of writing, too, is a central thematic concern of *Portrait du soleil.* In one passage the narrator describes her attempts to write an essay in English: she constantly produces two superimposed texts—one in Greek, one in English—and has only written two-thirds of a page when she realizes that she is late for a train going to "To-Lose" (Toulouse). She is burdened with a heavy suitcase, very difficult to carry. A taxi arrives, and the narrator, accompanied by her mother and brother, set out on a very crowded road but never reach the station. Suddenly the narrator finds herself alone inside a university, with female students, and she realizes that she has not written the right things. She encounters Hemingway, Jeor, and Dieubis and is invited to travel with Hemingway, although in the dream she is not sure what kind of relationship they have since she's not fond of his writing. At last the narrator finds herself in a strange house with an old man where she spends the night. Still looking for the train station, that narrator meets a young man who takes her there. His age seems to constantly change, as if, the narrator writes, time itself had two strings. Pulling on the left one, the young man appears to be 30; pulling on the right one makes the narrator seem 30. In the end there is no train.

Writing involves the textual braiding of all elements of the dream narrative: muguet (lily of the valley), sand, pearl necklace, flowerpots, marbles, balls. What and how do objects and words signify? "What the lily-of-the-valley says in a dream Mr K says with a jewelry box; what one says with flowers Papa says with pearls; what Dora did not say, her young man said with pictures; what she said to herself with her fingertips her doctor said with smoke; what Dieubis said with balls I no longer know to whom to say" (*Portrait du soleil,* 120). Dora's letter and its multiple readings, the narrator's dream of Madame J (a conflation of Jeor and Madame K from Dora's case), and intertextual allusions to the paintings viewed by Dora point to a key question addressed by *Portrait du soleil:* the definition and identify of self through gender.

Cixous's theoretical intertextual allusions in *Portrait du soleil* are to two philosophers, Friedrich Nietzsche and Georges Bataille. Through the appearance of Dioniris (a combination of the Greek god Dionysus and the Egyptian god Osiris) she opens the possibility of the discussion of the origins of philosophy itself and the birth of tragedy. Her use of Bataille marks, in the words of one critic, "a commitment to moving beyond the categories of the rational and the knowable, towards the site of creation, multiple subjectivity, and the bodily roots of human cultures."[10]

As Dieubis in the text is constantly associated with what is terrifying and traumatizing, Jeor seems to be associated with reintegration. Dioniris, with his dual geneology through Dionysus and Osiris, shares much with them. The parallels in their respective mythologies are clear: both are gods who arrive and whose cult spreads late through their respective cultures, where there are attempts to subordinate them into the existing pantheon. Both represent sacred kings who die and who are dismembered before rising from the dead. Both are popular with the lower classes and are associated with phallic rituals and cults. In Greek culture they are "the same," and Herodotus has written that the Egyptians equated the two as well.

Through the entire voyage of discovery the narrator suffers yet rejoices, finally concluding that "it's sad to learn that I am not the author of my biography, but it's delightful. It's delightful to know that I shall be the biographer of my author" (*Portrait du soleil,* 136). And much later in the text: "As the poet produces himself for being known by his metaphors, we are for being barred and liberated by our itinerary, as we are enlightened by being seen by the sun" (*Portrait du soleil,* 186). The narrator's quest mimes "the Dora effect": the effect of the explosive and irremediable disappearance of the object of desire—without the shadow of a hope for getting it back. This disappearance causes pain that is both doubly felt and reciprocal. The narrator, without the object of desire, cannot even console herself by "seeing herself": "Because I cannot see the object of my desire, I myself am no longer seen, and thus love's pain is doubled" (*Portrait du soleil,* 187).

The narrator's journey lasts "for centuries and hours," carrying her through both the most ancient and the most familiar territory where she sees the "allegory of her historicity." Colonization, decolonization, recuperation, exploitation, and usurpation are everywhere: "Everyone plays at History and refuses to recognize that it is they who are being played" (*Portrait du soleil,* 189). The narrator continues to search for a space in which she can find a stability for expressing what the patriarchal world has thus far denied her. She enters the home of the Prosecutor in order to present her case, only to find that he is away. When he returns, the text turns violent and ends with the sense of impossibility with which it opened: subjectivity for the female subject is elusive, and many attempts to go "beyond" are doomed.

Révolutions pour plus d'un Faust (1975)

Révolutions pour plus d'un Faust (Révolutions for More than One Faust) is a Cixousian text of transformations. In the foreground is the basic question everyone asks of History: What is "reality"? To this question History both gives and denies access, allowing furtive glimpses of partial "truth" but constantly screening it as well, thus obliging the truth seeker to requestion every provisional response received. The main "character" here is Faust himself, a Faust depicted as a traveler journeying toward "the Truth." The text constantly asks by which door, through which point, will he enter onto the scene of the real? A highly intertextual and allusive work, *Révolutions pour plus d'un Faust* provides multiple entry and exit points into the fugitive truth of History and time.

What kind of persons will we be who wish to imagine ourselves and imagine our own power to act? How will we feel pleasure? How will we be transformed when we find ourselves at the intersection of law, desire, the real and the imaginary, action and its representation? How do we move from the visual spectacle to action? What will our "revolutions" be? Just as Homunculus (the little man artificially produced by an alchemist) breaks his phial in order to rejoin the unlimited space of the real (even though it costs him his life), so will the pupil detach itself from the eye of the master, ceasing to belong to a single view or gaze, detaching itself from knowledge. In this way the pupil (read in its double meaning) finally flings itself into the movement of history, where it mingles with the future of all people, sharing in their struggles in all parts of the world. From Brazil to Vietnam, everywhere in the world, there will be new "communes."

A text about transformations, *Révolutions pour plus d'un Faust* is also always in the process of transforming itself, circulating through reflection, fiction, *récit,* and action on more than one level. *Révolutions* provides as well a textual space where the very act of writing is transformed, "revolves" into theater. The real is always a "stage," a place where writing is carried off into history. A "hymn to the forces of life," *Révolutions* moves forward in the fabulous wake of a Faust who is eternally plural, just as history itself. By leaps and bounds, ruptures and flights, the text in an infinite adventure moves us toward meaning.

Two epigraphs open Cixous's text, one taken from Hoffmann's *Kreisleriana* and the other from part 2 of Goethe's *Faust.* The Hoffmann quotation indeed sounds a familiar Cixousian tone: "Lacking a melody, singing, every instrumental ornamentation is like that rich vestment which in Shakespeare's *Tempest* covers no body and hangs from a string, attracting only imbecilic people." The quotation from Goethe is the Homunculus, speaking from his phial: "Come, press me tenderly to your heart! But not too hard—or I fear the glass will break. Here is the order of things. The universe is barely sufficient for the natural; for the artificial we must find an enclosed space." In the opening pages the narrator introduces readers to the great celebration of history, where they are invited to dance, dream, leap, and multiply: "And if, one night, or a day without sunlight, a demon, or a fool, or a devil in disguise, were to slip underneath your covers (reader) or mine, or slip into my solitude, or even into my doubt, and if he were to say, 'I have three voices: one for you, one for me, one for the other.'"[11] The narrator explains that in this case one would become the devil's marionette, and that probably the devil would claim that he had an eye that could travel through space and time, an eye that could read all the books. But there would be one eye that as yet he has not opened. And if he were to invite you to be the "pupil" of this eye, what would you do?

In the narrator's words, "Dream, reader, that here what comes after preceeds. That which will be now is before you. History, too, is a concept without a central core" (*Révolutions,* 12). Like other Cixousian texts, *Révolutions* is organized not into chapters but into fragmented passages of varying lengths that examine, in highly poetic language, virtually all forms of philosophical inquiry and the various relations of the human being to the cosmos. Taken as a whole, they present a restatement of Cixous's preoccupations with beginnings and endings, life and death, love and hatred, and the conceptual circularity and reversibility of all dualities. Among the philosophical appearances or apparitions in this text, we meet Kepler and Tycho, Ephèse, Empèdocle, Elli, Heraclitus, Socrates, Democritus, Dante, Faust, Anaxagore, Neptune, Thalia, Charon, Epicure, Alcibiades, Tc'hen, Egmont, Prometheus, Giordano Bruno, Euphorian—in sum, a kaleidoscopic cast of characters from both history and mythology.

Discussion and, indeed, subversion of various philosophical schools of thought are carried out in imaginary dialogues (between the Fool and the Subject, represented by the Eye and the Pupil) and in various sections of the text titled "Workshops" (*Ateliers*). In these passages multiple voices speak and echo across time and space. "Imagine," says the narrator, "the unimaginable: if you are able to think of a dream which dreams itself without a dreamer; invention without model, construction of destruction; or if you are able to see the moon coming out of the sun's matrice; or if you are able to be the material feminine principle, by uniting itself to its own conception of itself, can reproduce itself, then you as well will have created a wandering monster" (*Révolutions,* 21).

Many passages in *Révolutions pour plus d'un Faust* are drafted in dialogue form, a precursor of Cixous's later writing for the stage. Conversations (often with ironic reference to Socratic dialogue) between the ever-metamorphosing Fool and the narrator are interspersed with overheard dialogues between philosophers, often crossing boundaries of historical place and time. Ephèse argues with an atom and a proton; Agrigente and Elli are involved in a long discussion with the elements of Empèdocle; and Socrates, Democritus, and Heraclitus converse with Dante. Giordano Bruno (1548–1600), burned as a heretic for his beliefs that each individual's view of the world is relative to his position in it, that any absolute truth is beyond statement, and that possible knowledge is unlimited, speaks to Faust, while Galatea, Aphrodite, and other goddesses carry on a grand conversation.

The narrator continues with the quest for "truth" and "cause," wondering if there is a logic or a reason for Death (who has shown itself in many forms during the dream trips made in the company of the Fool) or if Death is part of history. Four horses (white, orange, black, and colorless) then appear, described by the Fool as the representation of the four moments of man in history: birth, construction, destruction, and death (*Révolutions,* 133). A fifth animal resembling a dark, very frizzy poodle, also emerges, the Dog of the Shadow, who leaps toward the narrator, ready for the attack. The narrator sees the other four horses (of the Apocalypse) charging back when suddenly the earth becomes sea, the narrator flings herself into the ocean where the horses can pass over her as long as her swimming movements and their running are synchronized. They pass over her, and the Fool then asks her if she is dreaming. "I think," she tells him, "that I dreamed of an Apocalypse. The earth was sea, and the sea was filled with earth and the four horsemen passed over my body which was swimming between two worlds. At first there was a dog" (*Révolutions,* 135). Laughing, the Fool points to the horizon, where four horses are being guarded by a very small curly-haired dog. "That's the watchdog of History," he tells her. "You dreamed a history of History" (135).

Révolutions pour plus d'un Faust presents the reader with moving depictions of international war and armed conflict—in Europe, in the Far East (the My Lai Massacre in Vietnam, violence in China), and South America (torture in Brazil). Revolution and revolutionaries, death, and destruction are presented, represented, and questioned in a cacaphony of the voices of history: "Histories, quavering voices, polyphonic, breathing which catches its breath and catches it again" (*Révolutions,* 221). Like other Cixous texts of this period, *Révolutions pour plus d'un Faust* is more about process than product, more about questions than answers, more about movement than stability.

Souffles (1975)

Souffles opens with a double epigraph: "Nun hast du mir den ersten Schmerz getan" (from Robert Schumann's song cycle *Frauenliebe und Leben*) and "When the child is to be weaned, his mother resorts to a stronger form of nourishment to keep him from perishing" (from Kierkegaard's *Crainte et Tremblement*) and ends with a repetition of the second epigraph, adding, "Now you have caused me my first pain." As always, Cixous provides readers with several clues as to the best reading process to follow when reading *Souffles* when she uses the paired words *halètement/allaitement* ("gasping for breath"/suckling, nursing). *Souffles* (the title can be read as breath or inspiration in both meanings of the word) is a text for the first voice, *"la première Voix,"* the voice of the mother, the one that touched the woman profoundly in the past. The text, constantly lyrical in its musical sonority, explores the mother-lover in her flesh, her sex, and her "luminous territories" which can no longer be called the dark continent. *Souffles,* published the same year as "The Laugh of the Medusa," is arguably the fictional companion piece to the theoretical manifesto on *écriture féminine.*

Souffles has been described by Cixous herself as "a meditation and a psalm on the passion of a woman." The text attempts to produce an answer to the question "What is it within woman that both suffers and feels sexual pleasure?" As woman journeys toward the source, she passes through her entire history, between Greece and Palestine, encountering along the way "the great mythical bodies in which the masculine and the feminine are blended into one: blind but all-seeing, she traverses her young erotic and bisexual countries."[12] *Souffles* is at once a mother-text, a child-text, and a love-text—a space of genesis and beginnings.

Souffles is "written" through the voice of an anonymous first-person female narrator, who at times uses the third person about "herself." This narrator is never described nor is she located precisely in time or space; she simply narrates a vertiginous variety of experiences in the present or in the past that may or may not be "true." As usual in Cixousian narrative, the feeling of the text is that of the dream state, or, more accurately, a waking dream state of semi-consciousness where past and present, verisimilitude and fantastic are interwoven and intertwined. There is an attempt to replicate to some extent the hallucinatory moment of dream and to allow intense erotic feeling (of a female nature) to be represented within the text. In the words of Dina Sherzer, "During these moments the narrator is free from the control of reason; she is outside the boundaries of normal life in which pragmatic, material activities are carried out. Her body and her mind are open to conscious physical sensations; she freely expresses unconscious, uncontrolled, and spontaneous drives."[13]

Long acknowledged as one of Cixous's most difficult texts, *Souffles* nonetheless presents a clear example of her efforts to undo the force of binary oppositional reasoning and thinking through the development of intricately woven textures of dream narrative—a narrative that is grounded in the continual undermining of those very oppositions. From the first paragraph of the book, a textual representation of the Freudian *fort-da* game and the key phrase "Here is the riddle: from strength comes softness" *("Voici l'énigme: de la force est née la douceur"),* to the final quotations from Schumann's *Frauenliebe und Leben* cited in the epigraph, we accompany the narrator through a multifarious series of female bodily experiences—graphic, poetic descriptions of sexual response located within a female body are common. And, as always, Cixous utilizes her own vast literary culture with intertextual references to Jean Genet, Novalis, the Bible, the story of Samson and Delilah (blindness, hair, and power), Milton's *Samson Agonistes,* and *The Arabian Nights.* "What connection is there between voice and hair and power?" (*Souffles,* 13), asks the narrator. Playing on the name Genet (*Je nais, Je n'*), the narrator explores in fictional form (in contrast to *La Jeune Née,* which presents the same argument in essay format) the quest for woman's voice, the voice of her subjecthood.

The process of birth is not only a physical voyage narrated from the dual position of "birth-giver/mother" as well as "child-in-process-of-being-born," but also in the sense of textual creation: "When he had reached some twenty pages (the child was a text), he became uncontrollable: moreover, I do not know even now if I created him, whole or partially, or if he is still out there, what form he has taken" (*Souffles,* 33). The enigmas posed by the narrator are typically Cixousian: gentleness is born of power; the outside is the inside (*Souffles,* 36); what is exposed is hidden: "By phrases like 'putting on the veils' and others whom I make my friends, I discover the ruses nudity uses to protect itself, the silences truth wraps itself in, the pleasures of interior descents; the taste for the void; and that if one gives oneself over to it, the abyss is generous" (*Souffles,* 51). The process of birth—whether to subjecthood, bodily knowledge, or textuality—is depicted in colors, natural and animal images as well as musical ones. It is also intimately connected to death: "in less time than it takes to be born, it is time to die" (*Souffles,* 66).

The narrator describes a dreamlike vision seen through a window: "a triangular bisexual place, with a tender green pubis, sculpted with Japanese care, and the vibrant stem of an erect pagoda, mixing maleness with feminine *phanères*—and the paths are bordered with genets" (*Souffles,* 80). She then speaks of receiving a small beribboned package (from Novalis, she is told), and she realizes that the art of No and the art of the German romantics are about to combine in order to create a "hybrid theatre": "East and West give themselves to each other in a poetic marriage" (*Souffles,* 80). From the flowers the narrator is drawn into the imaginary world of Genet—a sequence involving suicide, a shirt, and red boots.

LA (1976)

Cixous's writing in *LA* can be best described as existing at the intersections of feminist theory and criticism, philosophical writing, and "fiction." The text is based quite closely on Derrida's reading of Hegel's *Ethics,* and on the Hegelian heroic figure of Antigone, who "placed in a tomb, and dead before the onslaught of marriage, fixes herself, holds herself, benumbs and transfigures herself in this character of eternal sister charging off with her womanly desire" (Conley, 89). Antigone's mausoleum is the reassuring image of unity in Hegelian esthetics, "the most admirable and soothing work of art" (Conley, 89). Using Derrida's reading of Hegel, Cixous in turn will immerse life into Hegelian death.

LA opens with the Egyptian *Book of the Dead {Women} (Le Livre des mortes),* a text that points to the abysmal space out of which the woman writer will come. *LA* is permeated, as are many Cixousian texts of this period, with chants, songs, and lyrical dream texts, all underlining the primacy of voice. The operative thematic word in *LA* is "voyage": "And one travels. As if one had died for that. You flow further—the former ground has been engulfed—with no other destination than further away, where is the way?"[14] And the "object" of the voyage-quest is nothing less than "woman" herself. The introductory pages refer to someone who is "waiting," the possibility of a "new awakening," another language we do not yet speak, the recurring statement that "everything is desire" (*LA,* 10): "Another voice told me silence at night. This woman who so silkily identified herself was not me—but I felt it from the inside of her movement; she was the desire of herself looking for itself in the darkness, with such urgency, the urgent innocence of woman. What all women know not to know, in the body" (*LA,* 12).

The subsection titles Cixous assigns to the *Book of the Dead* are indicative in themselves of the fluid character of this text: "Appearance," "At First Death Dreamed about Her," "She Then Dreams of Death," "Being-in-I." Cixous appears to adopt Kierkegaard's view that woman is nothing but a dream before love awakens her: "She [woman] only awakens at love's touch and before that time she is but a dream. However, in this dream state, one can distinguish two stages: at first, love dreams of her, then she dreams of love" (*LA,* 25). The questions—What does woman know? What is she? What has she forgotten?—return again and again in this text as Cixous juxtaposes dream narratives focusing on strategies (*voler* means flying/stealing) that will enable the articulation of female desire through language (*language/tongue*) and through birth and rebirth via a uniquely maternal lineage.

As in many Cixousian texts, color imagery abounds. Red and blue predominate—red rooms and blue rooms, red blood and blue volubulis, with varying shades of each (carmine, pale pink, mauve, lavender, lapis lazuli). Sensual imagery as well plays a significant part in *LA*: the silken feel of cloth and skin; the taste of honey, salt on the tongue; the sight of brilliantly colored flowers and exotic animals; the sounds of ancient voices and music and the roar of the sea.

In a hypothetical dream state, what if a woman could "see" herself? Cixous describes the first woman "desperately following an unknown woman, having lost all her former pathways, it's unnerving. What this means is that the memory of her life is stripped from her. If her gait is synchronized with the other woman's rhythm, like a voice to the words of a song, that's a good sign. That means that the other life is saved for her" (*LA,* 36–37). What woman desires is the ability to go within herself just as a child might dream of joyfully reconnecting with the mother in dream painlessly (*LA,* 37). Yet to see herself—in a dream—is perhaps to see death but it is also to glimpse the amazing. Introducing the second major part of *LA,* Cixous announces to the reader that here begin the chapters about what it means to "be a woman"—how to explore, to learn about, to discover woman in the self, woman in the other (*LA,* 53–54). This second section of *LA* is entitled "Scope/Brood of the Unknown Woman" *("Portée de l'Inconnue"),* and, as the title indicates, it deals with woman's encounter with woman. Subheadings provide clues as to reading strategies: "Annunciation," "Parvis," "Lamentation against the Emaciated Mother," "Her Gift of Transfers," "En Croissance," "Who? Love," "The Miracle of the Bananas," "Her Art of Passage," "Help-of-My-Sanctuary!" and "Adoration in the Oven." Images of food, both spiritual and corporeal, focus attention on the construction of the female.

The third section is entitled "The Departure of Language to the Light of Day" and deals in a double sense with woman's relationship to language and to her own sexuality, constantly playing on the dual French meaning of *langue* (language/tongue). The exuberance and exhilarating freedom in the language of this section is distinctive. Woman's voice, heard at last through language, allows for the articulation of long-suppressed desire in feminine terms: "I have a tongue/language. I want my tongue/language to come, to experience sexual pleasure. . . . I want vulva. . . . Let her read me the books of my parts, and I myself will advance with the book of my body in my mouth and in my mouth I'll hold the volume that she works for me— . . . I want my tongue to invaginate me" (*LA,* 109–10).

The litany of doubled desire—desire for language, desire for sexual pleasure in terms of female body experience—takes the text up to the narrator's memories of "Osirisque." In this section the operative word becomes *voler* (flying/stealing), and the woman is reminded that where it is a question of the flight or theft of language, she must follow the memories of her very earliest childhood. The visit of the falcon (or the chimera) to the young female child represents the visitation of language and the possibilities it offers, even though sometimes frightening or terrifying, and it brings the narrator back to the question she has posed before: Where does woman begin? "If woman knows the next chapter, she will go out into the night in full light of her day, she will come along and go off into all the parts of her world, she will undergo all her metamorphoses at will. Gravity will be turned upside down! Pregnant and overflowing, she will fill the air with new melodies" (*LA,* 125). The woman who is seeking her identity must clear a path filled with numerous obstacles, traveling in dreams and nightmares "among" various bodies, in order to become "the one whose name is: 'it's you!'" (*LA,* 138).

The fourth section, "Her Preliminary Pleasures," deals with the etymological origins of the "material mother." The common root in *mater* and *materia* allows "woman" to become part of a "material chain"—sometimes hidden but sometimes visible—that allows her to be water, earth (*ma terre*), and forests, where her flesh, like bread dough, becomes the source of life itself. Recurring images of mazes and ladders allow the narrator to discourse on "affirmations of self" and on the art of "liberating her libido." Going forward always involves a contrary movement—one that drags the narrator back toward the terror and traumas of past lives and past experiences. Yet by risking the abyss and the dark labyrinth, she succeeds in the end by spiralling ever upwards, like the frozen upward movement of Gravida's foot.

The final section of *LA,* with the feminized adage "She who laughs last laughs best," speaks of the joyously multiple possibilities for woman and her newfound voice. The density of imagery and the multiplicity of writing styles in this text (one critic has identified 11 different ones) constantly pushes the reading experience to the edge of "stability." In the words of Morag Shiach, "Even in this audacious text, the burden of sustaining an identity which admits others without seeking to eradicate them, and acknowledges the sexual plurality implicit in the image of *'une belle mère masculine'* [a beautiful young masculine mother] is a heavy one" (Shiach, 90). Yet the power of identity "as woman"—what Shiach terms "the power that comes from collective identity, and collective transgression"—has always been of critical importance for Cixous. As she writes in "Castration or Decapitation?": "Culturally speaking, women have wept a great deal, but once the tears are shed, there will be endless laughter instead. Laughter that breaks out, overflows, a humour no one would expect to find in women—which is nonetheless surely their greatest strength because it's a humour that sees man much further away than he has ever been seen. Laughter that shakes the last chapter of my text *LA,* 'she who laughs last.' And her first laugh is at herself."[15]

Partie (1976)

Partie ("Gone," "Game," or "Portion") remains the most Joycean of any of Hélène Cixous's texts. Technically brilliant, this oversized volume is composed of two distinct parts, *Plus-je* (More/no more-I) and *Si-je* (If-I). The book is "reversible," but reading the title on the spine following French publishing custom (which is the reverse of English practice, the title being read from bottom up), the "first" way of opening the book provides the *Plus-je* narrative for some 90 pages, until we arrive at the upside down "ending" of the book's second part, *Si-je* (at page 66). Turning the book around and upside down, we then read the *Si-je* narrative (which has its own title page and a different typography). If we can characterize the *Plus-je* and *Si-je* narratives as ever advancing within the book each toward the other (the endings indeed "meet" at pages 90 and 66, respectively), it is fair to say that the *Plus-je* narrative is extroverted and multiple (more or less *I*), while the *Si-je* (the "iffy" I) is inverted, not open to capture, remaining totally divisible. *Plus-je* and *si-je* are indeed, as one critic has pointed out, involved in a mockery of the Homeric epic.

Rather than attempt an exegesis of this text—a text Cixous herself has said will probably never be translated in full—it is perhaps instructive to consider the following brief fragment translated by Verena Conley:

The alter-echo apostrophizes rudely:
Heguele: The fathermore goes out of him-
self in the other to come back to himself.
Plusje: Every auffher must take off in its
offher . . .
  A nounson bears not
  A nounson be-ears of his own desires
eguele: Forself of one depends on the forself of the offher.
Readhor: and how many states runs Plus-je?
Plusje: me I layover always surplus of nine
my nine
Hegueule: Thusleave a norfathernorson[16]

The philosopher Hegel has been transformed into "Hegueule" ("He shouts") while "auffher" and "offher" are derived from the English *author.* Playing on "mother," *Homère* (Homer) becomes *Ohmère* (Oh, Mother). The constant punning in French, English, and German make this text an incredibly rich one but one that demands a linguistic competence not readily available to most readers.

Angst (1977)

Hélène Cixous's preoccupation with Freudian psychoanalysis reappears again in *Angst,* a novel imprinted by the loss of the father. *Angst* (the title comes directly from philosophical writing on existential dread) explores, in a linguistically induced state of anxiety, the initiatory movement of the female narrator into the world of subjecthood. The novel, dedicated to "the Vital woman, to whom this text did not know it would lead,"[17] begins with a reenactment of the primal scene of angst for the child: "The worst is upon me. This is it: the scene of Great Suffering. During this scene the impossible takes place; my death attacks me, life panics and splits in two; one life tears at the other which has it by the throat, biting. You struggle. The body breaks, the sky shatters, the scene bursts into flames. You fall and the earth is no longer there" (*Angst,* 7). In more direct language the narrator explains, "Here is the unprecedented scene: My mother puts me down on the ground. The room closes in. 'Wait for me here. I'll be back straightaway.' My mother goes out. The ground closes in. I am outside. When *I* am not there *you* die. Betrayed. Everything starts to die" (*Angst,* 8).

The severing of the child's primary link to the maternal body, to the maternal presence, is always traumatic, and it is this basic problem of separation anxiety, most especially separation anxiety as experienced by the daughter rather than the son, which is the subject of *Angst.* As usual, much of the narrative takes place from within the dream state, and although Cixous would doubtless object to the term, the style is nonetheless often reminiscent of a kind of automatic writing or stream-of-consciousness technique that both propels and restricts the reading process. The intense anxiety states experienced by the female "woman-as-child" are described by the narrator in such a way as to signal both Cixous's ongoing connection to a literary father (in this case, James Joyce) and an attempt to use psychoanalysis in order to aid in the formulation of a female subject position. Herr suggests that in *Angst* Cixous asks us "to consider the absolutes of unity and separation as convenient fictions; . . . to imagine that the anguish of maternal loss (objective and subjective) and the subsequent repetition compulsion to replace the mother, which both is and produces anxiety behavior, can be placed, in the Derridean term, 'under erasure' by refiguring the terms of intimate relationality (parent/child, woman-lover)" (Herr, 201).

Interwoven with the anguished narrative of the female psyche's loss of the mother and the child-narrator's eternal *fort-da* games that constitute an attempt to reunite her with the maternal body is the parallel epistolary narrative of letters and telegrams sent, lost, never mailed, never written, imagined, and forgotten between the narrator and her absent lover/father. This absent lover, who is, we come to learn, ill and dying, finally does die, and proves to be an exacerbating source of anguish for the narrator. A third subtext of *Angst,* then, becomes the narrative of birth itself, which involves not only the anguish of birth as original trauma but also a reliving of initiatory trauma as she moves from childhood to adulthood. Angst describes the birth of the woman into her subject position as writer of the very text we are reading: "Being born! You never forget. Once you've learnt how to be born, it's like learning to swim, birth stays for ever in your body, a potential seed, always ready to make itself felt. You get up, move forward, part the waters with your arms" (*Angst,* 20).

On the way to self-discovery, the narrator explains, "It's the same old story: the right hand doesn't know what the left hand is doing. But it is more complicated than that: You aren't just one other self, but you have as many selves as fingers on your two hands. Plus the thumb. All different, no leader. No self is clearer than the others. You hurl yourself into hell ten ways at once. But it's not me who's burning—it's my other self. And among my others there are some I am closer to intellectually, others through passion, others through sexual confusion" (*Angst,* 69–70). She reminds us that there are strange moments in our lives that seem to be lived or experienced by another person (one of our own "others," the other within us). All these intensely painful psychic growing pains are described in minute detail, the text itself undergoing metamorphosis before our eyes as a chaotic case history of anxiety, anguish, and dread unfolds: "There are strange moments in the stories of my lives: whole days lived by someone else. In the dark, you take the wrong turning in time; you get up, unawares, slap in the middle of another story, which drags you far away from yourself, while our connections, relationships, memories, all our possessions, have stayed in the usual story from which we are now infinitely separate" (*Angst,* 70–71).

The symptoms of *angst* are well documented by the anxious narrator:

> You sleep. You serve. You do everything you thought you were incapable of doing. Fly. Jump. Speak a foreign language. Teach English in German. Teach pupils of both sexes skills you don't even possess. You go from the impossible to the impossible through all the possibilities of fraud; you fill all the places you have no right to. Whether you like it nor not, no one knows, and you don't forget you know nothing either. You are uneasy at ease, sorry, angry, negative. You owe the right to fill these places to someone else—it's the dark night of your soul—anguish is compelling you to do what fear wants to prevent you from doing. You plunge into the mountains as if they were paper curtains, at the helm of escaped monsters. You discover you have a talent for all kinds of delusions, falsehood,

> crimes. Everything you touch is tinged with remorse. That is not what you wanted: to do everything you didn't want to do, because you dare not disappoint someone you hardly know, whose name you can't even remember. You taste murder like a gourmet, almost faint with disgust. You drink blood and try to upset the glass under the table without being seen. Things gradually get harder and harder. You sink lower and lower. And you don't wake up. What suffering! (*Angst,* 71)

The narrator tries in vain to make sense of the dream narrative, but concludes that if she had "read the book of [her] life," she would certainly have been able to "prove that it was written by death: starting with my death, going backwards from suffering through absence, right back to the first disppointment" (*Angst,* 102). But why has the narrator chosen to write her angst? "You write in terror. Because of nostalgia: you are forced to admit to yourself that you cling to the room of your suffering as you would cling to the greatest joy. You write in hope and dread. You cannot brush aside the thought that dares to bring you back to the worst" (*Angst,* 116). She feels taken in by words themselves ("their web of metaphors, smothered innuendoes") and feels especially at a disadvantage, even to the point of exclusion from the game, as she "plays" with the masculine other: "He was playing chess with himself. He didn't place a word until he had measured his chances of protecting it. On the defensive. All the sentences calculated with an enemy in mind" (*Angst,* 127–28).

During her internalized conflicts centered on becoming a subject, the narrator often finds herself at various crossroads where "You are going to have to choose" (*Angst,* 134). This necessity of choice, this battle of ego and superego, is, of course, at once a further source of anguish and the inevitable result of living through time. The narrator not only feels the inner forces at war but is able to become a "third body" observing her selves in conflict. As death approaches and birth and separation anguish replay themselves again and again, the narrator attempts to learn how to lose, to learn how to let go: "Today, faced with life, close to life, to death, as if you have reached the way-in, way-out, passageway, and now I am not living, I am not dead: all paths lead you astray, the nights are endless, getting longer and longer—poor sensitive, willing being—you look around at those who do not know, supremely wise, supremely naive. Strangely joyful in your sorrow. And in that joy is the strange happiness of feeling yourself close to death. Death loves me. And that gentle, agonizing love deep in your heart, is life itself" (*Angst,* 172).

Shiach postulates that in *Angst* Cixous "feels able to describe the anguish of her past because she has rejected its inevitability for her future: she has looked god in the face and discovered that he does not exist" (Shiach, 91). It seems clear that in this period of her writing career, Cixous has been mainly preoccupied with confronting both her own past and the past of "the feminine." The collagelike structures of the texts from this period, along with their dizzying references to philosophical and literary intertexts, mark them as among the most difficult of Cixous's work. As she moves into a writing period where texts become arguably less narcissistic and more other-oriented, the reader's task becomes less daunting as well.

Chapter Four

From *Beyond the Abyss* to *The Flood*: The Generous Gesture from Self to Other

I owe a live apple to a woman. A joy-apple. I owe a work of apple to a woman. I owe: a birth to the nature of a woman: a book of apples. . . . The lesson of apple: of peace. The acidulous taste of the word on the tongue. The one-hundred savours of the different peels: the tart apple of the being-sweet-on-the-tongues, appelle apple apfel appeal a peal a-peel.

Hélène Cixous, *Vivre l'Orange/To Live the Orange*

Subtle changes in Hélène Cixous's writing are readily observable after the publication of *Angst* in 1977. During the 1980s and into the 1990s, Cixous shows a marked increase in accessibility to the reader, an accessibility accompanied by an ever-decreasing narcissistic tension. The 1980s can truly be termed an illustrative period in Cixous's own production for what *écriture féminine* can be. Having struggled to find voice, uncover female desire, and undo philosophical systems and beliefs that hold us trapped within stifling irrationality, Cixous turns her writerly attention to what we might term a celebration of the feminine libidinal economy.

This period in Cixousian production is marked quite prominently by her discovery, in 1977, of the works of the Brazilian writer Clarice Lispector. The subsequent interweaving of Clarice-Hélène is everywhere in the texts written in this period. It is certainly not the case that Cixous in any way abandons earlier concerns; it would appear, however, that having reached a certain point in her writing career, her talent and interests begin to lead her in slightly different directions—ones that allow for more openness in style.

Préparatifs de noces au-delà de l'abîme (1978)

The title of Cixous's 1978 work sounds the changes for the text that follows: *preparations, wedding, beyond, abyss*—all key words in the Cixousian fictional world. The book alludes to Kafka's story "Wedding Preparations in the Country," is dedicated *"Pour Vous, avec des femmes, mettre l'écriture à l'amour"* ("For You, with des femmes, to put writing in love"), and carries no generic marker on the title page. Obviously a text grounded within the feminine libidinal economy Cixous has described in *The Newly Born Woman, Préparatifs,* by its very typography, gives the reader a guide to follow in reading. There are no chapters, no divisions per se, except those marked off by occasional white spaces (seemingly arranged haphazardly) as the narrator's text jumps from one theme to another, sometimes in traditionally coherent fashion and sometimes arbitrarily, with no easily identifiable connection. Yet words in boldface type (most often entire sentences, but sometimes only the introductory clause) allow us to "follow" the flow of the argument: which is, in essence, another voyage by a female consciousness toward "the other side"—whether that "other side" is seen as death, love, or voice (or some of each).

Death, love, and voice are constants in the Cixousian world. They represent, as we have seen, concepts that historically embody an opposite (life, hatred, silence) but that in Cixous's text are opened up to new possibilities. One of the best images of the reception of a Cixousian text is to imagine the mind divided into compartments with semi-permeable membranes through which "feelings" or "concepts" that traditionally come to us in a culturally determined binary fashion manage to pass easily back and forth across the membrane barrier through a process of reciprocal osmosis. Reading Cixous can never be linear; the reading process itself must of necessity be circular, turning back on itself again and again—making links from one passage to another (or not), making links backward or forward to other texts.

The opening boldface passage in *Préparatifs* introduces us to our "heroine": "A woman bitten by a silence the day she attains her eighth year of love cannot survive. What is the cure?"[1] This woman, silent, sleeping like Sleeping Beauty, must decide which way to turn. Because both ways seem equally depressing, it is difficult to choose at all. Liberty to choose has led her to stasis. Then we learn that a woman with "a manbone stuck in her throat" has the following remedy at her disposal. She must search for the name of the "Invariable" (the constant, the first cause: Does the name start with *g* or *d?* God or Dieu?). She is not able to get beyond the first letter, but she does wish that there were such a constant and that it had "your voice" (*Préparatifs,* 18). Summoning sufficient courage, the woman is ready to pass beyond the wall. Possessed of a soul, desire, and the "powers of the bloods," she is ready to take the risk: to risk taking to the air, confronting the void, confronting absence, confronting the future. "She has everything she needs. Except a little *I*"

(*Préparatifs,* 18). With the problematic silence weighing heavily on her, the woman traveler is given some further advice and then continues on her way, finally arriving at the period of the "AntiSong of Songs" where, with references to the biblical text, the woman who has been bitten by silence is now "bitten by the belief that her bodies are in strange hands" as well. She tumbles into the abyss, and the narrator asks, "What are the signs?" (*Préparatifs,* 37).

The fact that this journey of preparation for union is a dangerous one is quite clear. Three dangers are referred to—anxieties, wrong routes, bad letters (*Préparatifs,* 49)—and can never be guarded against. Indeed, the three dangers are the very constituents of life itself: "It is written in the margin between my two pages: Life always awaits you where you are not waiting for it" (*Préparatifs,* 55). There are questions, eternal questions, which lead the fearful woman to the edge of the abyss. What she needs is "true strength: to know how to dis-pleasure (*un-jouir*). In order to thwart Death: contentment. Content yourself. Do not call Life by the names of death. Have the courage of each moment, even if it is not the last one. Live well, die well: pass through the deceptive duration which is Life in fine style. Not tomorrow, later, not today. One day. To live for Life, waiting for it" (*Préparatifs,* 67). Given that woman is only human, however, and not divine, there are things which make her forget her own advice.

Like the *fort-da* game of *Souffles,* the woman here is caught in a movement of "Go. Don't go: Go" (*Préparatifs,* 74). Yet if she allows herself to be frightened by the depth of Silence (and in Cixous silence is penetratingly deep), she will never be able to go beyond the barriers set in her way. She will never be able to force her way through walls. If she is one of those women who do not have the courage to receive silence, she will find refuge in whatever body, and will be pushed and pulled here and there by her anxieties. The narrator tells herself, "You are a being of flesh and words. You are a body overflowing with words. You are a girl overflowing with salivas and bloods. You are of the noisy race. You are of the species of questions. You are of the future species, you never stop starting" (*Préparatifs,* 76–77).

A feeling of repression and tension leads to the critical question, "What is it which still keeps you attached to yourself?" (*Préparatifs,* 88). And a certain impression of despair settles over the narrator as she asks, "Can I think all the days of a year, especially at the end of the day: 'Saved!'; when the entire body has lost?" (*Préparatifs,* 93). And yet, as in virtually every Cixous text, it is the quest itself that counts—the search for voice, love, and the other, as that search is complicated by flux of time and history: "In order to love well," claims the narrator, "it would be necessary both to forget everything—or at least to forget nothing, keep everything present and remember nothing" (*Préparatifs,* 94). Such a curious mixture of past, present, and future—the playing with oppositional time categories and mind-sets—is a marker for Cixous.

Still focused on love, the text turns to the problem of invisibility and inaudibilty of this emotion. If love is kept invisible, yet not entirely inaudible, then, it is argued, it is time to "take back the body a little" (*Préparatifs,* 97). The struggle to get "outside" the confines of woman's place, both corporeally and politically, and the risk that very movement represents, gives rise to a certain amount of perceived danger: "Once outside, it is not impossible that you will suddenly find yourself in the position of a young woman *mal morte,* who has just tried nine months running to re-enter her frozen body" (*Préparatifs,* 99). The link between maternal delivery and the French concept of untying (loosening bonds that constrict) (*délivrer* and *dé-livrer*) is a recurring theme in Cixous. Yet even if the risk is clear, it is also necessary, for once "outside," if you can resist being carried off along the first road, you find and "risk" taking the left-hand road, and in the end you will gain. Arrival, the eternal, and "getting there" are irrelevant in terms of the female quest. The energy from within constantly provides the desire for "moving through" and the need to "jump over time" (*Préparatifs,* 105).

The narrator points to causes that can prevent (either really prevent or in imaginary reality prevent) a scene of consolation. We should avoid spaces that place the various states of the body in danger, and we should flee places of regression. But the body is still the focus when the preparations are considered: "Then prepare bodies, in thought, to look like the body which decides your joys and your desires, make them without insistence? without restrictive precisions, make the portrait of the Mother without fault" (*Préparatifs,* 129). Being in pain, being the child in the pain of the mother leads to examples of the mother seen from the point of view of my "Absolute Need," one step away from the abyss (*Préparatifs,* 131). Finding herself in "hybrid space" (part-forest, part-construction), the narrator discovers that her most important talisman is the text itself: "A book will be able to stir you. A metaphor will be able to carry you off" (*Préparatifs,* 145). The book will be "the thing which is for me like my heart's bosom friend" (*Préparatifs,* 145).

The textual narration moves inexorably closer to the moment of crossing the abyss and considers the causes that slow the movement of clearing the "unthinkable" hurdle of love—a litany of questions and fears. Eventually the "sincere but divided soul" learns to expect the blows of the Law but not to flee (*Préparatifs,* 162), and the narrator finds herself at last "in that limitless room. You could enter without knocking" (*Préparatifs,* 164). Reaching out, reaching toward the other, involves resistance, however—"resistances of the pen" (*Préparatifs,* 171). As always, the arrival is not the final objective; the journey itself is the significant happening. What the preparations are about is the sea—"the green one, the great one, my innocent one, all entirely here" (*Préparatifs,* 179ff). The announced "marriage" is here as well.

On the back jacket of *Préparatifs* Cixous tells her readers:

> I see myself watching my truth face to face, my life remaining safe, a woman without a shadow of disappearance, I see the sea itself, its profusion, and life is not taken away from me, one step does not separate me from her great body of great disturbed light, she rises towards you from the depths of the abysses, her shining arrival, her powerful tendernesses, her sad infinitely gay eyes, "call me!," I hear her voice gently moving, it's still a young voice, a naked voice, issuing forth from my throat, which wanders, which says absolutely nothing, "call me," a stripped voice, a searcher, "make me come!," intimidated, "make me come all to you."

The movement toward writing we see in *Préparatifs* is a movement toward life itself. As Shiach points out, Cixous's narrator in this text eventually "comes to see the abyss as a necessary moment of confrontation that can lead her to the resources of her own subjectivity, and her own writing" (Shiach, 92).

Vivre l'orange/To Live the Orange (1979)

Vivre l'orange/To Live the Orange is an interesting example of one of Cixous's more accessible texts. The English version of the text (on the verso) faces its French "original" (on the recto) and was established by the author herself using the English translation done by two of her longtime collaborators, Sarah Cornell and Ann Liddle. As the critical discussions of how to read Cixous have progressed over time in the academe, it is interesting that very little attention has been paid to this text. Yet *Vivre l'orange* wonderfully illustrates the linguistic facility of its creator and further enunciates the ideas of *écriture féminine*, feminine libidinal economy, and the Clarice Lispector link; its autobiographical groundings are in Cixous's North African origins (we recall the blood orange of *Portrait du soleil,* the "Oran-je" of *The Newly Born Woman*). Because of its bilingual presentation, it gives the reader not only an *aide-lecture* but, because there is never a facile connection between the left- and right-hand side, the sense of the constant need to hold "the-two-as-one, the-two-as-two" in the mind during the reading process itself.

In *To Live the Orange* the first-person narrator is a woman, mostly the thinly disguised persona of Cixous. The text is situated historically at the time of the overthrow of the Shah of Iran (Iran appears as a chronological marker in the text) and at a time in Cixous's writing career when she has confessed to feeling that she had reached an impasse (hence the crucial moment of the discovery of the works of Clarice Lispector). The narrator begins by evoking the primacy of voice ("nothing is more powerful than the intimate touch of a veiled voice,"[2] linking the powerful attraction of the female voice to images of virtuoso fingers, birds' beaks, and flames. She then makes the specific reference to Lispector:

> A woman's voice came to me from far away, like a voice from a birth-town, it brought me insights that I once had, intimate insights, naive and knowing, ancient and fresh like the yellow and violet color of freesias rediscovered, this voice was unknown to me, it reached me on the twelfth of October 1978, this voice was not searching for me, it was writing to no one, to all women, to writing, in a foreign tongue. I do not speak it, but my heart understands it, and its silent words in all the veins of my life have translated themselves into made blood, into joy-blood." (*Orange,* 10)

The voice that comes to the narrator arrives "with an angel's footsteps" at a time when she is "so far from myself, alone at the extremity of my finite being, my writing-being was grieving for being so lonely, sending sadder and sadder unaddressed letters" (*Orange,* 10). But the voice of Lispector, audible in her texts (Cixous was given a copy of a translation of one of Lispector's works which Editions des femmes had decided to publish), provides for Cixous "a writing [which] found me when I was unfindable to myself" (*Orange,* 12). Indeed the writing was a writing which was Cixousian in essence, given everything she had previously written about what an *écriture féminine* could be: "More than a writing, the great writing, the writing of other days, the terrestrial, vegetal writing, of the time when the earth was the sovereign mother, the good mistress, and we went to the school of growth in her countries" (*Orange,* 12).

The narrator describes herself in images of aridity and smallness, her soul space reduced to the size of a tear, which contained "what remained of the woman I had loved being." "What have you in common with women?" the narrator asks herself. "When your hand no longer even knows anymore how to find a near and patient and realizable orange, at rest in the bowl?" (*Orange,* 12). The effect of Lispector on Cixous is to liquefy, in a sense, Cixous's own writing, to restore the "orange" of Oran and childhood: "She put the orange back into the deserted hands of my writing and with her orange-colored accents she rubbed the eyes of my writing which were arid and covered with white films" (*Orange,* 14).

The answer to the narrator's question comes from her encounter with Lispector. What she has in common with women is "the need to go to the sources. The easiness of forgetting the source. The possibility of being saved by a humid voice that has gone to the sources. The need to go further into the birth-voice" (*Orange,* 16). A return to childhood, to the source, "almost a young girl, an orange regained," allows Cixous to use her "speleologist's ears" to listen to the growing of still-subterranean poetry. And to all *amies,* to all those female friends "for whom loving the moment is a necessity, saving the moment is such a difficult thing, and we never have the necessary time, the slow, sanguineous time, that is the condition of this love," she dedicates three gifts: "slowness which is the essence of tenderness; a cup of passion-fruits whose flesh presents in its heart filaments comparable to the styles that poetry bears; and the word *spelaion,* as it is in itself a gourd full of voices, an enchanted ear, the instrument of a continuous music, an open, bottomless species of orange" (*Orange,* 18). "The orange," says the narrator, "is a beginning. Starting out from the orange all voyages are possible. All voices that go their way via her are good" (*Orange,* 20).

Before this voyage to the source becomes no more than a narcissistic quest, the narrator is interrupted by a telephone call (telephones appear often in Cixous's texts, seeming to have, with their ear/mouthpieces, long cords, and the invisible transmission of the voice over distance, a peculiar fascination) asking her what she thinks about the situation in Iran. Obviously a reference to "real life," to "real politics," and to "real women," the narrator makes the link between poetry and politics. One must never forget "real" struggle, and yet if one is a poet, a writer, perhaps courage is demonstrated by carrying on with that act: "a woman whose writing is courageous enough to dare to advance in a frightening movement of tearing away from all her being, to the truth of writing it, which is true madness, the madness of truth, the passion of approaching the origin of beings, at the risk of retreating from history" (*Orange,* 24). The love of the orange is political, too.

Qualities of the radiant Clarice (there are many wordplays throughout Cixous's writing about Lispector using the Brazilian writer's Christian name—Clarice, *clear, light, radiance*) involve two kinds of courage: the courage to explore the sources, the "foreign parts" of the self, and the courage to return to herself, "almost without self, without denying the going" (*Orange,* 28). Comparable to many of the Cixousian narrators from her own previous work (*Angst, Souffles, LA*), the important gesture is to follow one's fear to its origins ("recognized it unto death") and to come back from that experience, "not without fear, but henceforth capable of living fear" (*Orange,* 28).

Thoughts of Iran lead, via thoughts of Oran, Cixous's birthplace, to thoughts of the Jews, Cixous's heritage, and finally to the question of naming. Lispector called herself by various names—*panthera, gatta* (she-cat), pre-she-cat, egg of the hen (*huevo*), or egg (*ovo*), or even *o,* a simple sound. How was it possible for her to "move away from her lady-being"? wonders the narrator. "By what ladder did she descend to the depths of language down to the boiling center where the alloying of breaths takes place, to denominate herself Clarice, to forget herself, to re-birth herself . . . ?" (*Orange,* 36, 38).

This process of coming to life and to writing is a dramatic one as the narrator is transformed into a giant ear:

> [I]n the concentration of all my life forces, I was but an ear from feet to temples, a child-ear, tense, curled up, I listened, with all my pores, to the breathing of the sea that lives underground, with all of my palms, my conch-back, listening with the electric veins in the curves of my arms, the ears of my breasts attentive, I listened, stretched out at the foot of time, to the pulse of the embryos of things, with my ears in prayer, I heard the noise of the moon rising, the moon beating in the breath of the clouds, the sanguineous surge in the belly of the sky, I heard it, with all my inner ears turned towards the things of the world, those furthest away from our attention, with my intimate suns turned towards the radiance of the things of the body, those most removed from our care, I heard the furrowing of the blood, between the rocks, the warm life, I heard with my vegetal ears, and with my aquatic ears, the spirit of the organs stirring, life circulating in the mobile center of the world, the openings of the earth being made, tenderly, far ago, I listened to the sands rolling under the footsteps of light, with my primitive ears, my adoring ears, I heard the secret of things composing themselves, births being decided, the noise of births, the bursting silence of separations that multiply reached me, the musics of apparitions, I had almighty ears for attending the Encounters, inside, at the moments of grace, necessary, of repeated miracle, of the welcoming of things giving themselves to one another, giving rise to each other, echo, passage, continuation, one in the other, one near the other. (*Orange,* 42, 44)

Cixous's encounter with Clarice's texts is similar to an unmasking—what the narrator calls "Un-making up" (*Orange,* 50). The revelation of the face is "The Gift." And further to the gift of the face is the gift of the orange, "*naranja,* she translated it, into my tongue, and I re-discovered the taste of the lost orange, I re-knew the orange" (*Orange,* 52). The perfection or utopian power that Hélène attributes to Clarice is descriptive, in extrapolated form, of the power of *écriture féminine.* This perfection consists in having attained "such a development of the soul, to have reached inside of herself, an intelligence of her life-being, so profound, that she must have reached, way deep down, what is not a place, but is more than a region, in the infinitely extensible space which is the inner earth of life, at that state of being, that ripeness that prolongs the expanse, makes the life of life grow, really, spiritually, materially, deep down as the inner body of life grows, when its fertility is abundantly bathed by rivers of thought, until reaching this depth where the life of a life rejoins Life, the Great Mother-Life" (*Orange,* 60).

Images of flowers (Clarice has "orchid-force"), stars, lush vegetation, profusion ("entire museums of animated beings, fields of moments of being, of instants" [*Orange,* 66]) are combined with an almost Pascalian attention to the worlds of the infinitely small and the infinitely great. (Here, for example, is the narrator speaking of the crocus in March: "understanding the smallness of their greatness, the greatness of their smallness" [*Orange,* 72].) The importance of naming and calling of things in the physical world that surrounds us, through which we pass all too often unaware of their full power, is underlined in this text. But too often we "forget" and no longer know how to call or to name: "We speak silence" (*Orange,* 74). If we forget the orange, then the orange withers, and we find ourselves in darkness.

In order to overcome this sterile, arid existence, we must learn to see "with the true seeing, to see and undersee and see-over until being able to cry: 'in truth, I have seen!' We must train our eyes for this process of "unveiling, clariseeing: a seeing that passes through the frames and toiles that clothe the towns, the façades and armours, the images and curtains that efface and vanish the towns and translate them into Appearances-of-towns, into false cities, into a system of false constructions" (*Orange,* 74, 76). We must never forget the six million Jews slaughtered in the Holocaust, the three thousand nuclear warheads or a billion humans enchained and walled up as prisoners: "We must pierce the denseness of our inner immobility, find the ultimate force stronger than inertia, to pierce through the masses of oblivion, in order to go towards the memory of windows whose existence we had excluded in passing from life to Town" (*Orange,* 80).

The examination of a leaf can sometimes bring us to the edge of despair, for we have become afraid to think about life. We are frightened of being called back to life, "of feeling ourselves called back to it, no longer being able to avoid needing it, of no longer being able to bear keeping ourselves away from it, in forgetfulness or in recollection" (*Orange,* 82). We arrive at the leaf battered, soiled, bruised, ashamed, and we must engage in a battle with ourselves to move toward the leaf and the forest. The horror of this battle "lies entirely in its limits," says the narrator; "if I wage it, I win it; I lose it each time I don't wage it" (*Orange,* 82). Yet it is tiring and ultimately discouraging to realize that in order to "love a leaf in the middle of life" one is constantly obliged "to drive off death, to go back through hate and destruction again" (*Orange,* 82). In such cases, one has a tendency to abandon the leaf—and all the leaves in turn abandon the individual. It is the strength of a Clarice (of an Hélène) to be able to endow us with the force necessary to go and love a leaf.

Cixous tells us that "for the women who know how to believe, nothing is left but suffering, suffering. To have known how to think, to look, to smile in return, is a curse, to have known is a misfortune, to be human is the final catastrophe, now that murder is stronger than love" (*Orange,* 88). We become afraid of awakening to find ourselves once more alive. We dream a rose "so true that it awakens us" (*Orange,* 88). How could a rose have survived in the ashes of our world? It is possible, but we hold back. "For a true rose gives to a true woman the need to give to other women. A rose par excellence gives itself to be given" (*Orange,* 88). Yet we are afraid that if we look out the window we will see nothing but gas chambers. Is it possible that we can no longer look on a single rose? "Is it possible that we no longer know what to call an orange? How women are called? When they are unveiled?" Cixous cites the ultimate problem of our age: "For we no longer know how to not forget life while trying to not recall death, we no longer know how to save life from death, we do not know how to not forget the dead without forgetting life, we do not know how to live without forgetting" (*Orange,* 90). Because fear inhabits us, we "no longer approach: and the space wilts" (*Orange,* 92).

We are afraid of no longer being able to approach, as before, of never being able, to think a rose, quietly, to love, an orange, a child, without being afraid, of being "too heavy, too rapid, too slow, not slow enough, wounding" (*Orange,* 94). Yet in the contemporary horror chamber of history, the function of a Clarice (or a Cixous) is "to call life by its first name" and to bring us back to life: "And all women that remind us of life remind us of Clarice; call life by the name of Clarice. Life is called Clarice, but this is not its only name. I also call life by the name of Amie. Each time that we remember to love, Clarice comes back. Clarice is a rare but common name. A name that has never been mistaken. The orange name that unveils herself. Out of fidelity to herself. When a woman is called Clarice, she does not forget. Clarice unveils us; opens our windows" (*Orange,* 98).

Cixous's use of verbs in this text is typical of her—the choice is often the fluid present participle and this fluidity is maintained in the specific actions denoted: going, approaching, gazing, abiding, touching, calling, presenting, giving. Clarice's work, and by extension Cixous's work as well, passionately involves her (and us as readers) in "calling things forth . . . , giving things back to things, giving us each thing for the first time, giving us back each time the first time of things, giving us back the first times lost" (*Orange,* 104).

Finally, the images of orange, apple, rose, window, and garden merge as the text urges us to be strong enough "to leave the windows open without lying in wait" (*Orange,* 108). If we can use our strength to wait for the unexpected to happen, a garden will enter. "Seeing everything that comes in the clarice window, the marvelous quantity of things of all kinds, of all species, human, vegetal, animal, of all sexes, of all cultures, one feels with what loving force she holds herself open, with what frightened joy, to let herself by approached by the sudden" (*Orange,* 108, 110). If we can maintain openness to things, to the world, there is the possibility that we will be visited by beauty. Beauty, things of beauty, will take us by surprise, and will be "twice as beautiful for surprising us, for being surprised" (*Orange,* 110).

With *Vivre l'orange* we have entered the "generous" phase of Cixousian writing. The discovery of Lispector's work—in reality the work of a writer with many similarities in background and of concern, although with an entirely different style—made a profound difference in Cixous's life and writing. The encounter with Lispector produces a greater sense of opening out, of a freer play of metaphors and images, and an increased need to face head on the realities of death, silence, and forgetting. Yet there is a constant sense that in the very confrontation with the darker side of human experience—by being open to it and by embracing it—we find beauty and joy and love and life.

Anankè (1979)

Anankè (the Greek word for fate) was published by Editions des femmes in the same year as *Vivre l'orange.* Although in some respects it is linked with the increased open quality of texts like *Vivre l'orange,* in others it is more closely allied to a text like *Préparatifs des noces au-delà de l'abîme.* *Anankè* is "defined" on the text's dust jacket as a dance of transfer (transference)—a dance that leaps from unconscious to unconscious. The definition itself is printed beneath an amusing parodic Egyptian hieroglyph showing linked elephants and telephones, two recurring images of the text. The telephone is dear to Cixous because of its wires (*fils*) and connecting powers; *éléphants* for her become *éléfaunes (elle est faune:* she is a wild animal). Thus the major theme of *Anankè* is movement and, more precisely, movement toward. The inner traveler knows that "life awaits you at the school exit." The day of the *grand transfaire* ("the great transfer"/"moving across") is also (and simultaneously) the time of resistance to transfer. The question is always one of departure. How does one begin to travel? How does one begin to move toward knowledge?

Complicating matters further, the inner woman who is trying desperately to "leave" discovers that she cannot leave on her own; she is accompanied by other "unknowns" who live within her. Constantly pushed forward, then pulled back (by fate, by fear, by the unknown) the unified self (the *Une*) observes itself dividing into multiple "selves," all belonging to "her." The push-pull movement seems to be directly traceable to the problematic relationship between mother and daughter (within the female self the mother is constantly braking while the daughter steps on the accelerator). Sometimes it seems that the female traveler is walking on *les Eux* ("walking on eggs"—*oeufs*), very delicately so as not to break anything, but at the same time on "some men," *eux* (the disjunctive masculine plural pronoun). At other times the "Hombres" (a combination of men, in Spanish, and shadow) come back as ghosts to haunt her (*fanthommes*) and to pull her by her *chevaux* (horses rather than hair).

The central question asked of "fate" within this text involves the question, again, of identity, of "becoming." From whom must we separate, from whom must we find the material with which to create ourselves in order to have the best possible chance of becoming "women"? *"Quels fils de téléfaune couper?"* ("What wires/sons of a telephone/telephant/teleanimal should we snip?") The image of cutting refers us easily in several directions—to the fates who cut the cords, to the cutting of the umbilical cord. How, in the end, do we become "self," "one," "many"?

Anankè deals, as does fate itself, with questions of movement and questions of change—changing a step, a place, numbers, clothing, the body, the heart. *Anankè* is about translation, about transformation and transmutation. The female "translator" certainly has need of the unconscious's midwifery skills as she labors to give birth to the long-awaited "daughter"—herself. In the words of the author, "See, inner woman, your inner young woman, freed from a thousand ties on the edge of a brand-new History."[3]

Divided into six major sections (each title denoting a sense of color) with, as usual, several subdivisions within each section, *Anankè* is a text that possesses a kind of spiral movement. It is entirely nonlinear, never proceeding, either through action description or in any sense of marked time, toward closure but, rather, through constant to-ing and fro-ing, creating an impression of energetic movement which in the text's concluding pages leads to birth (rebirth) and the voyage already concluded to be undertaken again.

The first section, "Chapitre Pale," represents a beginning before the beginning, pale being not a color but the descriptor of some color not yet specified. The subheadings give us other important clues as to the organization of this section of the text. The subtitle listed in the book's table of contents is "Genesis of a Case of Female Exultation," and the two excerpts in italics that Cixous places as epigraphs are also telling: "—En route—A few difficulties (but small ones) in not allowing oneself to be stopped at the very outset by a translation of passions," and "What she could not attain at the wheel (or flying) (*au volant*), she could attain by desiring (*en voulant*)."

The second section, "Chapitre Orange," is reminiscent of the optimism of *Vivre l'orange* and begins with a passage explicating possible reasons for delay in beginning; under the heading "Detachments and beneath Detachments" we find two types of delays specified: those tied to the question of changing clothes (the person who is leaving is constantly changing her dress, sides, direction, means of transportation), and those tied to the question of composition (Who should go along? Should one separate in order to better maintain distance?). The female traveler does not leave. How can she?

"Chapitre Blanc," the third section, presents in its introductory passage "examples of figurations in the wandering toward the green present." We experience along with the narrator a series of dream sequences, a series of plays where all the actors know their parts except her. Given her textual ignorance, she appears to be a young neurotic come from afar and is surprised to find herself in the position of a "Sibyl whose god no longer telephones her." Nothing prevents her from visualizing herself in the same place as the Great She, if it were not for the logic of the "too-near-to-be-attained" (*Anankè,* 73). The narrator asks herself, What does my existence feel like in the present? And the answer: I feel like "a young women exterior to myself, who finds herself wandering in the world, pulled along by an incessant movement, in a series of scenes" (*Anankè,* 75). Doubtless there are invisible laws that push her along, she reasons. Yet she strongly senses her lack of history. History has been replaced by a series of random movements from place to place that only serve to organize her dislocation.

To illustrate this wandering existence toward the green present, Cixous moves through the following vignettes: "She wanders"; "She plays Phaedra, my labyrinth, my sister"; "First Elements of a *biografille*"; "A case of Sibylline neurosis"; "Entre la nouvelle, too good, la grande Nécessité trop bonne"; "the truest name of my Necessity"; and "the found letter."

"Chapitre Roux," the fourth section, uses the color *roux* (a shade of red that refers to hair color only—in animals as well as humans—hence Cixous's previous wordplay on *cheveux* and *chevaux* for red hair and roan-colored horses). References to the hour of *résistrance* (resistance/trance) and the reciprocal movement from translation of pulsations and pulsations of translation create space for the narration of other female fears.

The following section, "Chapitre Gris Perle" (pearl gray), introduces us to the *"fils du téléfaune"* (wires of the telephone, son(s) of the teleanimal) and asks questions of relationships. Again addressing shadows (*ombres/hombres*) and *les Eux* (eggs; masculine plural *them*), this section reintroduces the feeling of fear (fear of breaking—the eggs, the men), raises questions of feathers and shells, and interjects *"éléfantasmes"*—questions of taste, ears, trunk, defenses (*Anankè,* 147).

The color of pearl gray takes us as well into the color world of shadows. In this section, too, the typography and use of italics both to indicate subdivision and to set off the first sentence of some passages (without appearing to "separate") adds to our sense of dislocation. From the opening phrase "And now, what relationships are there with the gods?" to the first formal subdivision, *"Un K de nom fantôme"* / "A case with a ghostly name" (references at once to *cas* [case, case history], the letter *k* [for Kafka, Herr K from Dora's case]), the shadowplay of the fifth section leaves the reader perplexed. Yet the final section of *Anankè* recounts the narrator's eventual arrival in the green present. "Chapitre

Vert" with its epigrammatic "to create the child and interpret it" (*"faire l'enfant et l'interpréter"*) reminds us that although "confusions, divisions, and distractions" are numerous, it is only through them that we can explain birth or coming into being. The narrator certainly needs the help proferred by the midwife of the subconscious to attain the unattainable: "birth via the heart."

Illa (1980)

The cover of Cixous's 1980 text, *Illa,* shows the female figure of Spring, her back to the viewer, a basket of flowers cradled in her left arm, her right arm extended, and the fingers of the right hand gently picking a sprig of wildflower to add to her collection. She is barefoot and draped in loose, gauzy clothing, terra cotta against a green background. Her head, inclined slightly to the right, as she glances sidelong at the flower she is in the act of plucking, is set on a long graceful neck; her long hair is pulled up into a chignon, dressed with flowers. Cixous's introductory remarks allude to *Vivre l'orange* as she tells her readers that this "apple of a text," this "star" she has just placed on the ground, was not written by herself. The text radiates from "us," and we are reminded that writing comes not only from the self but grows and flourishes "within the constellation of stars formed by generous women."[4]

The title *Illa* derives from Latin, suggesting both "she" and, in French of course, the combination of he (*il*) plus the feminine article (*la*). The first fifty pages of the book involve a long poetic mediation on beginnings. The text poses a series of questions—Who am I? Who are we?—and introduces a character called "the third one," the one who is running along the edge of the earth, along the seashore. The relationship between mother and daughter and the combined forces of "happiness which is constantly fleeting . . . and feeling the self become unknown" (*Illa,* 7) provide the focal thematic material. Body parts (the hand, the ankle), comparisons with animals (white wolf, camel), and the continual evocation of the voice (by its presence or by its silent absence) bring the reader back again and again to the question of "Who?" Who is calling? And from what place?

Early on in the text we encounter Cordelia, whose name's initial syllable (*kor*) evokes not only Shakespeare's dutiful daughter but Koré and the old French *cor* (heart) and *corps* (body) as well. In *Illa,* as in all her texts of this period, Cixous seeks subject status for the female narrative voice, structuring her text in such a way as to reiterate favorite thematic material: the reciprocal movements of coming and going, the experience of desire and pleasure through the body, and the insistence on the process of writing as a way to accede to subject positioning. The young girl of the cover (Spring) is inserted within the written text: "Be careful of white flowers: it's just at the moment when a young girl picks a narcissus that the earth splits open" (*Illa,* 14). The mother, the daughter, and the third (absent) one, in their mythological entities are evoked by the writer-narrator within the story of Demeter (*Illa,* 18). Although there is silence in these woman-to-woman relationships, silence does not sever the connection between mother and daughter, daughter and mother. Illa, however, does not call. She *is* called.

Interspersed within the text of *Illa* are italicized passages labeled "notes." These notes provide a kind of commentary on the difficulty involved in the process of *écriture féminine*: "There is a game: a question 'what is it?' is given to a blind soul to feel. Its aroma of first apple. The question is tossed out over the edge of the world, outside. The *lâchée* soul must find it by tracking it down and bring it back in its mouth, even though it might be at the cost of blindness. The answer is found in this expedition: the abandoned soul goes out, the question returns: that's the answer. The *récit* of going-coming back and of the engendering of a sister by her twin is the matrice of fiction" (*Illa,* 25).

The eighth of August arrives, and a version of the narrator's meeting (with Clarice Lispector) is described thus: "I was distracted, not yet formed, at the time of ignorance, without writing, with a plan, nothing had as yet happened, I was struck, with the most precious violence, in the middle of the chest, in the midst of lethargy, by the bursting forth of the other, the door opened, I threw myself outside myself, adoration began, the récit, the quest, to write" (*Illa,* 29–30). The cake the narrator evokes (*gâteau de raisin*—called *pomme de lait* in some languages) is her grandmother's cake, and it produces a syllable (*lime*) that recalls a symbolic fruit:

> If a woman has experienced pleasure from it once, that is a good thing; it loses its name by transforming itself into sweetness, she keeps from its flesh only the gift of understanding the language of fruits, and all fruits speak sweetly to her; but if by happiness it happens that she taste it a second time, a long time afterwards, it is a tragic happiness, the taste of the flesh which she can forget one time becomes the unforgettable, it is life, death, which are spoken to her, all daily fruits rot, only one can give her life death, and deprived of its flesh, flesh melts, she can no longer stand upright, I can no longer take in the nourishment which keeps me alive,

> she can no longer do without the sublime taste, she can no longer vegetate, she can no longer be comforted with meats or fish, nor find sleep in the arms of the cedar nor peace on rocky mountain breasts, on hillsides covered with herbs. (*Illa,* 31–32)

At this point a vision of a woman appears—she is dressed in black with shining black curls. "You will not pass," she announces. "You were to ask for the Answer, not carry it away" (*Illa*, 34). This nightmarish scene (of dismemberment, of unveiling) is a kind of birth scene, "the moment at which what is not yet a woman is born" (*Illa,* 36). "Tell me, where does truth grow? / In the heart or in the head? / How is it born? How does it live? / Tell me, tell me!" (*Illa,* 37). The narrator imagines (within the casket inside her chest, behind her fertile lungs) a woman in the cradle, just barely conceived but already fully constituted as a woman. How does this living presence develop—engendered without a father, the fruit of love of her mother alone, in a pre-Oedipal moment when the mother-child union is total? "Tell me where the answer is hidden / Is it beneath the sea or the earth? / How can it be gotten out, how saved? / How can we make it return?" asks the narrator (*Illa,* 38). How does a woman become a woman? She is "multiplied by those others overflowing within her and outside her, gifted with triple wisdom: to say yes to fate, to say yes with her being to many persons" (*Illa,* 39). What this extraordinary woman possesses are tendencies that unite within her the most contradictory sensibilities: a tendency to bind up and to loosen, a tendency to move forward and to lag behind, and a talent for "thinking a thing and its opposite, composite words, in which the contrary syllables make a whole which expresses the sense of one of the contrasted parts but without excluding the others"—in short a way of being "lightdark, inside-outside, rapidslow, sereneagitated" (*Illa,* 40).

The text then turns to a reexamination of the celebrated mother-daughter story, the myth of Demeter. Demeter, the Greek earth-goddess of corn, harvest, and fruitfulness, was the mother of Persephone by Zeus. She and her daughter were chief figures in the Eleusinian Mysteries. The festival of Demeter—identified with the Roman goddess Ceres—was held in the autumn, the time of harvest. Persephone, goddess of fertility, became the wife of Hades, ruler of the underworld, who had stolen her away from the earth. Demeter, however, induced the gods to let Persephone return to earth for eight months each year, although she had to remain in the underworld for the remaining four months (since Hades had tricked her into eating four pomegranate seeds). Each time Persephone returned to earth, plants bloomed anew. She thus personified both birth and decay of vegetation. As queen of the underworld, Persephone was a stern woman, but as daughter of Demeter she was eternally a lovely young maiden with a horn of plenty as her symbol. The Eleusinian Mysteries, as the principal religious mysteries of Greece, symbolized yearly decay and renewal of vegetation and assured a happy afterlife to those who were initiates. Cixous's *Illa* recounts the stealing of Persephone by weaving her story within Egyptian hieroglyphs, the story of Narcissus (flower and myth), the fairy tale of Cinderella, and the Cixousian telephone call from afar.

"A typical difficulty: the choice of subject," the second section of the text, carries a duality within it—the search for the "subject" of the text (the text's own search) and the woman's search for the subject positioning in Lacanian terms. *Dies illa* and *dies irae* are combined with references to Leto, mother of Apollo and Artemis. Hera, in jealousy, caused Leto to wander, but Zeus chained the floating island of Delos to the bottom of the sea; here Leto bore the twins, who later took tragic revenge on Niobe for having insulted their mother. The narrator's dream text then shifts into the well-known "examination for which the candidate is not prepared."

The "transgression exam" demands of the candidate that she respond to the "question of questions," one that appears to her in a different fashion according to the time of day: the question of the "truth of her woman-being" (*Illa,* 48). Images of dismemberment (Humpty Dumpty is cited; a dismembered hand writes) and blue-green signs (ink, water, the sea) appear, as well as words written in other languages in reversed order (*detneserp*). The exam includes all the typical difficulties women have learned to expect: when asked to answer a question concerning their "being" as a woman (the objective and subjective truth), they become lost in patriarchal language, which holds them back and prevents a timely response. At the fourth hour mark of the exam, the woman has written nothing, although she has "lived a lot"; she has barely begun although she is "already old." She feels that she has somehow taken this exam brilliantly but in another memory. The answer the exam demands of her is at once retrospective and coextensive to her lived experience; it is a two-part response, consisting of, on the one hand, the story of her soul (her three libidos) and, on the other, the story of the portrait of each of her three grammatical "persons."

Another series of italicized notes contained in *Illa* refers to the initiation of the woman into the mysteries of the earth and of love—an initiation that, once completed, keeps her protected (or cures her) of vision or "fiction" problems or from imperfections and "infections" of language and libido, restoring to her all the powers of a femininity "stripped of impurities" (*Illa,* 59). What choice does a woman (who has two souls) make when faced with "two doors"—if she makes this choice "as a woman"? (*Illa,* 59).

Illa is a text that plays with the three singular subject pronouns, I , you, and she (illa). What Colette Camelin calls "the daughter's scene" is central.[5] The mother-daughter relationship, as seen through Demeter and Koré, is contrasted to various father-daughter relationships (Athena and Zeus, Hades and Persephone, and Lear and Cordelia). Arachne appears as well—a daughter who has no father at all. Camelin points out that even the mother-daughter relationship as depicted in *Illa* has at least three different episodes that correspond roughly to the text's three major movements (Camelin, 86). In the "first person" is the mother, mythically depicted through Demeter and characterized within the text as Clarice Lispector and Angela. The "second person" (*la deuxième*) is one kind of daughter, mythically depicted through Arachne and taken as a narrative character position by the narrator herself. The "third person" (*illa*) is a further working through of the daughter and is mythically depicted by Koré. This third person is characterized through the narrator as a child, later by Persephone, Cordelia, Portia, or Ariadne. She is characterized by the narrator as an adult and finally by a rediscovered Persephone, who then becomes the textual character of "*Illa délivrée*" (liberated Illa).

The action of *Illa* is nonlinear, with various scenes appearing in fragmented form (repeated, inverted, or variation on a theme) for the reader to reconstruct. If we consider *Illa* to be a text that revolves around the idea of initiation, we can organize the sequences into a rough "chronological" order—one that connects with psychic integration of the ego and development of the subject as a writing subject. In this reconstructed chronology, the earliest moments evoked within *Illa* are the perfect moments of pre-Oedipal childhood. We see the narrator in her shiny sandals in the luxuriant gardens of Oran and Demeter and her daughter Koré in the meadows of Enna. This is a time of orality, of total fusion between mother and daughter and total pleasure in the kind of basic elemental love.

The quest, however, must begin (the time of beginnings, the time of reluctant settings out), and the second kind of activity in *Illa* involves, as in all quest narratives, the time of trials. In these scenes we see Persephone as she descends into Hell (after being kidnapped), and the narrator's anguish as she finds herself confined within patriarchal order and language. Yet these trials—which include references to oppression of women and political struggles of women—also necessitate an *inner* quest, a need to go within oneself listening to and meeting with the other. Demeter's quest for her daughter, like the narrator's quest for writing, involves a necessary facing up to death, silence, and dismemberment but also to the possibility, quite optimistic, that once one "goes down" or "through" the horrors of Hell, one will encounter the other, one's other, one's self. This encounter successfully achieved leads to the third moment of *Illa*'s organization—one Cixous titles "Illa liberated." Set in a garden (reminiscent of childhood's garden but marked differently because innocence has been lost), which is given the name of "Jardin des Et" (Garden of the Ands), this portion of the text focuses on love and is the site of the growth of flowers, liberation (of all sorts), and poetry.

Illa is a sensual text. It speaks of sexual pleasure for females not only at the infantile oral stage but at the adult moment as well. The violence of fathers toward daughters (the father's rape or seduction of the daughter) makes them victims in some sense, but the kind of analytic work that comes through writing and through "connection" with that particular anguish (and anguish of absence) allows in the end for a full entry, as a initiate, into life.

With ou l'art de l'innocence (1981)

In the introductory words to *With ou l'art de l'innocence* Cixous tells us that she "would like to write like a fish in *écriture,* completely adopted by the sea." What she dreams of is being able "to surprise living *écriture,* by the other, to 'not take' it." The way to accomplish this goal remains unclear, however. The ideal situation, she suggests, would be to write far away from the self, far away from paper. *With ou l'art de l'innocence* is very much a companion text to *Illa.* Its title links quite clearly to *Illa*'s Garden of the Ands. Its 20-page prologue evokes, in highly poetic language, the recurring Cixousian themes of sun and sea, the confusion of elements—fire, water, earth, air—as well as meditations on language and the narrator's problematic relationship to it: "I have two joys—the joy of already-knowing and the joy of not-yet-knowing about all the rest, and I have the third joy, the joy of having the two joys which look out over the overabundance of 'there is.'"[6] The sensorial responses to the elements are, as always in Cixous, an almost surreal mixture ("I smell/hear/feel: the perfume of 'there is'" [*With,* 17]), and the initiatory aspects of the text are again evident: "I listen, I sniff, I smell the scent of the algae of first words which come from the mother tongue, I smell a word, the scent of natural language rises in my throat, how good is the scent of primitive words!" (*With,* 18). The importance of waiting ("One thing not to be forgotten: waiting is fragile" [*With,* 25]) provides the bridge to the first section of the text itself, in which we learn that "Waiting is a woman's art" (*With,* 27).

With, like *Illa,* is structured around a variety of female voices, which call to and are called by the writer-narrator—voices to which familiar yet strange names are given: Cordelia, Aura, Antouilya, Amyriam. It is important not to forget the work's "subtitle." Indeed, if one looks carefully at the text itself, the word *With* appears only on the title page and on the first page of the text. The title on the spine and cover and in the running heads of the text is "Ou l'art de l'innocence." So what is this innocence that possesses an art of its own? The narrator locates it in her childhood: "It was my good fortune: when a woman has spent her first year in paradise, she always has that year; the thing which is special about paradise is that one never loses it; one can leave it, but what you have you have forever, it's your piece of unlosable present, you will perhaps have even more, you will always have at least that" (*With,* 31). The innocence of childhood is not lost, but the act of writing involves waiting in order to recover what one has perhaps repressed or forgotten.

The narrator describes her waiting thus: "standing, pregnant, with whom?, straight and calm, soles of the feet glued like ears to the earth's chest, musical hips, at day's window, light is pregnant, with whom, you will see, waiting smiles, listens to the silence pregnant with things, with a delicate listening, listens to things growing which are preparing to appear, and always begins with A" (*With,* 35). *A,* says the narrator, is "the first sigh of life at the tenth of a second after conception" (*With,* 35). Everything that has to do with life itself begins with *a.* The waiting that is so crucial to the act of writing in *With* is linked closely to the idea of mystery. The path of writing is always a path to the unknown; it is always linked to mystery, and mystery is always linked to the body of a woman: "The secret of mystery is, like woman, at the origin already to be 'full of others.' The richness of mystery or 'of woman' is being inhabited by the unkown, being full of the mystery of You, in an unignorant ignorance."[7]

If *Illa* can be said to have developed a myth of writing that originates in the body, then *Ou l'art de l'innocence* is a further development of this myth—one that goes to the birthplace of writing itself. The writing subject is divided, as we have noted, into several voices: Antouilya, Amyriam, Aura, Cordelia, and Nuriel. These voices have no character as we would expect in a traditional fictional sense, but they do speak as parts of the writing subject. Often in *With* the text makes use of dialogue form as individualized voices (which we learn to recognize) ask questions and attempt answers (often contradictory, often ambiguous). Given Cixous's interest in music, this polyphonic approach allows us as readers to structure the text in a circulatory movement "organized in accordance not with a narrative order but with a melodic movement" (Salesne, 123). The text is produced following a double rhythm, "one metonymical in which a word, a thought, leads to another, the other making us hear the hammering of repetition" (Salesne, 123).

Whereas *Illa* can best be described as an initiatory text in which the quest revolves around the female subject, *Ou l'art de l'innocence* takes the trajectory of writing itself as both the object and subject of the quest. In both texts, however, we observe a new myth of writing—one in which, as Verena Conley tells us, "women are attuned to each other through the body. . . . *'Corps appelle corps appellent corps,'* can be said to rewrite Gertrude Stein's famous declaration that 'rose is a rose is a rose'" (Conley 1992, 75).

Limonade tout était si infini (1982)

The entire text of *Limonade tout était si infini* springs from this sentence, which remains "meaningless" but contains the last words spoken by Kafka before he died: "Limonade es war alles so grenzenlos" ("Lemonade it was all so infinite"). Cixous divides her poetic meditation on this phrase into two main parts: "The First Letter" and "The Last Sentence." The first section is set off by stark white letters on a single page that spell out "PARCE QUE" (BECAUSE). The narrator explains that what she wishes to give to Elli (her daughter) is "freedom par excellence"—a liberty that is more than liberty. Because she already possesses it, Elli has no need of receiving the gift of freedom. What the narrator wishes to give her instead is "the freedom of freedom," what she terms a "marvelously succulent gift." To taste and to know (*goûter* and *savoir*) are entwined here as the text explores various senses of thirst, adoration, and Passion.

Moving from spiritual or emotional thirst to more mundane moments over coffee on the balcony at the beginning of a new day, the narrator asks how she can accomplish her task: if lightness also has weight and if even the word *lightness* has weight, "there is no word light enough which would not make the lightness of lightness heavier."[8] The question the narrator has been considering for some time now is whether one can give "without giving notice." "How can one give notice without speech? Silence, too, is speech" (*Limonade,* 19). She confides her thoughts to a diary (red, Chinese) which she calls "Kohelet," noting that it is always difficult to know for whom one is writing, "because I don't know how to say what I need to say: that is what I try to write to myself" (*Limonade,* 20).

The narrator buys a small seashell in an antiques store, a symbol that has "everything to please her," noting especially the two halves with their delicately fluted edges of a pale yellow color, "which does not exist on our planet" (*Limonade,* 27). She refers to the eternal yellow voice of the Androgyne and finds fascination in the shell's Latin name, *Tridacna squamosa.* She rises at six, knows she has a difficult day ahead of her, but realizes that for her, just as for the biblical Sarah, the miracle is to give birth when there is no longer enough time. The miracle is that the word *impossible* also means *possible.* Making the impossible a reality, however, demands incredible strength and a spiritual competence that one only acquires with daily apprenticeship. Her thoughts moving in "excessive circles" and relating again to original paradisical innocence (the operative verb is *serpenser*—serpent thinking) leads to the conclusion that she does at least have a goal: "I want only to live as close as I can to real mysteries. I want to rip my life away from false charms. I want to study, my whole life long, the mysteries of the delicate arts. I want to work near the mysteries which ensure the life of life" (*Limonade,* 41).

Yet discovery of the mysteries is difficult. At first it is the thing itself that takes us by surprise, but then if we are lucky, we surprise it, and it is only later that we begin to understand. Like a dragonfly with shining wings that sparkle in the sunlight, the surprises of existence are seen, and not seen, in the blink of an eye. It is difficult for us to understand how something we have just seen give off a spark of light can suddenly become invisible (*Limonade,* 45). The mystery of mystery revolves around the fact that it can suddenly appear totally devoid of mystery, yet even then there remains within it something that disturbs us, a sense of "mystery vanished."

The equation discovered by the narrator ("life = the most delicate = the most invisible") "exists" in the shell she holds in the palm of her left hand. One discovery leads to another, the act of discovery continually carrying her forward. Discovery is a promise that produces energy in the searcher and a new direction in the world. And this is why the act of discovery is so shattering: "at the very instant of arrival, you find out that departure is imminent" (*Limonade,* 50). Another of the narrator's pressing questions is that of "where": "In order to think you have to begin without a watch, without a deadline, without reserve. Without asking yourself: 'Who?' but 'Where?'" (*Limonade,* 51).

The narrator sees everything in nature ordered by "the Great Logic of Destruction," and she has difficulty understanding how any kind of life can be drawn from such a chain of death (*Limonade,* 77). She understands that death is a necessary part of survival and that the chain of destruction is impossible to break but becomes exhausted by the effort of attempting to find the fault in the chain that would cause it to break. The notion that life can actually *give* life to some forms of death and vice versa, however, leaves her a pleasant sensation of madness. The letter she sends to Elli is described as a kind of "butterfly of art," again reinforcing the gossamer and fragile images of this text (*Limonade,* 83). Yet this happiness—the happiness of love for Elli—is also terrifying because happiness is always that which has escaped, that which has almost not come into existence and is still trembling. The choice now for the narrator becomes another one of taste: the choice between peach or pear. A political choice, a sexual choice. She really wants a pear although what she wanted at first was a peach. The narrator has learned how the mistakes of women and men are different, and she has also learned that "not a single piece of knowledge about existing can be 'said.' It must be lived" (*Limonade,* 95).

The narrator takes a peach (her fruit of choice) and goes onto her balcony to think about "men-men," those who do not dream so that they can exist more comfortably in the world. Dreaming, says the narrator, is not in their interest; in fact, it is in the "masculine interest" that this civilization *not* dream. It is not part of their "feminine interest," however, as one can die from lack of dreaming. And humanity does have a "feminine interest." Rather than living "near their savage sources," men-men possess. And what do they possess? Ideas. Yet individuals who do not renounce their "feminine interest" are able to go directly to the source and hold living things in their hands. They touch life itself. There are "real men" among the creatures of this group, but "men-men" are not part of it. They continue to have no time to have time. Those, however, who come to the source, are bathed in the source and "are" (*Limonade,* 98–99).

The peach finished, the narrator meditates on the nature of what she terms "the most interesting fruit." The peach is a fruit that makes one see and think. A treasure is hidden within a peach—a treasure that provides inspiration to painters, poets, and women—for all those, indeed, who search for life. The peach (unlike the pear, which is entirely consumed) contains the seed of the future. In that sense the peach is eternal. Since the peach pit contains the new peach tree, one must be careful not to crack it: "Peaches are like women, they are infinitely tender beings and certainly decided about resisting destruction" (*Limonade,* 100).

In this text Cixous presents life as a series of explorations. Each thing, each person, offers itself to us to be known *on the inside.* We can refuse the offer and remain on the outside of the world. Or we can live by flinging ourselves into the other's moment: "It's like when you were jumping rope and when your friends were turning it, and the rope went up in a circular movement and you had to jump in. And to do that you had to leave the inert exterior, and in one leap adjust your movement to the movement of the rope. It's a question of rhythm: adjust yours to the rhythm of life and jump!" (*Limonade,* 131). To the narrator's shell collection is added a black jumping rope with canary yellow handles.

The narrator returns again and again to the question of a benediction or blessing. When does one discover a benediction? The conditions, the narrator discovers, involve the constant movement toward life. To meet the other, to go to the other, to meet the world. Thus benedictions are always linked to points of encounter (*Limonade,* 153). "I'd especially like to take care of the peonies because they are so fragile" (*Limonade,* 171), she tells us. The narrator knows that if you have once found the secret of simplicity, it will come back to you and lightness will return. Beginning to live and not merely continuing to exist is the essence of human happiness (*Limonade,* 173–74).

The second half of *Limonade* is a meditation on the last words spoken by Franz Kafka before his death. The narrator awakens after a night of dreams (at the end of part 1) and finds herself eager to write. "My baroque pearl"—a phrase that calls to mind Rembrandt's portrait of Saskia—sends her toward not a work of art (*oeuvre d'art*) but rather to a work of being (*oeuvre d'être*). The narrator then recounts an anecdote from Kafka's life, on 10 October 1904: three people form the cast for this story. The one who watches is named Max; he is also the one who makes the introductions. Max has spoken about the other two, to each about the other, in advance. He has told Franz that O is blind. When the introductions are made, Max says the two names: "The word 'blind' is in the room, but mute" (*Limonade,* 240). Max introduces Kafka by name. Kafka bows to O, without a word. Is that all? What makes the scene so fragile (and *fragile* is a word that returns again and again in this text—*fragile* happiness, *fragile* peonies, *fragile* meeting) is that it happened within the invisible. The unspeakable delicacy of a gesture—to make a sign of seeing in the presence of a blind man—is one that generously gives the most precious mark of respect. In bowing to O, Kafka literally gave him back his sight. The marvelous element within this story is the invisible gift of Kafka to one who was apparently not in a position to receive it. When O tells the same story later, he describes the moment when Max pronounces Franz's name. Because Franz knows that O is blind, the act of bowing is perhaps, according to O, a formality devoid of meaning for someone who could not see it. Yet when Kafka bowed, a lock of his hair had brushed against O's forehead and he had experienced a special kind of joy (*Limonade,* 244). The secret dream of writing, the narrator tells us, is to be as delicate as silence itself (*Limonade,* 252).

The narrator then turns to another anecdote and another date from literary history. On 22 December 1849, Fyodor Dostoyevski is in prison awaiting death, yet at the last minute he is given a reprieve. On that day, says the narrator, Fyodor died and lived (until his "actual" death on 31 January 1881). But for the writer what is significant are those things that happen during the moments immediately preceding "death." It is in facing death that we are given access to life. Dostoyevski, in prison and among the condemned, is truly a "dying" man since he knows the term of his life (it has been decided by others) and is not a toy of nature's whim. The secret of transparent "last" sentences is that they are just that: final. To write "last" sentences the writer needs a self that is as light as a dragonfly. As translucid as a young grasshopper, almost invisible, like the palest touch of green in nature. "I fear writing the book," says the narrator. "I want to write the last book which would be the last book. I want, I need to write such a book" (*Limonade,* 262). The last sentence—"*Limonade tout était si infini*"—is parsed poetically, and the text concludes with a trilingual poem:

Limonade es war alles so grenzenlos
C'est pour cela qu'on aime les libellules
Darum liebt man die Wasserjungfrauen
Et le lilas au soleil
Wo ist der ewige Fruhling?
Un oiseau est entré
(E que voce nao sabe o quanto pesa uma pessoa que
nao tem força)

Und Flieder in die Sonne
Mais pour l'instant il y a assez de fleurs
Ein Vogel war im Zimmer
Limonade tout était si infini

Le Livre de Promethea (1983) and *La Bataille d'Arcachon* (1986)

Le Livre de Promethea should be considered as a companion volume to a book that appeared three years later, *La Bataille d'Arcachon.* Both texts deal with the relationship between language and love, writing and "life," and they involve a complex narrational structure—narrators including Hélène and HC (in first and third persons), with the introduction of a feminine Prometheus figure (Promethea) who is central to the text's love story as well as to the metanarrative on the act of writing itself. *The Book of Promethea* is a rarity in contemporary French writing—the story of a love between two women told in a multiregistered fashion.

In Greek religion, of course, Prometheus was the Titan who gave fire and arts to mankind. Zeus's punishment for this action was to chain him to a mountain where an eagle devoured his liver. He was eventually freed by Hercules. This is the story told in Aeschylus's *Prometheus Bound.* Many other writers have used the story of Prometheus or the theme of bringer of fire, bringer of arts. One of the best known is Shelley, whose poem "Prometheus Unbound" celebrates the theme of mankind's deliverance. Cixous has in turn taken the Greek male god but transformed him into a female figure, a woman who loves and who lives in the moment. *Promethea* belongs to what one of Cixous's translators, Betsy Wing, has called a "fiction of presence."[9]

The Book of Promethea is the first Cixousian fictional text to be translated since *Inside* in 1969. It is an accessible text and one of which Cixous remains fond. The epigraph, as usual, tells us something of the attachment between author and text: "I am a little afraid for this book. Because it is a book of love. It is a burning bush. Best to plunge in. Once in the fire one is bathed in sweetness. Honestly: here I am, in it" (*Promethea,* 4). The text's opening tackles head on the problem of the "who" of narration, "I" announcing that the introduction must be done by someone since "neither of the two who really made this book can bring herself to do it" (*Promethea,* 5). The two who really made this book are then identified as "H" and Promethea. The first-person narrator lets us know that she is an author, that she is female, and that she will attempt to keep the textual threads untangled as we move through the text: "My aim is to slip as close as possible to the two real makers' being until I can marry the contour of these women's souls with mine, without, however, causing any confusion" (*Promethea,* 5). H is described as having had problems with producing a text since, after her encounter with Promethea, her "old ways are no longer possible." In the words of H, "What am I going to do with my theories, all so pretty, so agile, and so theoretical, and now so obviously surrounded by reality in person in the specific person of Promethea, which they did not expect at all?" (*Promethea,* 6). H even refers to Cixous's own bibliography in her references to theory ("From the first, the one about bisexuality, which I always had some qualms about, up to the newest and supplest, the one that carried me dancing to a tune by Rossini in a single, unbroken gallop from Argel by way of Santiago to Jerusalem" [*Promethea,* 6–7]).

The generous gesture involved in the writing of *Promethea* is demonstrated by the increased vulnerability of the author/creator/narrator/I/H as she attempts to get to the center of the onionlike structure of writing itself, always remembering, always reminding readers that she is "just a woman who thinks her duty is not to forget" (*Promethea,* 9). And this duty, she tells us as well, is "'as a woman' living now I must repeat again and again 'I am a woman,' because we exist in an epoch still so ancient and ignorant and slow that there is always the danger of gynocide" (*Promethea,* 9).

The "problem" H and the narrator are having with the text of "Promethea's book" are problems centered on the creator and not the creation. The book—a book "of love," a "raging book," a "book about now," a "fearless book"—is lit by Promethean fire. "Promethea is my heroine," says the narrator (*Promethea,* 10). "But the question of writing is my adversary" (*Promethea,* 10). The narrator explains that she cannot do without H: "I do not yet have the mental courage to be only *I.* I dread nothing as much as autobiography. Autobiography does not exist. Yet so many people believe it exists. So here I solemnly state: autobiography is only a literary genre. It is nothing living. It is a jealous, deceitful sort of thing—I detest it. When I say 'I,' this I is never the subject of autobiography, my I is free. It is the subject of my madness, my alarms, my vertigo" (*Promethea,* 19).

The narrator has promised Promethea that she will write that Promethea loves her, yet she has been thus far in the text unable to keep her word. She is particularly concerned with the problem of "translation": "Translating oneself is already serious—I mean putting life into words—sometimes it is almost putting it to death; sometimes dragging it out, sometimes embalming it, sometimes making it vomit or lie, sometimes bringing it to climax, but one never knows before beginning whether one's luck will be good or bad, whether this is birth or suicide. But translating someone else—that requires extraordinary arrogance or extraordinary humility" (*Promethea,* 21).

Because the narrator is "not Promethea," she cannot bring herself to act as if she were; thus she cannot bring Promethea's words to the text. She decides that perhaps she can simply transmit Promethea's words as if they had been dictated:

> Promethea's speech is very simple and high and very pointed like a mountain. She uses few words because there are few at that altitude but they are sparkling and transparent like glaciers at the very top. Her vocabulary comes always from the guts, hers or the earth's. It comes out smoking and violent, with roots still permeated with blood, with earth, with salt, with oil. But she also uses gentler forms, ancient recitations that ripple out along the road, in airy notes, in rainbowed bubbles of sound, leaving silver traces in the air. Generally, her languages are ancient and fresh and lightly limned as the paintings at Lascaux. They are all clairvoyant. She speaks in evocations and eruptions more than in metaphors. Whereas I, I drill, I dig, I sink in, I plow even the sea, I want to turn it over. No, we do not speak at all the same languages. Things she lets bubble up in a shower of sparks, I would like to collect and bind. She burns and I want to write out the fire! Luckily, I'll never succeed. (*Promethea,* 23–24)

The narrator shows Promethea her introductory pages, which include Promethea's words; but Promethea responds that she doesn't like them at all since they are "literature" and as such now totally unrecognizable to her (*Promethea,* 25).

The narrator then finds herself in a forest, having taken a different path from that chosen by Promethea. "Writing," she thinks, "is a translation." She enters a small dark inner room in which she confronts her three memories—the Paleolithic, the biblical, and the poetic. The narrator evokes the presence of Clarice Lispector and Lispector's creation of Macabea, while Promethea is equated to the narrator's Bradamante. The writing of Promethea's book is also related to Gilgamesh, the hero of the Babylonian epic that tells of his adventures. She admits, however, that she has perhaps been confused, admitting that she now recognizes "Ariosto's style"—

Ludovico Ariosto, the Italian epic and lyric poet, famous for his *Orlando Furioso* (1516), an epic treatment of the Roland story. Finally acknowledging the impossibilty of tracing the source of the book, the narrator confesses that "for me, the closest to the pen, well-placed, I think, to decide: it is Promethea. Consequently: everything that follows has moved through my hand and onto the paper when there was real contact with Promethea. I have often put my left hand between her breasts and with the rapid motions of my docile right hand it was written. I am only that cardiograph" (*Promethea,* 53). The image of the writer as cardiograph is striking—and, indeed, expressive of the overall Cixousian project.

Written in two notebooks, *The Book of Promethea* traces not only the progression of love but the progression of the writer in relation to the text: "I used to call what I now call generosity, dependency, and I thought it was bad. It is not my way of thinking that has turned upside down, it is my life which has suddenly turned toward death and smiled at it. Now that I am going in the direction of death with Promethea, I think of it [death] altogether differently. I have far more respect for it. I do not forget it" (*Promethea,* 55). Love as a form of cannibalism, love and marketing, love and reading—these preoccupations haunt the narrator: "Promethea discovers garden cucumbers and ancient rites, and the whole market suddenly takes on the brilliance of a Shakespearean comedy. That is why sometimes I want to go to the market the same way I want to reread *Les Illuminations.* . . . In the market things to eat are so alive, so meaningful, so eloquent and young, that one starts loving the things one will end up devouring. It is a love sotry that is both magic and absolutely real; it is our history. The story of love" (*Promethea,* 58).

Although the love affair with Promethea is not all passion and physical connection ("Because in love not all is love. But also: injustice, anger, hunger, delicate hunger and raging hunger, innocent hungers and cruel hungers proud of being so and ashamed of being so and even prouder" [*Promethea,* 65–66]), *The Book of Promethea* is still, above all, a book about love—a celebration of the passion of meeting and and the pain of separation that are bound up together in this most elemental of human experiences. "We go beyond ourselves with love's help," says the narrator. "Sometimes we leap over our own limits and we land unhurt on the moss. But sometimes the leap is not magical enough, we have forgotten a word, a heartbeat, and we stay put with a heavy shudder" (*Promethea,* 87). The "ordeal of Paradise" is that one cannot bear to spend a season there "without crying out in instant nostalgia: never will we have the strength to endure such intoxicating agony a second time" (*Promethea,* 86).

Writing and love have an anchor in the present: "I want to know the present as presently as possible" (*Promethea,* 92), the narrator tells us. "I do not believe in magic or parapsychology, as I have said elsewhere. But I do believe in poetry. I believe that there are creatures endowed with the power to put things together and bring them back to life" (*Promethea,* 103). And the most wonderful belief of all is the belief in Promethea's love: "But what astonishes me most, and so often astonishes me least (and I still wonder how to speak of it if I decide to try), is that Promethea loves me and I know it" (*Promethea,* 103). In the past, the narrator confesses that although she thought she knew something about love, she had contented herself with loving, thinking that that was sufficient. But Promethea draws her attention to the other aspect of love, the receiving of love. "Giving requires no courage," she tells the reader, "but to receive love so much strength, so much patience, and so much generosity must be extended" (*Promethea,* 105).

The first notebook is one of springtime, "of growth, of restoration, of meals, of promises, of tasting, of driving-growing-certainty," what the narrator calls "love defending itself" (*Promethea,* 120). Following the first notebook, however, love changes and is transformed into a kind of vampirelike relationship. Counting the days (the fifty-third, the sixtieth), the narrator notes the metamorphosis of love: "Rereading this book I notice that it has a unity: a book on relinquishment, dispossession and possession" (*Promethea,* 136).

The second section refers directly to metamorphosis but in a dual sense. Metamorphosis relates not only to the transmutations of feeling but also to the growing confusion of the identity of the narrator and Promethea: "I no longer know if 'she' is Promethea or me, in these notes" (*Promethea,* 139). In the second notebook as well, "up and down are frequently turned upside down, things are frequently reversed: one into the other, one sort into another, fire into ice, blood into stone, and stone into tears" (*Promethea,* 141). It is "full of fantastic incidents, both fascinating and painful" (Promethea, 141). The narrator calls it a "hippogriff."

The story of Promethea and H is continued in the 1986 *conte, The Battle of Arcachon,* the only one of Cixous's books to be published outside France. In *The Battle of Arcachon,* Cixous's first-person narrator takes up the tale in Arcachon, at a time when H and Promethea are separated. The chapter titles give us a clear indication of Cixous's themes and symbols: the departure of H, beneath the sand, the arrival of Promethea ("I'll not release you until you've blessed me"), the glow-worm, the lake, the meadow, the return of H, and the botanical garden. Once again the reader participates in the passionate relationship between H and her lover Promethea, a relationship filtered through often ambiguous narration: "As I expected," says the narrator, "they are still there. Nothing has happened. Nothing that I could tell in a simple way. . . . How am I going to be able to relate that which goes beyond? These last few days they've lived too fast. They're exhausting each other! They're making each other dizzy. I like it better when they're arguing: then they mark time, they go round in circles, and I have time to note everything down."[10]

One of the joys of the relationship between H and Promethea has always been that, by a series of strokes of fate, Promethea has introduced H to many pleasures and pains, both large and small—cappuccino, for example, which serves as the pretext for the narration of H's departure, or ginger chicken, the dish prepared by Promethea for H the night before she leaves. When H arrives in Arcachon, it is raining and she has problems with the lock on the door. She feels dirty from the trip and is prey to strange emotional states, perhaps understandable given the fact that her current reading material includes Ariosto, *The Arabian Nights,* and the Roman plays of Shakespeare. H is incapable of reading a newspaper while in Arcachon—something the narrator feels would alleviate her emotional distress. But one of H's problems involves the loss of her desert, the necessary desert for her poems.

During the week that follows H's arrival in Arcachon, she works "beneath the sand," always searching for traces of Promethea. For five days and four nights she manages to work without Promethea's presence. Finally, however, the weekend arrives and with it Promethea—by air. The reunion of the two lovers in Arcachon marks a kind of return to Paradise, a return to peace. Love "surprises" them, as always. The narrator, from the vantage point of her flying carpet (this is a story about *The Arabian Nights,* after all), takes us, in a flashback, to a previous Sunday that Promethea and H had spent in Paris. H, who is in a bad mood, makes a list of all the things which Promethea does to make her angry. The terrible secret H discovers on this day is that we can never possess another person. She ought to have known that, but she realizes that there are times when one does not really know what one knows.

Promethea and H spend the day and night arguing (the narrator coyly announcing that she has taken her model from canto 19 of Ariosto's *Orlando Furioso,* "when the two champions equal in force and in chivalry no longer know how to finish their battle"; *Arcachon*, 52). H ends the chapter, begun with the list of her lover's failings, with a list of her own needs: a desert, sunrises, eyes with which to see the world (which is always beautiful even when it is horrible), the world's waters and milk, infinities and silences, music, a little casserole, and of course Promethea, "her bread" (*Arcachon,* 57). Along with these things, however, H needs something for which she has always been searching—she calls it truth; Promethea would call it "the essential." Compared to a luminous gazelle, the truth, the essential can never be captured. Yet from time to time, as if the gazelle were somehow struck by love for those who seek her so passionately, the animal turns to look, "transformed into water of joy" (*Arcachon,* 57).

The glow-worm, the firefly, of truth or life's essence, is the title for the following section, and the narrator watches as Promethea and H spend their precious two days together looking for it, loving each other. Before Promethea leaves, she asks the narrator if she has finished the list of all the things H has done "for the first time" with Promethea. Embarrassed, the narrator admits that she has not had time to do so yet—and that the rhythm of the text has not seemed appropriate for the insertion of such a chapter. While Promethea and H are packing, however, the narrator inserts a short section on that very subject.

In both *The Book of Promethea* and *La Bataille d'Arcachon* Cixous confronts the tension between total identification with the loved other and separation from the loved other. As Morag Shiach reminds us, "Total identification with an Other threatens the subject with annihilation, while separation leads to unbearable grief" (Shiach, 100). Although the Cixousian textual world could hardly be called one of moderation, it is fair to say that the tension provided from extremes generally propels the narrative forward.

Manne, aux Mandelstams, aux Mandelas (1988)

The small gaps between the production of Cixous's fiction in the 1980s (*La Bataille d'Arcachon* appears three years after *Promethea; Manne* two years after *Arcachon*—an unusual rhythm if compared with her career up to this point) are explained by her increasingly concentrated work in theater. Indeed, during this particular "fictional" period, her involvement with the Théâtre du Soleil and Ariane Mnouchkine grew substantially. The text of *Manne* marks as well a more abrupt shift in style than previously observable throughout the earlier years of her writing career. Consonant with a certain contemporary literary shift to overt mixture of "fact" and "fiction," *Manne* makes use of two real-life characters as well as true historical dates in order to anchor a narrative that concerns itself, not surprisingly, with what it is like to live in exile, to live in prison, to love, to rescue, and to suffer. *Manne* has been called a "mythical exploration of the power of individual and collective resistance" (Shiach, 101), and is a text in which Cixous "attempts to find a form to move beyond the contingencies of contemporary history toward the more universal narratives of myth" (Shiach, 101).

The text's title evokes the words *manna* (holy sustenance), the German *Manne* (people), and *man* as the shared syllable of both Mandelstam and Mandela, "two names which knot the text with their common syllable, 'two almonds in the breast of the world' (deux amandes)."[11] Although the two never knew each other, the Russian poet Osip Mandelstam and the South African leader Nelson Mandela shared the same pain—the pain of exile and the pain of condemnation. The quotation Cixous uses as an epigraph is also indicative of the focus of attention in *Manne*: Dante's *Paradiso* (canto 18).

Two dates are key as well in this text: 1 May 1938, the date on which Osip Mandelstam was sent to a gulag in exile, and 12 June 1964, the day on which Nelson Mandela was condemned to life in prison. In 1986 Cixous contributed to a French-edited volume of essays titled *For Nelson Mandela,* a literary homage to honor the South African leader who had become a symbol of justice and the struggle against apartheid in his country. Cixous's contribution, "The Parting of the Cake," later becomes the centerpiece of *Manne.*

"The Parting of the Cake" begins with the evocation of an imaginary journey to South Africa—a journey that is only possible through the articulation of the "real name" of apartheid, "apart-hate."[12] In the imagination of the author, however, the putrid breath of apartheid is countered by the aroma of "milky almond," a scent characterized as "a perfume of the soul, the strong yet delicate perfume of the great loves, the almond perfume of the Mandelas. The perfume of a love stronger than death" (*Mandela,* 203).

Cixous traces an evocative and richly poetic story of the relationship of Nelson and Winnie Mandela from the moment of their first meeting in 1958. Winnie's African name, we learn, is Zami, which means "test" in Zhosa. The Mandela love story is in many ways a parallel of the difficult but always vibrant struggle for freedom from apartheid within South Africa's history: "It was not easy having a life of destiny and Africa for a family name. For, even so, he was just a man, she just a woman with a desire to cry. They have labored so hard, but unheroically, especially she. With difficulty, with terror, with such pities. But, I believe, being tested and crying out unheroically is what heroism means. And also laughing whenever possible" (*Mandela,* 210). The moment comes, however, when Nelson and Zami are to marry: "It would be a perfect marriage, the marriage of the future. Both traditional and modern, it would unite east and west, heaven and earth, Xhosa kin and Thembu kin, ancestors and descendants, fire and rain, lachyrmal salt and salivary sugar, hope and certainty, ostrich and hunter, faith and science, black learning and white learning" (*Mandela,* 210). The wedding cake, too, is both functional and symbolic within the marriage celebration: "All these vows went into the dough for the marriage cake. The first half of the cake is to be eaten with the family of the bride, the other half with the family of the groom. When the dough is fully blended with the human dough, the force of the cake of desires begins acting. Zami and Nelson's cake was uniquely magical" (*Mandela,* 210).

The Mandela story is a tale of separation, both physical and emotional (Nelson and Winnie Mandela were apart even from the first day of their marriage—he in prison, she from time to time under house arrest or in prison as well). They endured individual suffering, shared suffering, but in the end "the cake had the best of it. The dough proved stronger than all the forces of decomposition and dispersion. Not a crumb was lost" (*Mandela,* 212). Cixous brings us up to date with the Mandela–South Africa saga thus: "Today the cake is twenty-eight. All the crumbs are in safe-keeping in Orlando. Nelson has been in Pollsmoor Prison in Capetown since April 1982. I am writing this in April 1986. All the Mandela crumbs are living" (*Mandela,* 212). Playing again on the almond-Mandela pairing (almond cake is traditional for weddings, *amande* contains the "seed" of Mandela's name), Cixous describes the tender almond, like the flesh of a child, hidden within the bitter and inedible shell, the tender almond the "secret" of Mandela.

Cixous claims that because she cannot write as a man in *Manne,* she has approached the narrative through the "character" of Winnie Mandela. *Manne* thus becomes the extended story of the Mandela wedding cake: the first half eaten but the second half uneaten because of the force of history. Themes of parting and splitting, separation and loss, death and life, absence and presence return again and again. The "real" separation between Winnie and Nelson Mandela exists because of the South African prison and the South African political system, yet psychic closeness and intimacy are still possible. As Verena Conley reminds us,

"Praising an ethics of distance in proximity, Cixous brings together body and soul" (Conley, 1992, 92). Cixous has chosen in *Manne* to write about an idealized couple and about a love affair that goes "beyond ordinary bounds of time." "Beyond the misery of which she is most aware, [Cixous] chooses to enter the scene of history with extraordinary characters with whom she identifies" (Conley 1992, 95).

Yet *Manne* is only partly concerned with the idealized and fictionalized character of Nelson Mandela; it is also very much a text about a dead poet, Osip Mandelstam. And in this perhaps strange but typically Cixousian juxtaposition we see the other key feature of *Manne*: its focus on the question of writing itself. *Manne* continues the meditation begun by Cixous in the 1970s on the relationship between politics and poetry; it is a text that articulates the inherent difficulties of describing or representing the atrocities of contemporary society: torture, murder, famine.

Osip Mandelstam—persecuted by the Soviet government for many years because of his poetry, eventually dying of starvation in prison—his wife, Nadja, and the Russian poet Anna Akhmatova form the trio around which the Mandelstam portion of *Manne* revolves. Like Nelson Mandela, they are exiled; however, in their case it is their poetry that carries them beyond the body. The manna here is poetry itself or, as Conley points out in a more general sense, "Poetry is the ultimate manna that links those in exile. Real political transformations would occur through the testing of the soul. It is the soul that gives shape to the body" (Conley 1992, 112). Cixous's identification with poets and poetry leads her recurringly to the question of the "place of poetry" in contemporary society. She imagines "generations of poets, touching each other, communciating somatically, through bodily vibrations produced by their poetry, their lights glowing in the darkness of the world" (Conley 1992, 113).

The titles of the text's 16 chapters are "Dedication to the Ostrich," "The Posthumous Poem," "The Face of Abandon," "The Marriage Proposal," "The True Portrait of Nelson," "The Visit of the Ostrich," "Akhmatova's Egg," "The Separation of the Cake," "The End of the Unfinished Poem," "En Route," "Osip's Last Letter," "The Song of Roads," "Everything Which They Could Not Do," "The No-Good-bye of May 1," "The Day of Condemnation," and "A Life of Letters." *Manne* is certainly, as Morag Shiach has pointed out, a courageous text, since it was written at a time when Nelson Mandela was still in prison and when the fact of open support by a writer for the African National Congress was very unusual. Shiach points as well, however, to the ambiguous implications of Cixous's commitment. Obviously Cixous has chosen both Mandela and Mandelstam as poetic figures of resistance. But, says Shiach, "writing poetry and waging a guerrilla war are not the same, yet *Manne* deals with both at a level of abstraction that renders such distinction almost irrelevant. We are thus left with a slight feeling that some important questions have been evaded by the sheer virtuosity of Cixous's metaphorical associations" (Shiach, 104). In this postmodern blend of fiction and history, the questions remain: "If it is a fiction, to what extent does its factual accuracy matter? If it is a history, can it also, productively, be a myth? Can the emotional power of a mythic text be the means of transforming our historical knowledge, or does it simply supplement or refine it?" (Shiach, 105).

Jours de l'an (1990) and *L'Ange au secret* (1991)

Cixous's most recent fictions are also clearly very closely related in substance and style to *Manne.* They continue to show, in their variations-on-a-theme style, the ever-present concern she has both for the act of writing itself and for the relationship between writing poetry and political gesture. Unlike the earlier twinned texts of the 1970s, *Les Commencements* and *Le Troisième Corps, Jours de l'an* and *L'Ange au secret* are not so obviously linked. Yet the cycles of life and death, lived experience and memory are played out in very similar fashion in both texts, as is the recurring meditation on the act of writing. Unlike her political positioning of the 1970s, Cixous "no longer sees herself at the head of an avant-garde, but rather, as a part of a group that holds onto, and defends, a culture about to disappear" (Conley 1992, 123–24). The act of writing has now become the act of witnessing history and preserving memory. The meditative style used by Cixous in both *Jours de l'an* and *L'Ange au secret* places her writing on the margins between life and death, in an eternal present that is constantly in motion. It is a style that deliberately leaves her previous work behind her: "That is how I left behind me, one two three four dead (and perhaps others of whom there remain only bones and dust), of which one is a mummy, and one could be my woman-friend. The other two, I hate."[13]

The title *Jours de l'an*—"days of the year" or "New Year's Days"—underlines Cixous's preoccupation with time and dates, with the recurring nature of our joys and sorrows, and with the writer's obsession for holding the instant in language while liberating it at the same time. "Why," asks the narrator,

> do I speak of the author if she is not me? Because she is not me. She comes from much further away and from a more outside place than all my outsiders. She leaves me behind and goes where I do not wish to go. Whereas I, since February 12 of this year, have tried with all my might to capture some small glimpses of the truth, the author has only been busy with the story she has to tell. *An Ideal Story.* Off she goes—so slowly that in the meantime I could tell ten stories. I write underground, like an animal, burrowing in the silence of my chest. One difference between the author and me: the author is the daughter of dead fathers. I come from the line of my living mother. (*Jours de l'an*)

The text of *Jours de l'an* is divided into seven parts, each section recapitulating Cixousian themes and allusively integrating thematic preoccupations of several other writers who are most currently among Cixous's favorites: Paul Celan, Thomas Bernhard, and Anna Akhmatova. The text begins with the time marker "Thirty years ago" (*Jours de l'an,* 5), which points to Cixous's own entry into writing. Thus there now exists for the author a present that is 30 years old: "And for thirty years I've been writing, carried along by writing, this book, that book; and now I suddenly feel, among all those books, the book that I have not written, the book that I have never stopped not writing. And it's now that I feel it, today, a day after the twelfth of February, when I learn now, not before now, that it's the book I miss" (*Jours de l'an,* 7). The eternal dream of the writer is to write the book that has not been written, or using another favorite example of Cixous's, to dream of painting Mount Fujiyama: "If it happened that you managed to paint what you had dreamed of painting since the first brush stroke, everything would immediately perish: art, nature, the painter, hope, everything would have happened" (*Jours de l'an,* 17).

The second section, "The Principal Character in this Book Is . . . ," returns us to a now familiar Cixousian concern with death. Death, says the narrator, is the principal character in this book (*Jours de l'an,* 49). A brief bridging third section, "Thinking Is Not What We Think It Is," leads us to the fourth section, "Mes Berceaux Tombeaux/My cribcrypts." Dates—for Cixous, 9 December, 1 October, 27 July, and 12 February—bring us the end of the world: "Another ending. Another ending. And the ending of an ending. The first among them, the one which blazed the trail of dates in my forest," the narrator tells us, "is February 12. The twelfth of February is the arrow which pierced the beyond within me, twelve times bloodied it, clawed the cells of my memory, and when I have been an atom for generations, a twelfth of

February will somewhere still produce a slight trembling of atoms in Asian jasmine" (*Jours de l'an,* 63).

The twelfth of February, the date of Cixous's father's death in 1948, also recalls an experience of 12 February 1989. Cixous is sitting in a room with her mother, reading Thomas Bernhard's *The Child* (the fifth volume of his autobiography), when her mother glances up from the newspaper and announces that Bernhard has died. Cixous says to herself that perhaps Bernhard has died for her birthday (since the death of the father is closely connected to the birth of the daughter), "because this twelfth of February day for forty years had never been lived in this world, but in the other world" (*Jours de l'an,* 86). The twelfth of February is always a different day, a day marked differently, "a window opened on eternity" (*Jours de l'an,* 86). Just as death is always present in life, so is life always present in death: "Who can say what happens to me on February 12?" asks the narrator. "Perhaps it's a June 5 [Cixous's birthday] that happens to me on February 12. Today, says my mother, is your father's anniversary. Yes, it's the anniversary. My father in his red granite cradle. And now it's my cradle every year. It's my anniversary" (*Jours de l'an,* 65).

The next two sections, "Knocking Down a Wall Is an Angel's Work" and "At Night my Strange Life," are both fast-paced mixtures of many things already familiar to readers of Cixous: Clarice Lispector (and her significant "days of the year"), the author's passion for doors (open, shut, as passageways), a short meditation on the nature of reading, a consideration of Rembrandt and several of his paintings (*The Jewish Fiancée, The Anatomy Lesson*), and more deliberate descriptive passages about the significant times we spend in dream worlds.

The seventh section, "Self-Portraits of a Blind Woman," returns us to the question of the author and recapitulates material from the introductory portion of the text. The author, says Cixous, is not me. "The author" indeed often disappears and goes into territories where the I-narrator cannot follow: "Often she is as if she were dead when I am alive and vice versa" (*Jours de l'an,* 153). "There is a difference between myself and the author—the author is the daughter of dead fathers whereas I descend from the living mother. Between us everything is different, unequal, shattering" (*Jours de l'an,* 154). Photographs of Clarice Lispector and Marina Tsvetaeva serve as reminders to the narrator that writing and reading are intimate acts that connect us in the deepest way. In the words of "the author," "I need to speak of these women who have become part of me, they have struck me, they have hurt me, they have awakened the dead within me, they have blazed the way, they have brought me wars, gardens, children, strange families, mournings without grave markers, and I have tasted the world through their languages/tongues. Within me they have lived their lives. They have written. They are dead. They continue to live, never ceasing to live, nor to die, nor to write" (*Jours de l'an,* 162). Other anecdotal imagined scenes between dead writers or literary characters (Marina Tsvetaeva and Rilke, Pushkin's Tatiana from *Eugene Onegin*) lead eventually to "An Ideal Story," which is the final section of the text.

Two "characters," Clarice and Isaac, move closer, then farther away from each other—seeking connection, seeking communication, seeking (as the author promised us in the text's introductory section) "truth." Truth, however, like intimacy or "love," is always "farther away." "I want farther away," says the narrator. "Where I'm afraid to go is where I want to go. The life I'm seeking is hidden behind fear. Fortunately [though] fear is there with its black and red banner to show me the way" (*Jours de l'an,* 228). Death, too, of course, becomes an integral part of Clarice and Isaac's "ideal story": "the mystery is that we confuse inventing and believing. We create the word Death, and the word becomes our master, and we do not un-create it" (*Jours de l'an,* 255).

Just as Cixous has habitually had difficulty in beginning a text, so she has expressed difficulty in endings ("I'm going to make a confession. For ten days I've been trying to write a last page for this book" [*Jours de l'an,* 274]). But just as the writer's journey from textual beginning to ending is trying, so is existence, so is life itself. "A journey threatens our existence. We do not get up in the same book every day. In the midst of life we are carried off into another life. Only to return to ourselves a month, a year, a country, later. . . . Eventually one always ends by beginning, yet to end, no, (and so many lives are going on beyond us), to end ends nothing" (*Jours de l'an,* 276). "If I wrote a book," says the author who has just written one—the one we have nearly finished reading—"I would begin with a garden at dawn, pink, at the foot of a mountain. I would do absolutely everything to prevent the book from turning against me, so that it would travel towards the south, towards the pink, towards the sea, which are my true directions, if ever I were the one who wrote a book" (*Jours de l'an,* 276).

L'Ange au secret (The Secret Angel) continues in the meditative tone established in *Jours de l'an,* concentrating, however, on a slightly different version of the writer's project as it relates to the description of lived human experience and the experience of living as a common journey toward one's "secret crime." Divided into 10 chapters, the text opens with an introductory section written "*In extremis*" from the swamp of the Apocalypses. The constant image of the Apocalypse serves to remind readers of the biblical Book of Revelations (derived from the Greek *apokalypsis*), the last book of the New Testament, which is rich in allegory and subject to numerous interpretations. The Book of Revelations was written in order to prepare Christians for the final intervention of God into human affairs, and Saint John, its author, deliberately chose a literary vehicle that would tend to conceal his message from the enemies of the church. This vehicle was apocalypse, a literary form characterized by an often elaborately symbolic interpretation and prediction of events. The key to the original symbolism of the text has long been lost, but the Book of Revelations is valued today for its literary qualities and for its depiction of a historical crisis in Christianity. Cixous's text takes on its own special revelatory power as the narrator moves from swamplike apocalyptic space outward in an exploration of guilt, evil, and human connectedness.

The old house of childhood, "the house of yesterdays," allows the narrator to articulate her four fears: "I fear what will happen. I fear what will not happen. I am afraid, here, of the dead. I am afraid of the love of the dead."[14] In dreams she explores the possible "characters" for the book she is attempting to write and is gradually drawn to the inescapable conclusion that "one does not leave without angels" on such a perilous journey. The second chapter thus introduces us to some of her "angels"—names with which we are already quite familiar: Dostoyevski, Clarice Lispector, Ingeborg Bachmann, Anna Akhmatova, and Thomas Bernhard, with brief appearances by Virgil and Dante. The narrator admits that her narration moves like a beetle and that trying to follow along behind it "one could die of frustration" (*L'Ange au secret,* 45). By this time, however, the text has taken over: "I am in the mouth of the book, I feel it biting me everywhere, on the back, on the nape of the neck, on my feet. It's a multilingual mouth. I won't get out of here without harm" (*L'Ange au secret,* 47).

Chapter 3 focuses on "Having the Label T.B.," a reference to tuberculosis (the disease that killed Cixous's father at age 39), Thomas Bernhard, and, in French, the school notation "Very Good" (*Très Bien*). Franz Kafka, Kathleen Ferrier, and Thomas Bernhard—all favorites of Cixous and all victims like her father of tuberculosis—appear in this chapter. The act of writing is equated to the breaking free of shells that "protect" us from the world; the writer's dream is "to take a photo of my dreams" (*L'Ange au secret,* 71). Yet if she could actually take a photograph of her text, "we could see almost the whole book in a single glance, just as after the fact we can today see at a glance the Apocalypse, letters, angels, trumpets, books, visions, harvests, plagues, punishments, escapes, regrets, arrivals of the future, publication, all included" (*L'Ange au secret,* 72).

Chapter 4 turns to the question of fear ("Schumann's Finger or Each to His/Her Own Fear"): of dictatorships, cancer, and AIDS—all move through their stages of development, one plague replacing another. Yet mankind demanding its rights, its beastly rights in the name of "mankind," is ever-present in the world. The narrator confesses her usual difficulty in writing ("My first difficulty: drafting revelation; then, too, nobody really likes the apocalypse, myself included" [*L'Ange au secret,* 89]) and acknowledges that even in writing an apocalyptic text she is aware that not everyone is seduced or struck by the same terror, thus "to each his/her own taste, to each his/her own fear" (*L'Ange au secret,* 89–90). Each of us must, however, search for that primal fear, either within the silences of our childhood or within a text that pushes us to the edge of discovery. Within this chapter are woven references to Robert Schumann (whose injured finger cost him his concert career as a pianist), Dostoyevski's *The Idiot,* and Pushkin.

"We Need the Scene of the Crime," declares the title of chapter 5, which centers on a long discussion of the nature of and need for confession. The temptation, reveals the narrator, is to confess, yet "we must not confess our crimes to anyone, since every crime confessed becomes a kind of boastful act. Confessing a crime is bragging—it becomes an ornament to the personality. . . . If we confess, we commit the most insidious of crimes" (*L'Ange au secret,* 103). It is Stavrogin, Dostoyevski's protagonist from *The Possessed,* who serves as Cixous's model in this section as she explores the nature of evil, its doubling with good, and our eventual hope as represented in the text by the small red glow of a geranium.

"Follow the Geranium," says the narrator in chapter 6, using again the works of Dostoyevski as the principal theme around which a discussion of torture and criminal intention revolve. Quotations from Dostoyevski's *Notebooks* (written in conjunction with *The Idiot*) and reworked incidents extracted from *The Possessed* lead to chapter 7's "Murder Attempt by [Pear] Core," in which Cixous weaves a remembered incident from childhood (offering a pear core to another little girl, on the Snow White model, believing that this would be a fatal gesture, only to have the little girl's mother explain that the pear core is not edible, toss it out, thus robbing the "criminal act" of its realization—although of course not removing the action's "criminal intent"). These imaginary or fictionalized murder attempts, these temptations toward evil (lying, jealousy, hatred) lead the narrator to the realization that serves as her title to chapter 8, "Our Dead, Our Killers": "Life revives through mysteries. Murder descends down from body to body, down to the roots. We die. Then we live again. Thanks to crime. After our death, sparkling images rise up from our cadavers. Each one in turn nourishes the world" (*L'Ange au secret,* 159).

It is again obvious that Cixous, in this period of her writing career, has made very little effort to maintain the barriers between the autobiographical and the literary. An anecdote about her mother, a lengthy discussion of her father's illness and death are interspersed quite freely amid references to literary works. One often has the impression that for Cixous her literary "angels" are as alive to her as the flesh and blood persons who work with her or study with her:

> Without Shakespeare with Poe, at first—and then without Homer, without the Old Testament, Kleist, Kafka, Dostoyevski, and then afterwards, without Clarice Lispector, Marina Tsvetaeva with Anna Akhmatova, without Thomas Bernhard with Ingeborg Bachmann, without Nelly Sachs and . . . I would not have been able to live. Without the daily and certainly strange conversation with them, I would not have lived and I would not live. It has been like this for forty years, not a day goes by without getting the news of the world from one or another of them, not a night goes by without having one or another of them accompany me to the edge of dream; and we have always talked about things which have excited and intrigued us anew, and that has gone on and on, time, decades, centuries have never weakened the energy of human enigmas. (*L'Ange au secret,* 155)

Without books, says the narrator, without the books written by her guides, she could not live. The authors of these books, persons with whom she has had no "real" contact, still represent for her nurturing presences—"despite their death and its consequences, and, too, thanks to their state of absence, surely thanks to the goodness which follows from that, the great blind goodness of the dead we have never known. A dead person who does not forbid, who grants permission" (*L'Ange au secret,* 161). Yet the narrator is forced to admit that she feels she is losing truth. She sees it shining, like the geranium, in shadow, but then the glow is extinguished. Perhaps Dostoyevski was right, she concedes, "the human being is too vast, illusions of truth speak endlessly, truths are always too much for words" (*L'Ange au secret,* 190).

The penultimate chapter carries the title, "Someone Has Killed Ingeborg Bachmann," and continues the discussion of abandonment as it relates to relationships ("the hatred of love") and to the crimes of the human heart. The final chapter, "To Write, to Walk on Fire," sums up—again with myriad allusions to Dostoyevski, Bernhard, and Schumann—the ultimate revelation of this text: that writing is like a game of Russian roulette, like playing with fire. The temptation is always there for the writer, the temptation to "taste the fire": "To caress the flames, to let the flames, with the sharp tips of their tongues, lick at our hearts" (*L'Ange au secret,* 224). Pulled eternally between the need to plunge downward (toward a revelation from our past, toward an important "truth") and our angels' aspiration for the heights (a pull between "roots" and "blooming," says the narrator), we find ourselves in a place described most aptly by the narrator as "I desire-fear-desire" (*L'Ange au secret,* 232).

What we must do, above all, is to move toward the place of execution while thinking about our secret crime: "We must commit it, we shall go to the rosy, the red, the yellow of the fire, to the black, in full consciousness, dreaming with every step we take of what we are about to discover, of what we are about to lose, thinking about the pain with fear and courage which become more and more intense, in full consciousness up to its limits . . . and then we shall cross" (*L'Ange au secret,* 232). In the end we are forced to content ourselves with our fear as "an instrument of progression, if not of revelation" (*L'Ange au secret,* 255). "I am afraid," confesses the narrator. "Afraid of lying, afraid of speaking the truth" (*L'Ange au secret,* 255). This final confession represents, of course, the ultimate challenge of writing (and reading). The narrator (and the reader as well) contemplates with a certain nostalgia those things she will never be able to write: "Even I would have liked to have known them," she believes. "Everything is there, at least all science and all revelation. I could have known everything. You have to admit it, we shall die without having written 'the truth'" (*L'Ange au secret,* 256). But the final words of this text belong to the readers: "Stop now, everything depends on the readers: truth is there. It's getting away from me. Please, catch it! On the fly! There! There! There! It's yours! (Do you have it? Tell me, do you have it?)" (*L'Ange au secret,* 257).

Déluge (1992)

The central theme of *Déluge (Flood)* is, as always, a preoccupation with death and life, loss and mourning. The watery image of the flood is recapitulated in the torrents of tears unleashed in response to the return of memory of loss. "Where does the flood surprise us?" asks Cixous:

> On an April evening, at the corner of the street, suddenly Mourning falls over her with the violence of a storm. The wheel has turned. Again Mourning has been unleashed. Mourning cries and she can do nothing. Without limits, without. One has never seen so many tears. They find no resistance. It's not within our control. They rush forward. As for us, we don't want to cry, but Mourning listens only to its own desires, which are so powerful, so ancient. An infinite affliction carries our tragedy into its unfolding. A hundred mournings throw themselves into this one. No, it's not you we're weeping for, it's not us who are weeping for you. Mourning weeps within us the best of ourselves. Weeps Eternity. The next day the same waters give birth. What agonizes in this book is Mourning.

Divided into 11 loosely connected "chapters," the text begins with a Cixousian meditation on the *entredeux* ("between two," "in-between"). Similar to the opening passage of many other Cixous texts, *Déluge* sets its readers down into a space between East and West, constantly dividing itself between two camps. The first-person narrator speaks from a site where history is moving very rapidly as the narrator is plunged within the experience of reading the *Nibelungenlied,* which has washed over her like a flood. In Germanic myth, the Niebelungen were an evil family who possessed a cursed and magical hoard of gold. A long epic poem in Middle High German composed around 1160, the *Nibelungenlied* tells the story of Siegfried, who obtains the Nibelung gold, marries Kriemhild and procures Brunhilde to be the wife of King Gunther, his brother-in-law. Brunhilde, however, conspires to plan Siegfried's death at the hands of Hagen, who buries the treasure in the Rhine. Kriemhild then marries Etzel and contrives to avenge Siegfried's death. Out of the final slaughter only Etzel and a few others survive. The Nibelungen material has also come down to us through Richard Wagner's operatic tetralogy, *Der Ring des Nibelungen.*

"I want to write a book full of kings and queens," says the narrator. "The music of mourning is happy: we are killed in the midst of celebration."[15] Recurring references to the *Nibelungenlied* punctuate passages on the perceived need in the narrator to weep and to be free of a world that has become "dry" and "without mourning." It is the hour between day and night, and the narrator sets the readers on their way as she stretches out with the *Nibelungenlied*: "My characters will soon enter," she tells us. "What will happen?" she asks. "What I know is that the most unexpected will happen. . . . [T]hat's the theme of this story" (*Déluge,* 19). Her character's name announced as Clarice, we move on to the second section, "Be It Day or Night."

A voice, which we have learned to recognize as Clarice's, speaks of the necessity of finding a door. A friend, Alia (or "Others"), who has written a book, asks the narrator to correct the text: interestingly enough, the book is called *Entredeux.* The narrator continually refers to the search for "a kind of door, a kind of movement, a kind of strength" (*Déluge,* 25). Yet the search evokes memories of Cixous's Algerian childhood, of her white sandals: "What I'm looking for are the traces of that year, the young year, the last year, it's still farther away, there, farther away, after memory? I rush out into streets filled with the past" (*Déluge,* 27). The beginning of forgetting occurs, and the narrator identifies a key problem she has with verb tenses: "The person about whom I was going to speak is a danger to me. However, I was she. As recently as yesterday, it seems to me, I was noting everything in the first person. But at this moment, right here when I want to enter the book, it's not right, there is a rupture/break, deafness, secession, as if many weeks had gone by during the night within myself" (*Déluge,* 30).

What about "she"? What about Amélie or Ascension or Apparition? Will Ascension maintain her position as protagonist of this story? Who will die? Even though the book is not going to be a "mere tragedy," it is nonetheless the story of a killing—yet even though the woman is killed, she does not die because of the joy that keeps death always at bay. "Is it day? Is it night? Both. You have to be able to write while sobbing and smile through your tears," says the narrator (*Déluge,* 33). "Ascension is in front of it (her story), like those poets who are born for happiness and who by chance have had the Wall as the background for their entire lives. In everything they write there is the Wall at the bottom: they can neither rip it nor swallow it. They write sometimes in front, sometimes to one side, sometimes in back, sometimes to the other side. Rosiers, clematis, honeysuckle assail the Wall. This does not prevent stones form commemorating. Stones which carry the names of victims find exaltation in roses" (*Déluge,* 37).

The narrator speaks of treason and joy, which live together in the same life. Passing quick in review Dostoyevski, Ferdinand and Miranda from Shakespeare's *Tempest,* and the biblical David and Bathsheba, the narrator finally fixes on a provisional title for her book: *The Tempest, Sequels.* She says, "Mourning and joy I do not coincide. Write both I say to myself. Both of them" (*Déluge,* 41).

The third section of *Déluge,* "Going Back Is an Impossibility," begins with a description of the position of the narrator: "To return home becomes an obligatory action and an impossible one for the person who has been expelled from herself through an abandonment. To leave abandonment it is necessary to move from a broken period of time to the next period via an excessively narrow slit between the inside and the outside" (*Déluge,* 45). It is now a question of textual departures, of taking the train, of beginning to move. Clarice's voice interposes: "I want to try, as a woman, and as a person having been betrayed, to escape from the prison of treason" (*Déluge,* 55). Ascension approaches the door, and we discover as readers that "no, this is not a book on treason. This is a book on joy. Which escapes" (*Déluge,* 59).

The fourth section brings us to the heart of Cixous's text: "Tragedy with Comedy: *The Tempest,* Sequel 1." David has promised to phone Ascension, but as she awaits the telephone call she has a vision of a dog, which leads her to the last step on the staircase, the one metaphorically we have the most difficulty with. And finally we, along with Ascension, discover that we are in mourning: "In Mourning—there is where our sick ones are, in the Grey Country—where there is no 'me,' no I am. In Mourning we live without being. It is a country without land. The only things which happen there are events which are twisted and backwards. Country of the realization of fears, no, of horrors. We have entered the Unbelievable, the Worst Country. Here it's not our enemies who attack us, it's our loved ones. Our own flesh detaches itself from us and sinks its teeth into us. There where we lay our head in a dear lap, this is where the lap opens onto hells. You don't know where the bottom is" (*Déluge,* 69).

Ascension spends the next day with Paolo, and we share the arrival of the surprise character of the story, Ascension's chance or fate: "the heroine in dark blue silk, soft hair, clothing and voice which recall the day, everything is silken" (*Déluge,* 72). But depression, described as a kind of black merry-go-round, makes us less able to carry on: "On the black merry-go-round you lose all memory of hope. The sun does not rise. The sun has never risen. The sun will never rise. The sun is not of this world. The sun is not a source of light. It is a source of nostalgia. On the black merry-go-round the mind is cut off from all of humanity" (*Déluge,* 78).

The difficulties of communication (Ascension's troubles with the "down staircase" or Titus and Berenice's inability to speak to each other, for example) and the issue of language and loss are also primary in *Déluge:* "I am in the process of creating a strange bitter language, my next language. I am in the act of invoking the language of the country to come, life without you, life which you will not inhabit, life which I enter without you, books without you, life in which you will be the most outside of outsiders" (*Déluge,* 87). "Trying the world's doors from both sides," the narrator makes use of dreams in her quest: "It is so dark here where I am seeking a language which makes no noise in order to whisper what is neither living nor dead. All words are too loud, too rapid, too confident. I seek the names of the shadows between words, the names of things which remain. The name of the love which remains after love. . . . What are the names of the things which resist, the sentences which begin and remain unfinished?" (*Déluge,* 111–12).

The issue of "point of view" is a reassuring one: "Everything is a question of point of view. But no one sees himself or herself. Moreover, no one sees that s/he is seen" (*Déluge,* 122). Point of view here involves total reversibility of position. Is one the agent or the recipient of abandonment, for example?

The next section of *Déluge*, "Underneath the tablecloth," involves a kind of passing to the other side and the beginning of yet another story recounted through the heroine's letters to her sister, Elisa, about her love for Isaac. "We are all characters in a story," she tells us, "which gives us enormous freedom, the freedom of narrating as our heart tells us" (*Déluge*, 136).

Isaac is in turn no one, "the proper name of her mysterious half; or the name of her existence, or perhaps the name of her personal country." He is all the inner difference of Ascension. As she explains to Elisa, "We cannot live without 'him,' without 'her,' without the person . . . the secret person who protects us against death, who saves our life, the danger-life, the life-which-kills, the today-life" (*Déluge,* 139).

According to the narrator, we believe that the events in our lives happen at the moment they take place and that "the end comes when they explode" (*Déluge,* 145). However, for Ascension this is not the way of things: "What happens on that day in our house, in our body, is rupture and betrayal. And we believe that time is held all of a piece within the body of this drama" (*Déluge,* 145). The round sapphire "ring of writing" worn by the narrator protects her in the life of writing: "Life is a secret legend. With words we try to imitate it" (*Déluge,* 149).

In the seventh section of *Déluge* ("Points of view 2, 3") we shift from Brutus to Caesar: "But from Brutus's point of view only Caesar can kill us. This is also the point of view of Shakespeare and thus ours, and it's Ascension's as well" (*Déluge*, 195). The story of David and Bathsheba and the description of the difference between cataclysm and catastrophe lead to Ascension's disappearance. However, the voice of Clarice returns to provide a kind of character sketch for David, Ascension, and Isaac, and to discuss as well the function of the writer (a view shared by Hélène Cixous as well): "I do not know my characters better than myself. I know them by feeling, by music. Knowledge of a blind person, by their breathing. Through my heart. I use my heart to discover them, to live them up close . . . I listen, I depict their steps. I write the interior. I write by advancing toward the inside. One day I shall advance toward the inside of the outside and I shall write a novel" (*Déluge,* 164).

Part 8 introduces the second sequel to *The Tempest*, "One Always Loses the Child." The first sentence refers to the death of Siegfried and the mourning of Kreimhild and the theme of what it means to grieve: "To leave death behind one, you have to start out running very fast, straight ahead, with the lightness of a deer, being yourself speed and lightness" (*Déluge,* 171). Yet no matter what strategy we adopt to avoid it, mourning continues to take us by surprise: "The flood is our condition, but not our end, {for} while it rains in torrents on our feathers, on the inside the dream lights a candle" (*Déluge,* 177).

Ascension's dream takes her into the world of hair. The hairdresser of the dream is named Saul, and as he cuts her hair the curls drop slowly to the ground like tears. If this is the last day of life, what should she be doing? Writing. Yet what a constant struggle it is "to avoid lying when one is searching for the truth" (*Déluge,* 185).

The dream scene becomes a scene of driving in a car with no headlights and with a broken throttle, yet at least in this territory of dreams death is held at bay. "Dreams made her think of life which is never what we think it will be . . . life which is always much stronger and young and audacious and tireless than we are. Living was not simply in the straight lines of the days " (*Déluge,* 188).

Opera music (from *La Forza del Destino*) and a cat enter the dream world as we arrive at the fourth "point of view" section, which describes the "guilty innocents." This section addresses the question of what it means to be a "witness" and how the concept of witnessing is linked inextricably to point of view: "One never knows who will cast the first stone. And yet as soon as there is a story, we can hear the stone fly through the air" (*Déluge,* 196). In a discussion of the process of loving and of love's intimate relationship to guilt, the narrator says: "As soon as we love, even when we love reciprocally, as soon as we kiss, someone is going to die, someone is going to kill, someone is going to eat, someone is going to be swallowed, whole or in small mouthfuls. The necessary cleverness is to believe that in our exceptional case there will be no butchery" (*Déluge,* 199).

The dream car careens out of control but stops short of disaster, just at the edge of the abyss. Within the shadows of the dream world, truth is evanescent, always fleeting, changing. There remains a longing to write "the other [truth], the truth of clarity" (*Déluge,* 218).

In the text's final section, "After," we discover that death departs as rapidly as it had come to Ascension. In both worlds, the world of the dream and the world of reality, there is a danger of belief: "To know that one day I will die and that he will die one day is enough to defuse my anger and my illusions. . . . One hundred years from now, we will never have existed, 20 million years will have gone by, our two-person civilisation will have disappeared" (*Déluge,* 223).

"The play is over," she says. "Now I am going to go out into the night my impersonal mother. There I shall take my indistinct place among the plants, stars, cars, and passers-by. I shall taste the solemn and ever so simple taste of time" (*Déluge,* 223). The text ends in familiar Cixousian fashion with the narrator preparing herself to be born, as a woman having in some profound manner successfully escaped the attacks of the tragic.

Chapter Five

From the Scene of the Unconscious to the Scene of History: Writing for the Theater

> The theatre can give us back our true dimension, our depths, our heights, our interior Indias. It's there where we have a chance/hope of rediscovering the gods. The atmosphere of the theatre is full of them. Gods? I mean what goes beyond us, what pulls us along, that to which we blindly address ourselves. I mean our own portion of divinity. Because we are divine the moment we cease being marionettes of our own machines. And when we communicate with the stars without restraint, the secrets of the world, and those of the heart, yes, when we are part of creation, as human atoms.
>
> Hélène Cixous, "Le Chemin de légende"

Thus far we have considered the work of Hélène Cixous in what might be called the more private forms of reading discourse—the academic critical essay on various authors (Joyce, Kleist, Poe, Hoffmann), various autobiographical texts (short story, novella, novels, and "fictions"), and several purely theoretical works. Of course this writing belongs to the public domain in that it is openly published, read, reviewed, discussed, and analyzed. It remains, however, in very significant ways, nonperformative, as the basic reading contract is concluded between the text and a single reader. It has always been evident, however, in our discussions of her work that the dramatic element is a key one in both overall structure and metaphoric content of Cixousian texts.

Since the early 1980s, then, it is probable that there are many more who recognize the name Hélène Cixous much more readily for her writing for the stage than those who identify her as a Parisian intellectual and academic author of fictions published by Editions des femmes. In short, it is fair to say that the oeuvre of Hélène Cixous, although still very much "in progress," has undergone an important transition, from private theater to public theater. Cixous's career has seen, accordingly, a deepening and expanding emphasis on the dramatic text.

It is interesting to note the difference discernible between her texts of the mid-1970s and those of the early 1980s (the period that effectively marks her entry into writing for the theater). Whereas the earlier texts could be said to be marked by an insistence on the subject, or, rather, the passivity of the subject (as Cixous often claims that one is traversed by language or languages), the texts that coexist at the time of theatrical writing (especially those that concern themselves with the linkage of writing and painting—*L'Approche de Clarice Lispector,* for example) are more or less marked by "the search for the third person and the passage from 'I' to 'he.'"[1] The question could certainly be asked if it is the theater itself that has been a kind of accelerator for Cixous in this period of her "other" writing.

While Cixous has not denied the observable change in her writing over the course of the past decade, she has also made it very clear that her "other" writing (her *écriture originaire*) has in no way been abandoned. It is still that writing which is "her": "It is in that writing where I recognize myself without difficulty, it's that writing which reassures me, it's my ground(ing); without that writing, I wouldn't dare to write otherwise" ("L'Auteur," 46).

What theatrical writing has done for Cixous (as opposed to her *écriture originaire*) is to allow a kind of separation of self from "self": "I need myself, thus I need this *écriture originaire,* to start, to engender. Then afterwards it becomes separate from me, since there are all these others. And there begins, if you can put it that way, the drama. Not the theatre, the drama" ("L'Auteur," 46). Asked if the metaphors of pregnancy and childbirth would be applicable to her theatrical creations, Cixous has replied in the negative, stating that for her, even though there is indeed a period of gestation required in order to bring her characters into the world, at a certain moment they do detach themselves from their creator—in a very permanent way, thus making the maternal metaphor a tenuous one.

From *La Pupille* (1972) and *Portrait de Dora,* (1976), a reworking and revisioning of Freud's famous case history, to her most recent collaborative efforts with Ariane Mnouchkine of the Théâtre du Soleil, Cixous has become progressively engaged in a far more "political" praxis than she described in earlier discussions on the relative importance of poetry and politics in her work. One can observe, over the 15-year period in question, a gradual shift away from what one might call the scene of the female hysteric (on a personal level, then on a demonstrated psychoanalytical level) toward the scene of history, wherein the hysterical family drama is played out for the whole world. Indeed, the essay penned by Cixous in 1980, "Poetry Is/and (the) Political," would today be more aptly entitled "Politics Are/and (the) Poetical."[2]

According to Jeannette Laillou Savona, Cixous's "initial distrust of the theatre's 'means of production and expression' has now given way to an enthusiastic rediscovery of the playwright's 'metamorphosis' while writing her play, and of the 'archaic complicity' between performers and spectators, or between hostile members of an audience."[3] Cixous provides further indications of her authorial evolution in the essay "The Place of Crime, the Place of Forgiveness," included as part of an appendix to her 1987 play, *L'Indiade ou l'Inde de leurs rêves.* One of the key questions she addresses there is the way in which the poet can "open his universe to the destinies of a people."[4] Because the poet is "first of all an explorer of the Self," how is she/he able to move beyond the ego into the realm of the other? The corollary question asked by Cixous in this essay is, of course, that of appropriation: "How can I, who am of the literate species, ever give speech to an illiterate peasant woman without taking it away from her, with one stroke of my language, without buying her with one of my fine sentences? In my texts would there never be but people who know how to read and write, to juggle with signs?" ("Writings," 121). For a long time, Cixous tells us, she thought her texts would only live in "those rare and desert places where only poems grow" (121), yet when she came to the theater "there was the stage, the earth, where the ego remains imperceptible, the land of others. There their words make themselves heard, and their silences, their cries, their song, each according to his own world and in his foreign tongue" (121).

La Pupille (1972)

Cixous's first writing for the stage, *La Pupille,* is an adaptation written in 1971 of parts of her fictional text *Révolutions pour plus d'un Faust.* Although *La Pupille* has never been staged, it nonetheless contains all the essential elements of Cixousian dramatic writing. Two characters from *Révolutions,* the Fool and the Subject (also the Eye and the Pupil, Virgil and Dante), accompany us through three major scenes extracted from *Révolutions.* Act 1 represents the My Lai massacre of Vietnamese civilians by American soldiers during the Vietnam War; act 2 takes place in Brazil, depicting torture and atrocities related to political upheaval there during the years following the May 1968 uprising; and act 3 moves backward in time to the nineteenth century, focusing on the struggles of the Communards in Paris.

In *La Pupille* Cixous creates a character whom she christens "The Voice of the Theater" and who will appear in later plays as well.

Reminiscent of allegorical theater, *La Pupille* sees Money, Death, and multiple representations of police brutality parade across the stage. Faust and Helen arrive (from Goethe's play), as do other literary and historical figures from *Révolutions.* The Voice of the Theater announces at one point that history comes from the East, which, as Shiach points out, "relates interestingly to Cixous's later interest in cultures of the East as sites of resistance to the dominance of hierarchical and dualist thought" (Shiach, 112). Cixous has referred to *La Pupille* as "nothing really . . . a very intellectual, heavy, conceptual piece,"[5] yet it is a text that demonstrates early on in her writing career a certain fascination for creating in the dramatic mode. It is an ambitious text as well through "its attempt to represent contemporary social forces and struggles," and it prefigures the work that Cixous will undertake a decade later with the Théâtre du Soleil.

Portrait de Dora (1976)

In 1976 at the Théatre d'Orsay the Compagnie Renaud-Barrault staged Cixous's *Portrait de Dora,* a theatrical representation of Freud's famous case study, *Dora: A Fragment of an Analysis of a Case of Hysteria,* first published in 1905. Obviously one of the classic (and most interesting) of Freudian case histories, the Dora study ("Dora" was a woman named Ida Bauer) has had in contemporary critical circles a wide-ranging response from feminist, literary, and psychoanalytical critics. As one literary critic has pointed out, "The case reads like a detective novel, with Freud weaving ever more complex and startling interpretations around the clues he uncovers in the hysteric's symptoms and dreams."[6] Obviously the need to "tell the story," or, rather, to translate Dora's symptoms into narrative, becomes the focus for Freud the analyst. But there are gaps within Freud's narrative (his acceptance of a heterosexual analytic framework that blinded him to Dora's homoerotic attachment to her father's mistress, for example). In many ways the gaps, the "spaces between," are what Cixous attempts to deal with in her script.

Willis reminds us, too, that in making a case of Dora, "Cixous's text enters a peculiar bind: its efficacy depends on the spectator's knowledge of its pretext, and more generally, on some idea of the historical status of hysteria and its importance for the origins of psychoanalysis" (Willis, 78). Such a risk might not be unreasonable were it not for the question that casts its shadow across Cixous's text: Why should theater be the arena in which such a meeting of theoretical discourses is staged, in which such an interpretive rereading is enacted? Willis argues that because *Portrait of Dora* reframes Freud's text in a way that puts into question the theatrical frame, and the body staged within it, it becomes "exemplary of the critical operations of certain feminist performance practice, particularly in its steadfast refusal of the categories of theory and practice" (Willis, 78). To date, *Portrait de Dora* has probably been the most critically discussed of Cixous's plays, although of all her work for theater it remains curiously "readerly" in many respects. Written in 1976 and first produced in Paris, it was translated into English by Anita Barrows for Simone Benmussa's staging of the play in London.

As we have noted, Cixous has never been a disciple of the twentieth century's *maîtres à penser,* as the French like to call them. Nonetheless, she has always insisted that one lives in culture and that, accordingly, one must take on in some way the thinking and feeling of that culture in order to criticize it, to subvert it, and, finally, to transform it. Thus, Freud's very literary dealing with the "hysterical" female provides a cultural critic like Cixous with evidence that phallocentric and logocentric discourse is now and has always been the law in Western culture. Yet Cixous would also argue that, in a positive sense, Freud, in his reliance on the narrative strength and structure of the dream, and in his willingness to privilege "talk" and to trust somehow the narrative voice, has contributed a way in (as opposed to a way out) for writers who are looking for the voice of *écriture féminine.*

The compositional origins of *Portrait de Dora* are also interesting. Cixous has stated that *Portrait de Dora* was not written originally as a play; it "emerged" from *Portrait du soleil,* a fictional text in which it had been hidden even from the author herself. In the process of rereading *Portrait du soleil,* Cixous felt she could discern "scenes" within the fictional text: "I said to myself, 'look, there are scenes in there,' it was very odd" ("L'Auteur," 45). Then fate seemed to intervene in the person of Simone Benmussa, who, on meeting Cixous, told her that she should write for the theater. And in short order *Dora* was born. In Cixous's words, "I didn't even know what writing for the theatre was. So I cut apart and restitched bits of text, under the professional eye of Simone Benmussa. I didn't consider that a theatrical experience strictly speaking, but like a kind of oblique coming to the theatre. It didn't give me the feeling of being a playwright. I had the impression of having done it in an oblique manner, a bit illegitimately. A naive impression, for that too, that obliqueness, is theatrical" ("L'Auteur," 45).

The "real Dora" of *Portrait de Dora,* Ida Bauer, was born in Vienna in 1882 and treated by Freud when she was 18. Her father, Philip Bauer, was a wealthy industrialist who had also been a patient of Freud. Dora's mother seems to have suffered from what today we would call an obsessive-compulsive disorder—she was obsessed with orderliness and cleanliness. Dora's father had a mistress (Frau K in the case history) who had previously been his nurse during an illness. In Dora's "case," Dora remembers and dreams about an incident, or several incidents, in which the husband of Frau K attempts to seduce her, once by the lake and once on the stairs. Dora exhibits many of the physical symptoms that Freud and others considered emblematic of hysteria (aphonia, or inability to speak, as well as a persistent cough and difficulties in swallowing). The precipitating incident for her treatment with Freud was a draft suicide note that she had "accidentally" left in her father's desk and that had been discovered.

Dora underwent the "talking cure" with Freud for only a few months. When suddenly she announced that she was abandoning treatment, however, Freud himself then became obsessed with writing a complete case history of Dora (indeed he added a long series of notes to his first account) and so historically the story ended. What became more and more interesting to later analysts and literary critics (once Freud's writing had become as legitimate an object of analysis as any other text and as "literary" as "literature") was the perverse way in which he had co-opted Dora's narrative.

Cixous takes the idea of "frame" and the ancillary concept of "portrait"—the person frozen within a frame and given over by the artist/creator to the viewer as a representation of the "real"—and revises it in a dramatic setting. As in all dramatic writing, the reading of the play is not sufficient to give full due to the innovations conceived of by the playwright. Plays are written to be performed, not read, and we can learn a great deal about Cixous's writing for the stage through those who have actually produced her work. Simone Benmussa[7] is helpful in this respect in her notes on the London production of *Dora:*

> For the stage work on *Portrait of Dora,* some questions seemed of prime importance. But this had more to do with impatience than with intellectual judgment or procedures. . . . What we did no doubt was allow free rein to our own images, our own fantasies, though when we later analyzed what we had done, a logical connection or an association would always appear. We had to proceed step by step, from image to image, from association to association. If the actors' instinct is sound, the details will fall into place either instinctively or empirically, and their meaning will be discovered later. (Benmussa, 10)

Benmussa explains that in the production procedure in London it was important to express what the characters do not reveal of their own accord:

> We had to enable the spectator to perceive what lies behind the thoughts and words, to imagine themselves on the obscure, reverse side. The problems occurred haphazard, unchosen, in no sort of order: where were we to place the voids that corresponded to the visual silences, how were we to disorientate the spectator's gaze from what seemed real, how light the dream to make it appear real, and not a romantic or poetic illusion? The acting had to be real, for if voice and gesture had poeticized the text, the play would have been immured in the nineteenth century, whereas Dora is on the threshold of the twentieth century. (Benmussa, 10)

Portrait de Dora is constructed, as are many Cixousian fictional texts, like a jigsaw puzzle. It was originally written for radio (with Cixousian privileging of the voice), but when Benmussa founded her actors' workshop at the Théâtre d'Orsay in Paris she had thought it would be interesting to start with a text that was not theatrical, "as it would enable us to avoid the habitual theatrical yoke, the yoke that constricts the actors' freedom and forces them to keep on the rails of theatrical 'language'" (Benmussa, 10). *Portrait de Dora* was just such a text: it "came from 'elsewhere.' If this kind of theatre is to succeed in upsetting the everyday, restrictive ordering of space and time imposed on us by the powers that be, then it must exist and assert itself as political theatre. It is radically opposed to the great edifying and reproductive machines we see all around us at the moment" (Benmussa, 10–11).

In her staging of *Dora,* Benmussa conceived of the play as having four different levels, each of which must, in her words, always remain "readable": memory, reality, dream, and fantasy (Benmussa, 12). These four distinct levels—by "breaking things up, slowing down the time of appearances or disappearances, as when we watch a roll of film being developed"—allowed Benmussa to slow down the process, to change theatrical time. She used slides in the production (projecting them onto a scrim—itself an invisible substance), which showed life-sized images of the actors and also served to represent their placing and movements. "These images," according to Benmussa, "in which duration is broken down in a fluid and continuous manner, are the necessary counterpart of the disjointed structure of the text, to the breaks in the narrative" (Benmussa, 13).

Benmussa's insistent counterpoint between breaks and continuity was an attempt to convey a state of conflict in scenic terms. Yet continuity was necessary for the audience's understanding, she tells us:

> for one can only hold on to something that is held out to one, just as tension can only exist in something that is extensible. We had to have visual unity so that it could be broken up—like angles, like that alternation of light and shade. We also needed unity of costume and place—the park by the lake (with garden furniture, and people walking in a garden). It was on these unities that the characters' other meeting places would be superimposed, such as Dora's sessions with Freud, her talks with Mrs K, the confidential dialogues. . . . Breaks in the lighting were also necessary. [I]t had to be split up, meticulous, fluid; it had to play with chiaroscuro, the ever-present yellow light coming through the doorways contrasting with the white light of day. Also necessary was a unity that gave the actors a path to follow in order to adopt the different angles and detours of their roles. (Benmussa, 13)

Benmussa adopted a staging where one sequence is often interrupted by other sequences, only to continue later on, thus establishing a same-yet-different pattern in the play. Directions to the actors were given by means of the association of words or images, in order to "follow the route that leads through the subterranean passages, comes up to the surface, goes down again" (Benmussa, 13). In short, Benmussa attempted to create within her production a unity that would show Freud's social attitude toward Dora—one firmly entrenched in masculine ideology.

The stage itself in *Portrait de Dora* is divided into sections that delineate a specific character's spatial home. Frau K's space includes the stairs and the bench, while Dora's space (when she is talking to Freud) is downstage op side, the chair in front of Freud, or the little slope in the foreground. Freud never leaves his chair except to watch the other characters. Herr K's space is by the doors or walls on the op side (places forbidden to Dora and which she is afraid of). Dora's father's space is by the Venetian blind, the house, or near Freud. The Venetian blinds are an important prop because they open for someone to be seen behind them, and then close, at the same time keeping a secret and creating a break in the image: "Open or closed, [they] reveal, efface, repeat the process, both seen and not seen, both separate and present" (Benmussa, 14). This physical opening and closing of the blinds is a powerful visual representation of a constant in Cixous's style—the insistent urging toward an acceptance of ambiguity as a possible ground for truth-seeking. That is a constant thrust in all Cixous's texts—movement toward the "both-and" rather than the "either-or."

In *Portrait de Dora,* which is presented with no scene or act breaks but with a fragmented and interrupted wholeness, the passage from real to dream to fantasy to memory involves the audience in passing from seeing events through Dora's eyes, then Freud's, then through those of her father, Herr K, and Frau K. As in Freud's narrative, Dora's mother is notable by her absence. Dora's stories about Herr K, retold by Freud to Dora, objected to by Dora, are represented on stage by a kaleidoscopic movement of monologue and dialogue.

Morag Shiach reminds us that *Dora*'s main focus is "the presentation of the disruptive potential of female subjectivity and the female body for the familial structures of patriarchy, and for the specular relations of theatre" (Shiach, 112). In *Portrait de Dora* Cixous has attempted to represent in dramatic form the "energies and forces that lie behind Dora's hysteria" and to then "relate them to the circuits of exchange and desire so tantalizingly sketched out by Freud" (Shiach, 112). Most critics who have engaged in discussion of Cixous's *Dora* have focused on how Cixous's version relates to the original case study; Shiach, however, suggests that more emphasis should be placed on "the originality and power of Cixous's engagement with the politics of theatrical representation itself" (Shiach, 114).

In the Anglophone world, *Portrait of Dora* remains the most well-known of Cixous's plays (among her theatrical works it holds the same position as "The Laugh of the Medusa"). Even though it is innovative and has been well received in its productions all over the world, Cixous has said that the play is not truly "theater," according to her present notion of the dramatic genre, which is closer to the Shakespearean or Aristotelian definitions (Franke, 117). The creative path leading to this present notion has certainly traced an interesting trajectory from "literary" to "theatrical."

L'Arrivante (1977) and *Le Nom d'Oedipe* (1978)

L'Arrivante (the title reminiscent of the essay collection *Coming to Writing*) is composed of a series of passages lifted from Cixous's 1975 text, *LA*. Like several other of her dramatic works, it was first staged at the Festival d'Avignon (in the summer of 1977 by Viviane Théophilidès). Just as the fiction *LA* is focused on the problematic process of creating a feminine subjectivity or the articulation of femininity itself, *L'Arrivante* places the very same search into dramatic form. In the Avignon production, the multiple voices of "woman" are depicted through the use of seven different actresses to play the various "roles." The production was an interesting one, yet the text, it can be argued, remains still too grounded in the readerly rather than in the dramatic to be successful as theater. The performative element is still lacking.

A second Cixous production from the Festival d'Avignon (one year later, in 1978) is the operatic text *Le Nom d'Oedipe.* The stage version was adapted from a longer text entitled *Le Nom d'Oedipe ou le chant du corps interdit (The Name of Oedipus or the Song of the Forbidden Body)*; music was added by André Boucourechliev. The play finds its obvious literary source in Sophocles' *Oedipus the King,* but it is indelibly marked with Cixous's concern for "voice" and the thematic importance of identity. Cixous describes *Le Nom d'Oedipe* as "written for the ear, for music, not for action. It was a kind of huge lyric. I like that text, but I don't consider it theater, it needs the music" (Franke, 172).

La Prise de l'école de Madhubai (1983)

Cixous calls *La Prise de l'école de Madhubai (The Taking of the School at Madhubai)* her first "real play," as she wrote it directly in dramatic form. It is not, like *Portrait of Dora, L'Arrivante,* or *Oedipe,* a play developed out of a piece of fiction. Although Cixous christens the play's heroine Sakundeva, the plot is based loosely on the life of India's Phoolan Devi, who was jailed without trial in 1983 and who is commonly characterized as India's most notorious modern-day *dacoit* (or bandit). She and her gang, members of India's lowest caste, committed scores of robberies and murders, including a massacre that left 20 dead, from 1978 to 1982. It is important to note, however, that she was then and still remains a potent symbol of rebellion for many women and for members of the lowest and poorest castes because in her criminal acts she lashed out mostly against those in higher castes. In the end Phoolan Devi managed to negotiate her own surrender, and though her original release from prison scheduled for 1991 was delayed until 1994, she was expected to participate in Indian politics in the ranks of a left-of-center coalition led by the Samajwadi (Socialist) Janata party.

In "Le Chemin de légende," her brief essay introducing the 1986 published version of the play, Cixous reminds us that to write for the theater "it is necessary to distance oneself, to leave, to travel for a long time in darkness, until one no longer knows where one is, who one is, it's very difficult, up to feeling space become a terribly strange country, until one arrives lost in a region which I cannot recognize, until waking up transformed into someone whom I've never met, like a beggar woman, a naive divinity, an avise old man."[8] Following this transformation, we may ask, what remains of the author once she has become the beggar woman or a minister of the government? "Almost nothing," says Cixous, "except the beating of surprise within my chest" (*Théâtre*, 7). The epigraph chosen for the play is taken from Kleist's novella *Michael Kohlhaas:* "In a word, it would have been . . . for the world to honor his memory had he not overstepped the bounds of a virtue: the sense of justice made of him an outlaw and a murderer." The story of Sakundeva is a story, like that of the partition of India, which has its origins in historical fact.

The play opens at the home of Pandala in northern India, where the rain will not stop. Pandela announces that she feels like a woman about to give birth (fearful but still ready to laugh); in her long opening monologue she lets the audience know that the police are searching for Sakundeva, "queen of the rebels," and we understand that in the life of this fugitive there is still someone who remembers her with tenderness and love. Sakundeva herself then arrives and asks for asylum for two or three days so that she can have time to decide what to do. She who has killed to give herself rebirth, she who owes her little bit of liberty to murder must now decide how to leave these "circles of blood." In order to survive what she names the three "violences" (hunger, injustice, and rape) it will be necessary to at once forget pain and not forget it. She will have to exchange shame for honor and transform memory into hope.

Sakundeva's rebellion remains a compelling story to Cixous: "I wonder by what combat this is possible. For Sakundeva, as for so many women, is this possible? For Sakundeva, as for so many women, is this not the wildest dream, the most dangerous, the most desirable gift?"[9]

L'Histoire terrible mais inachevée de Norodom Sihanouk, roi du Cambodge (1985)

It is important to note the situation of two of Cixous's plays, *The Terrible but Unfinished Story of Norodom Sihanouk, King of Cambodia,* and *The Indiade,* in Eastern rather than Western culture. Lispector has been one influence on this choice, but as Verena Conley points out, there is also Cixous's "distaste for the dehumanizing effects of Occidental civilization," where the way of living has been less expansionist and destructive

(Conley 1992, 96). Both plays, however, take us to two very painful moments in contemporary Asian history—to Cambodia during the period 1955 to 1979, when the country was literally cut up by other nations, and to India in the period 1937 to 1948, at the time of independence and eventual partition of the country into India and Pakistan. Rather than base these "historical" plays in the realm of battles won and lost, Cixous has chosen to look to the larger questions of the "struggle between good and evil, in the very quest for 'truth'" (Conley 1992, 96).

The "terrible but unfinished story" of Cambodia's ruler, Norodom Sihanouk, is the tale of a king who is a person of integrity but one who finds himself in a tenuous position and is sometimes guilty of making wrong, self-serving decisions. The division between good (the Cambodian people, who, during the time of the play, are interned in camps by foreign powers and robbed of the happiness they enjoyed in the time before the invasions of outsiders) and evil (foreign nations, those who wish to take over the country and industrialize, modernize, and otherwise force change) and the ambiguous nature of each world gives the play its dramatic energy.

Cixous's remarks relating to the writing of this play are useful in our understanding of its basic themes. "The first character from *L'Histoire terrible* to come out of my heart was King Suramarit," she tells us. "Dead and quite alive and right away remarkable for his extreme vitality. He was the first, and I knew at once he would always be there, the most vivacious, the most faithful, the most immortal. I loved him and I needed him. Afterwards came the thoughts, mine and those of the others. Mine? I thought: here is the ferryman, father and contemporary of the dead and of the living, *the* wet-nurse, true king of the theater, he who upon entering the stage suspends the combat between the spirit of legend and the spirit of realism, and who responds to our most ancient desire: that of traversing death, quite alive" ("Writings," 129).

L'Histoire terrible was the first production resulting from the collaboration of Cixous and Ariane Mnouchkine and the Théâtre du Soleil. In describing the origins of this joint working relationship, Cixous recalls that Mnouchkine asked her to write something for the troupe but that the request had come as quite a surprise, as Cixous considered her writing very different from the style with which Mnouchkine would be pleased. Yet when Mnouchkine asked her to try to write something for the company, Cixous agreed. She began her work in 1983, and the production was staged two years later. It was Mnouchkine's great dream to do a play about contemporary history, especially Asian. Early on Cambodia became their historical site, both because of the almost larger-than-life character of Prince Sihanouk and because Cixous was "completely taken by the story of Cambodia" (Franke, 154).

Yet there were problems in writing about contemporary history and writing about and creating lives for characters who are "real": "I was afraid to deal with the present, with people who are alive. I think it's impossible to do that. First, have you got the right? You can make huge mistakes, you can mistreat people, you can say things that will hurt them. To do that would be a kind of sin, unless you can find a posture that is delicate enough, tactful enough not to hurt the other. But you can never be sure of that" (Franke, 154). *L'Histoire terrible* was Cixous's first experience in writing for a specific group (the Théâtre du Soleil is a large repertory group of some 40 actors), and it was her first epic play. After choosing a direction (a global generality like Cambodia is only the beginning), she must then "find the subject" in order to write the story. "You can write history from so many points of view," she reminds us, "and choose different levels and invent different characters, since one half of the characters are fictitious" (Franke, 155).

Most critics have been quick to note that *L'Histoire terrible* is very much in the tradition of Shakespeare's history plays. "I wrote Sihanouk under the sign of Shakespeare," Cixous has said. "I worked across and through Shakespeare in order to write it. The textuality of Sihanouk can be said to be worked by a Shakespearean symbolicity. His influence in my text has to do with the kind of political gestures across history which his texts exhibit. In a fundamental and founding way it's true that Shakespeare is like the ground for my text" (Franke, 156–57).

Cixous notes that she, too, considers her theatrical enterprise, which consists of attempting to recount contemporary history in dramatic form, to be in a direct line of descent from Shakespeare, who remains for her "synonymous with historical drama" (Franke, 157). And yet in many ways Cixous is original in her use of the historical form. She herself cites the moments of pause in her plays—moments when there is a sense of stopping, of stopping history itself, moments when there is no history. "These moments when history stops are to me very poignant," she tells us, "because in fact history doesn't stop, that would be impossible. But from time to time we want to stop it. We want to sit down and look at the stars. It's as though, through these scenes, I were trying to inscribe the nostalgia on the part of human beings for eternity. If we could stop history, then there would be a constant peace, a constant rest, whereas this is not the case: there is no rest, there is only war" (Franke, 158–59). Moments of absolute solitude (the soliloquy) and tragic irony are two other Shakespearean traits Cixous has identified in her works. It is important to note, however, that although the connection with Shakespeare is certainly there, the Cixousian style is also very much in evidence.

Cixous has a clear idea of the interrelationship between characters presented on-stage and spectators seated in the audience:

> The characters on stage are blind, they think they can see, they act, but at the same time they are seen by us as not seeing what is going to happen to them, not suspecting that which is being prepared for them, they're late in relation to the announcement. Whereas we are in on the secret, the spectator is in the know about what's going to happen to the character. I call this the representation of human blindness. We the spectators are blind also. We see Sihanouk's blindness, we see that the Cambodians are blind to what's going to happen to them, that which we the public can see rising up to meet them. What this should inscribe is that we, the public, don't see what's going to happen to *us,* only someone behind sees it, God sees it, maybe you see it. That's the secret, we don't see our own blindness. (Franke, 159)

Of course Cixous takes liberties with historical "fact," opting at times to present scenarios that are at variance with "historical reality." She reminds us that the most important scenes in her plays in this respect are those in which we are shown what could *not* have happened. "Consider, for example, the moment in which Sihanouk must decide whether or not to return to Phnom Penh," she suggests. "He's in Paris, and keeps receiving loads of telegrams, and he becomes the plaything of those telegrams, which are like the gods. The gods are telling him: 'return, no don't return, return,' etc. It's at this moment that we see the tragic machine starting up. We wonder why Sihanouk doesn't open his eyes, and we know it's destiny, it's Sihanouk, it's blindness. And, as twentieth-century spectators we can also add, it's the unconscious" (Franke, 160).

The kingdom of Cambodia, a former state in the colonial world of French Indochina, is situated on the saucer-shaped plain of the Mekong River; it is in a tropical climate and is completely surrounded by mountains. Cambodia was prominent during the Khmer empire but became prey to Siam and Annam from the fifteenth to the nineteenth centuries. In 1854 the king of Cambodia asked the French for protection, and Cambodia eventually became a French protectorate in 1863. After World War I the French restored Cambodia's western provinces; following World War II the country was granted more self-government. In 1955 France recognized Cambodia as an independent kingdom under King Norodom

Sihanouk. During the Vietnam conflict, Cambodia pursued a policy of neutrality and received military aid from the United States. Border disputes with South Thailand and South Vietnam, however, remained unsettled and kept the country in flux. For Cixous, the possibility of writing a play about a people threatened with disappearance in the modern world (*"l'un des peuples menancés de disparition par notre monde moderne"*)[10] led her to the history of Cambodia. And in her description of the fatality of Cambodia's geography and political situation, Cixous also recognized the importance of her protagonist, Prince Norodom Sihanouk, so remarkably theatrical both in the circumstances of his life and in his living of it. Setting out to tell a modern-day legend ("Once upon a time there was a very peaceful, happy and ancient people"), Cixous's dramatic text covers the entire historical upheaval of Cambodia—from the 1955 restoration of the kingdom to the arrival of the Vietnamese in 1979. During this period Cixous attempts to show how unhappiness insinuates itself within happiness and how the net of fatalities squeezes ever more tightly.

L'Indiade ou l'Inde de leurs rêves (1987)

"When history is at work," Cixous tells us, "one realizes how time makes fun of us, how time reinscribes things, how time jests with our desires, which have been played out or maybe realized. It is in these moments that time says to us, oh, you thought that such and such a thing was going to happen, well, as a matter of fact it's exactly the opposite which is going to take place. Just as [Jawaharlal] Nehru says at a certain moment in *The Indiade*: 'Nothing will ever separate us,' and one act later India and Pakistan are definitively separated. Time makes fun of everything we have imagined, or undoes it, or inversely it realizes it. But in history, in general, time undoes more than it accomplishes" (Franke, 161). One of the themes of *L'Indiade,* Cixous's 1987 play, is that of fidelity and its paradoxes: "In *The Indiade* everyone is unfaithful to everyone else, and yet the only desire on everyone's part is for fidelity. . . . Fidelity is almost an abstract value. It's of the order of the heart. It's not keeping one's promises, because after all no one ever keeps his or her promises. Fidelity is rather not lying, day after day, moment after moment. Fidelity contains infidelity" (Franke, 164–65).

Cixous, who refers to Mohandas Gandhi as "a naked bird, an angel without feathers," has stated in *The Indiade* that Gandhi was not more important than the other characters. He is more remarkable, more original than the others, and for many people more enigmatic, "because he belongs to the level of the absolute" (Franke, 165). When questioned about a "higher level of realism" in *The Indiade,* Cixous has answered that there is no insistence on realism for the Théâtre du Soleil but rather an insistence on truth, "which is just the opposite of realism." "Realism for me," she says, "is the worst thing in the world, it's television, it's documentary, it has no soul. Realism is only facts, and facts are nothing. What the actors have achieved in *The Indiade* is beyond realism, it has to do with truth. Realism doesn't touch anybody. You can watch a massacre on television without realizing it's true, that people are really dying, suffering, etc. If you can catch the truth of it, then you start crying" (Franke, 166). The she-bear that recurs in the play is, in Cixous's words, "a metaphor for the play, for innocence and guilt, for innocent guilt, for guilty innocence, for intelligence and wildness" (Franke, 167).

L'Indiade evokes the period of history between 1937 and 1948 and gives the spectator scenes taken "from real life." *L'Indiade* is also, however, the story of "excessiveness, excessiveness in the formidable desire for independence by a people . . . also in the tragic partition which created Pakistan, and which could be seen after the act as being the price to be paid for independence."[11] For Cixous, the play was a natural outcome of the Cambodia play that had been mounted the preceding year by the Théâtre du Soleil. Originally the play on India was to have centered on the figure of Indira Ghandi, yet the proximity of Indira Ghandi's life in time made the work extremely difficult. The events were still much too close and, for Cixous, not easily transposed to the stage. In order to explain the present she was constantly obliged to return to the past, which made her feel that she was writing backwards: "Each time I produced a scene which was going on in the immediacy of theater, I had to do the historical background for the scene, present new characters, and unpack each one's baggage from the past" (Golfier, 81). She spent over a year researching India—going through documentation on the country's history, geography, and politics—but she finally decided to renounce the work on Indira Ghandi and focus only on the events of 1937–48. This play, like the Cambodian piece, is a stunning example of the movement and growth in Cixous's writing over the past decade.

La Nuit miraculeuse (1989)

Again collaborating with Ariane Mnouchkine, Cixous wrote the screenplay *La Nuit miraculeuse* for television, to celebrate the bicentenntial of the French Revolution. A script that "equates freedom and deliverance with artistic imagination," *La Nuit miraculeuse* also shows a Cixous who seems to identify with a small group of writers and artists who have become contemporary society's defenders of culture. In this film, according to Verena Conley, "politics and ambition are set against another kind of politics and poetry, an innocent child and his animal are set against corrupt adults, rich capitalists against the poor artists" (Conley, 117).

On ne part pas, on ne revient pas (1991)

On ne part pas, on ne revient pas (You Never Leave, You Never Return) had its premiere on 24 November 1991 at La Métaphore. It was mounted under the direction of Daniel Mesguich and André Guittier by the Théatre National Lille-Tourcoing Région Nord/Pas de Calais and had in its cast four well-known French actors—Nicole Garcia, Christele Wurmser, Daniel Mesguich, and Bernard Yerles. The four characters in this play include Nathanael, a world-renowned orchestra conductor; his wife, Clara; Clara's friend Lucie; and the orchestra's first violinist. The three-act structure focuses, in order, on three different characters in turn: act 1, "A Woman"; act 2, "The Child"; and act 3, "A Leader" (the reference here is to Nathanael, the conductor).

In act 1 the focus of attention is on Clara, and the action takes place at night in Clara and Nathanael's home. The intimate conversation that takes place is between two women, as Clara speaks to Lucie about the horrible prospect of leaving her husband. Leaving or staying—this choice has been an agonizing one for her for over a year. She has finally decided that this is the only action remaining to her and has opted for leaving during the night, before sunrise. Clara tells Lucie that like Tsvetaeva, Mandelstam, and Rimbaud, she has always liked those who left. Lucie, ever reasonable, reminds her that you can't really "leave"—but as the two friends pack Clara's books she reassures her that "I'm your friend, I'm listening to you, I'll make sense of it all later. I hear you, I'm worried about you, the wind is blowing and I see you unhinged. I also see the hour growing later, later, you want to leave but I see you staying here."[12] Lucie tells Clara that for the 20 years that they have been friends, Clara has been "the most elegant, the most secret, the most controlled woman." This is the first time she has seen her friend like this, out of control.

Act 2 is played out in the same space, and the same characters continue their conversation. The focal point, however, is no longer the role Clara has played more or less successfully over the past 20 years—that of wife to the great man—but rather the empty space that exists in her life where "the child" ought to be or ought to have been. Dates, as always significant for Cixous, are important here, as Clara mentions the approaching date of 31 July, which is that of little Franz's death, five years before. "Obviously a child from a story," says Clara, "the genius of the impossible, such a child who cannot exist except in stories, suddenly you see him arrive in reality, come from nowhere, come from a village" (*On ne part pas,* 62).

After the somewhat mysterious presentation of the wife in acts 1 and 2, the focus of act 3 is on the figure of the conductor, the "Maestro" husband, Nathanael. As the all-powerful leader of the orchestra, the conductor holds "the celestial spheres" within the power of his baton (*On ne part pas*, 130). Admired and beloved by all, he feels nonetheless that no one understands what his position of power actually costs him. He, too, speaks of Franz and of his desire to leave him a gift of "art and gold." The gift which he would have wished from Franz in exchange is nothing less than his own "forbidden and suppressed childhood" (*On ne part pas*, 130). And if this childhood were indeed to be regained, as a kind of lost paradise, the conductor would then in turn become the composer or "creator." "One always kills the child," the narrator told us in *Déluge*, and the same theme has returned in *On ne part pas, on ne revient pas.*

While a storm rages outside, the first violin (traditionally the orchestra's concertmaster) arrives. He explains to Nathanael that he feels worthless and that for over a year he has been sensitive to "the smell of death" emanating from his own instrument (*On ne part pas*, 143). He has been playing Schumann concertos with no emotion at all and can barely look the Maestro in the eye. To Nathanael's ironic rejoinder that he had simply thought the concertmaster "hated Schumann," he replies that he can no longer make music, that he has become the "First False Violin" and the "First Genuine Liar" as well. Nathanael assures his colleague that this is merely an illness which will pass.

The concertmaster, however, continues to describe his overwhelming feelings of universal guilt and the utter solitude of his present isolated existence in a large empty house. His wife, who has been dead now for more than a year, had in the past offered him a certain protection from the world but now he has no one in his life save his son, who is filled with "tyrannical anti-artistic opinions" (*On ne part pas*, 148). And his son, too, has recently deserted him, with the result that inside his cavernous house there is now only the battle between music and silence. "The truth is," he confides, "that I come home, I open the door, and I am dead" (*On ne part pas*, 149).

The conductor's advice to the concertmaster is clear and commonsensical: sell the house and buy another. Stop saying that you are dead. "To change your existence you must change your address—to cure, to heal, to become another man" (*On ne part pas*, 150–51). "When you are tired," Nathanael advises the concertmaster, "think about Mozart, don't think about yourself, don't think at all" (*On ne part pas*, 151).

The concertmaster then asks Nathanael about his own personal secret for survival after more than thirty years as a conductor. Nathanael responds that his only mark of distinction is his baton, yet to his puzzlement everyone seems to flee from it. No one desires it, and no one ever attempts to pick it up, even when Nathanael leaves it quite openly on his stand. No one, that is, except "the child."

The concertmaster with his bow and the conductor with his baton then hear the faint sound of a whistle from offstage. Nathanael immediately rushes off but soon returns, having missed the one he was seeking.

"You have to run, you don't get there, you don't leave, you don't return . . . humanity has no luck, the race isn't the race," mutters the concertmaster (*On ne part pas*, 154).

Yet Nathanael assures the first violin that he will find what he is seeking even though he is always struggling against "absence, forgetfulness, abandonment" (*On ne part pas*, 155). But when the last room is reached he knows that no one is ever there. There is only silence. Everything, all of life, is really just "Shakespeare."

Nathanael and the first violin leave, one after the other, and Clara and Lucie, the two characters who began the play, return. Clara is now obviously unable to see, and she confides to Lucie that she has always been afraid of losing her sight but that she had never truly believed this could happen to her, since fear was in fact a kind of denial. She asks Lucie to make the light brighter, and her friend obliges until finally Clara can "see" via the "feeling" of light in the room.

The concertmaster returns to let the two women know that the car has arrived. Clara and Lucie leave, Clara "seeing" herself in another life, "neither leaving nor staying, going forward" (*On ne part pas*, 162). And the concertmaster, left alone, delivers the final soliloquy as the curtain falls.

To the overall question of character development and narrative pace, Cixous has stated that her theatrical characters have not been as "slow-going" as the characters she has created in her fictional works can be. What is less important, less active, and less present in her writing for the theater is her constant meditation on the work language does on itself: "When you write chronicles, histories, the history is essential, the analysis comes second" (Franke, 176–77). Cixous has also stated that writing for the theater has changed in some way her fiction writing, that she has begun to have a "different relationship to the other in [her] fiction because of the relationship to so many others in [her] writing for the theater" (Franke, 178). It is clear that Cixous's latest work—drama and prose alike—is under the sign of constant change.

Conclusion

> But there is no "conclusion" to be found in writing.
>
> Hélène Cixous

In the spring of 1990 Hélène Cixous delivered the Wellek Library Lectures at the University of California at Irvine. The three lectures, published collectively in English as *Three Steps on the Ladder of Writing* (1993), present, in highly condensed and poetic form, Cixous's current yet long-standing preoccupations with the relationship of life and death to poetry and politics, the writers with whom she feels the greatest affinity (Clarice Lispector, Jean Genet, Thomas Bernhard, Ingeborg Bachmann, Franz Kafka), and the crucial question of the act of writing: Why do we write? How do we write? From where do we write? What informs the writing that we do? She begins with the concept of writing as analogous to going to school: there are three schools to be attended by writers and readers (because readers are always writers as well): "The School of the Dead," "The School of Dreams," and "The School of Roots."

From her earliest writing in the 1960s—which shows an incredibly well-grounded knowledge of psychoanalysis and philosophy and a concomitant narcissism that makes this writing less accesssible than her more recent publications—to her most recent writing for the theater, Cixous's works demonstrate that writing is both discovery-as-process and discovery-as-product. Cixous's work represents a kind of living textual production of the process lived by her as an individual creator.

Cixous's critics tend still to read her work as being (for feminists) too essentialist, (for pragmatists/activists) too utopian, (for political experts) too naive. The latter criticisms are leveled most especially against her theatrical representations of Cambodia and India, which, according to some, oversimplify complex political situations. The overall concern for Cixous is, however, as in Shakespeare's drama, for the eternal human frailties—conflicts between good and evil, the ambiguity of barriers between the masculine and the feminine—and this would appear to be a constant in her work.

In the Wellek lectures Cixous addresses the basic questions of writing—questions that have informed her career from the outset and that sum up the body of her work to date. Taking a very personal look at her career, she begins with "The School of the Dead" by sketching the image of a ladder and evokes the names of her own chosen voices—the voices her readers are accustomed to hearing (Clarice Lispector, Thomas Bernhard, Marina Tsvetaeva, Ingeborg Bachmann). Linking herself to this family of fellow creators, she allows that they have all frequented the same ladder: "To us this ladder has a *descending* movement, because the ascent, which evokes effort and difficulty, is toward the bottom. I say *ascent* downward because we ordinarily believe the descent is easy. The writers I love are *descenders,* explorers of the lowest and the deepest. Descending is deceptive. Carried out by those I love the descent is sometimes intolerable, the descenders descend with difficulty."[1] Cixous signals two possibilities for descent, or "clambering downward" as she calls it: "plunging into the earth and going deep into the sea," and neither, she reminds us, is easy for the writer (*Three Steps,* 5).

The ladder is the figure Cixous uses to describe her search for "the truth"—"what calls me, attracts me magnetically, irresistibly." Of course, she tells us the word *truth* must be circled "with all kinds of signs, quotation marks, and brackets, to protect it from any form of fixation or conceptualization, since it is one of those words that constantly crosses our universe in a dazzling wake, but is also pursued by suspicion" (*Three Steps,* 6). "Truth," says Cixous, "is what writing wants."

Cixous's constant interest in the presence of death in life and the critical position of death in each of our lives as it allows us access to the door that leads to the other side of life. Having the desire and the courage to open the door is critical—for writing, for living: "The first dead are our first masters, those who unlock the door for us that opens onto the other side, if only we are willing to bear it. Writing, in its noblest function is the attempt to unerase, to unearth, to find the primitive picture again, ours, the one that frightens us" (*Three Steps,* 9).

Cixous acknowledged that her first books came from the death of her father: "And I said to myself that I wouldn't have written . . . I wouldn't have had death, if my father had lived. I have written this several times: he gave me death. To start with" (*Three Steps,* 12). She also reminds us that we don't know, either universally or individually, exactly what our relationship to the dead is. For each individual death constitutes "part of our work, our work of love, not of hate or destruction; we must think through each relationship. We can think this with the help of writing if we know how to write, if we dare write. Also with the help of dreams: they give us the marvelous gift of constantly bringing back our dead alive, with the result that at night we can talk with our dead. Each of us, individually and freely, must do the work that consists of rethinking what is your death and my death, which are inseparable. Writing originates in this relationship" (*Three Steps,* 13).

Echoing a sentence by Kafka, Cixous urges that we "should only read those books that 'wound' us and 'stab' us, 'wake us up with a blow on the head' or strike us like terrible events, that do and don't do us good, that don't do us good in doing us good, a book 'like the death of someone we loved more than ourselves' or that is 'like being banished into a forest far from everyone' or books that are 'like a suicide'" (*Three Steps,* 17). Or, quoting Kafka again, "a book 'must be the axe for the frozen sea inside us'" (*Three Steps,* 17). Only those books that "break the frozen sea and kill us" give us joy. She reminds us that the writers she has always felt closest to are those who play with fire, "those who play seriously with their own mortality, go further, go too far, sometimes go as far as catching fire, as far as being seized by fire" (*Three Steps,* 18).

But not content with speaking merely of the act of writing, Cixous then turns her attention to the corollary action of reading:

> As soon as you open the book as a door, you enter another world, you close the door on this world. Reading is escaping in broad daylight, it's the rejection of the other; most of the time it's a solitary act, exactly like writing. We don't always think of this because we no longer read; we used to read when we were children and knew how violent reading can be. The book strikes a blow, but you, with your book, strike the outside world with an equal blow. We cannot write in any other way—without slamming the door, without cutting the ties. (*Three Steps*, 20)

Reading, Cixous reminds us, is "eating on the sly." It is "a provocation, a rebellion: we open the book's door, pretending it is a simple paperback cover, and in broad daylight escape!" (*Three Steps,* 21). "We are no longer there: this is what real reading is. If we haven't left the room, if we haven't gone over the wall, we're not reading" (*Three Steps,* 210). Reading is eating the forbidden fruit, making forbidden love, changing eras, changing families, changing destinies, and changing day for night. Reading is doing everything exactly as we want and "on the sly" (*Three Steps,* 22). And the books we often choose to read in this solitary, secretive activity are those that "teach us how to die." Like Montaigne, like Thomas Berhnard. Like those of Cixous herself.

Notes and References

Preface

1. Nicole Ward Jouve, *White Woman Speaks with Forked Tongue: Criticism as Autobiography* (London: Routledge, 1990), 91.

2. In *Coming to Writing and Other Essays* (Cambridge, Mass., and London: Harvard University Press, 1991), 194–95; hereafter cited in text.

3. Verena Andermatt Conley, *Hélène Cixous: Writing the Feminine* (Lincoln and London: University of Nebraska Press, 1984), x.

4. Susan Rubin Suleiman, in *Coming to Writing and Other Essays,* xi.

5. *Readings with Clarice Lispector: Seminaires, 1982–1986,* ed. and trans. Verena Conley (Minneapolis: University of Minnesota Press, 1989), 3; hereafter cited in text as *Readings.*

Chapter One

1. "Difficult Joys," in *The Body and the Text: Hélène Cixous, Reading and Teaching,* ed. Helen Wilcox, Keith McWatters, Ann Thompson, and Linda R. Williams (New York: St. Martin's Press, 1990), 2.

2. Jacqueline Sudaka, "Avec Hélène Cixous," *Les Nouveaux Cahiers* 46 (automne 1976), 92.

3. Unpublished typescript notes provided by Hélène Cixous.

4. Quoted in Alice Jardine and Anne M. Menke, "Exploding the Issue: 'French' 'Women,' 'Writers,' and 'the Canon'?" *Yale French Studies* 75 (1988): 238; hereafter cited in text.

5. "Writing the Feminine: Hélène Cixous," interview with Verena A. Conley, in *Hélène Cixous* (Lincoln: University of Nebraska Press, 1984), 139.

Chapter Two

1. *Writing Differences: Readings from the Seminar of Hélène Cixous,* ed. Susan Sellers (Milton Keynes, England: Open University Press, 1988), 144; hereafter cited in text as *Seminar.*

2. One contemporary Joyce critic has noted that Cixous's thesis still is, along with Richard Ellmann's biography, the biggest book written on Joyce by a single author (Geert Lernout, *The French Joyce* [Ann Arbor: University of Michigan Press, 1990]; hereafter cited in text).

3. In Lernout's bibliography we find under the name Hélène Berger one translation and three articles: "Stephen, Hamlet, Will: Joyce par delà Shakespeare," *Etudes Anglaises* 17 (1964): 571–85; "L'Avant-portrait ou la bifur-

cation d'une vocation," *Tel Quel,* no. 22 (1965): 69–76; and "Portrait de la femme par l'artiste," *Lettres Nouvelles* 15 (196?): 41–67.

4. *The Exile of James Joyce or the Art of Replacement,* trans. Sally A. S. Purcell (London: John Calder, 1976; New York: Riverrun Press, 1980), 737; hereafter cited in text as *Exile.*

5. "The Laugh of the Medusa," trans. Keith Cohen and Paula Cohen, *Signs* 1–4 (Summer 1976): 279; hereafter cited in text as "Medusa."

6. Sandra Gilbert, in *The Newly Born Woman,* trans. Betsy Wing (Minneapolis: University of Minnesota Press, 1986), x; hereafter cited in text.

Chapter Three

1. *Le Prénom de Dieu* (Paris: Grasset, 1967), 153; hereafter cited in text.

2. *Inside,* trans. Carol Barko (New York: Shocken Books, 1984), 5; hereafter cited in text.

3. *Les Commencements* (Paris: Grasset, 1970), 28.

4. *Neutre* (Paris: Grasset, 1972), np; hereafter cited in text.

5. *Un vrai jardin* (Paris: L'Herne, 1971), 10; hereafter cited in text.

6. Gilles Deleuze, "Hélène Cixous ou l'écriture stroboscopique," *Le Monde,* 11 August 1972, 10.

7. *Tombe* (Paris: Editions du Seuil, 1973), 11–12.

8. Claudine Guégan Fisher, *La Cosmogonie d'Hélène Cixous* (Amsterdam: Editions Rodopoi, 1988).

9. *Portrait du soleil* (Paris: Editions Denoel, 1975), 5; hereafter cited in text.

10. Morag Shiach, *Hélène Cixous: A Politics of Writing* (London and New York: Routledge, 1991), 81; hereafter cited in text.

11. *Révolutions pour plus d'un Faust* (Paris: Editions du Seuil, 1975), 9; hereafter cited in text as *Révolutions.*

12. *Souffles* (Paris: Editions des femmes, 1975), np; hereafter cited in text.

13. Dina Sherzer, "Postmodernist Feminist Fiction," in *Representations in Contemporary French Fiction* (Lincoln and London: University of Nebraska Press, 1986), 147.

14. *LA* (Paris: Editions Gallimard, 1976; Editions des femmes, 1979), 9; hereafter cited in text.

15. "Castration or Decapitation?" trans. Anette Kuhn, *Signs* (Autumn 1981): 55.

16. "Partie," excerpt trans. K. Cohen, *Tri-Quarterly* 38 (1977): 95.

17. *Angst,* trans. Jo Levy (London: John Calder, 1986), 5; hereafter cited in text.

Chapter Four

1. *Préparatifs de noces au-delà de l'abîme* (Paris: Editions des femmes, 1978), 8; hereafter cited in text as *Préparatifs.*

2. *Vivre l'orange/To Live the Orange* (Paris: Editions des femmes, 1979), 8; hereafter cited in text as *Orange.*

3. *Anankè* (Paris: Editions des femmes, 1979), np; hereafter cited in text.

4. *Illa* (Paris: Editions des femmes, 1980), np; hereafter cited in text.

5. Colette Camelin, "La Scène de la fille dans *Illa,*" *Littérature* 67 (October 1987): 85; hereafter cited in text.

6. *With ou l'art de l'innocence* (Paris: Editions des femmes, 1981), 8; hereafter cited in text as *With.*

7. Pierre Salesne, "Hélène Cixous's *Ou l'art de l'innocence*: The Path to You," in *Writing Differences: Readings from the Seminar of Hélène Cixous,* ed. Susan Sellers (Milton Keynes, England: Open University Press, 1988), 125; hereafter cited in text.

8. *Limonade tout était si infini* (Paris: Editions des femmes, 1982), 17; hereafter cited in text as *Limonade.*

9. *Le Livre de Promethea,* trans. Betsy Wing (Lincoln: University of Nebraska Press, 1991), x; hereafter cited in text as *Promethea.*

10. *La Bataille d'Arcachon* (Québec: Editions Trois, 1986); hereafter cited in text as *Arcachon.*

11. *Manne, aux Mandelstams, aux Mandelas* (Paris: Editions des femmes, 1988); hereafter cited in text.

12. "La Séparation du gâteau," in *Pour Nelson Mandela* (Paris: Gallimard, 1986), 203; hereafter cited in text.

13. *Jours de l'an* (Paris: Editions des femmes, 1990), 124; hereafter cited in text.

14. *L'Ange au secret* (Paris: Editions des femmes, 1991), 16; hereafter cited in text.

15. *Déluge* (Paris: Editions des femmes, 1991), 13; hereafter cited in text.

Chapter Five

1. "L'Auteur entre texte et théâtre," *Hors Cadre* 8 (1990): 46; hereafter cited in text as "L'Auteur."

2. "Writings on the Theatre," trans. Catherine Franke, *Qui Parle?* (Spring 1989): 116.

3. Jeannette Laillou Savona, "In Search of Feminist Theatre: *Portrait of Dora,*" in *Feminine Focus: The New Women Playwrights,* ed. E. Brater (Oxford: Oxford University Press, 1989), 542.

4. Reprinted in "Writings on the Theater:" hereafter cited in text as "Writings."

5. Catherine Franke, interview with Hélène Cixous, *Qui Parle?* (Spring 1989): 172; hereafter cited in text.

6. Sharon Willis, "Hélène Cixous's *Portrait de Dora*: The Unseen and the Un-Scene," *Theatre Journal* 37 (1985): 77; hereafter cited in text.

7. *Benmussa Directs "Portrait of Dora" by Hélène Cixous; "The Singular Life of Albert Nobbs" by Simone Benmussa* (London: John Calder, 1979).

8. *Théâtre (Portrait de Dora, La Prise de l'école de Madhubai)* (Paris: Editions des femmes, 1986), 7; hereafter cited in text as *Théâtre.*

9. *The Conquest of the School at Madhubai,* trans. Deborah Carpenter, *Women and Performance* 3 (special feature) (1986): 59.

10. Véronique Hotte, interview with Hélène Cixous, *Théâtre Public,* no. 68 (1986): 22.

11. Bernard Golfier, "Le Tragique de la partition" (interview with Hélène Cixous), *Théâtre Public* (June 1988): 81; hereafter cited in text.

12. *On ne part pas, on ne revient pas* (Paris: Editions des femmes, 1991), 55; hereafter cited in text.

Conclusion

1. *Three Steps on the Ladder of Writing*, trans. Sarah Cornell and Susan Sellers (New York: Columbia University Press, 1993).

Selected Bibliography

PRIMARY WORKS

Fiction

Le Prénom de Dieu. Paris: Grasset, 1967.
Dedans. Paris: Grasset, 1969; Editions des femmes, 1986.
Le Troisième Corps. Paris: Grasset, 1970.
Les Commencements. Paris: Grasset, 1970.
Un vrai jardin. Paris: L'Herne, 1971.
Neutre. Paris: Grasset, 1972.
Tombe. Paris: Editions du Seuil, 1973.
Portrait du soleil. Paris: Editions Denoel, 1975.
Révolutions pour plus d'un Faust. Paris: Editions du Seuil, 1975.
Souffles. Paris: Editions des femmes, 1975.
LA. Paris: Editions Gallimard, 1976; Editions des femmes, 1979.
Partie. Paris: Editions des femmes, 1976.
Angst. Paris: Editions des femmes, 1977.
Préparatifs de noces au-delà de l'abîme. Paris: Editions des femmes, 1978.
Vivre l'orange/To Live the Orange. Paris: Editions des femmes, 1979. Bilingual text.
Ananké. Paris: Editions des femmes, 1979.
Illa. Paris: Editions des femmes, 1980.
With ou l'art de l'innocence. Paris: Editions des femmes, 1981.
Limonade tout était si infini. Paris: Editions des femmes, 1982.
Le Livre de Promethea. Paris: Editions Gallimard, 1983.
La Bataille d'Arcachon. Québec: Editions Trois, 1986.
Manne, aux Mandelstams, aux Mandelas. Paris: Editions des femmes, 1988.
Jours de l'an. Paris: Editions des femmes, 1990.
L'Ange au secret. Paris: Editions des femmes, 1991.
Déluge. Paris: Editions des femmes, 1991.
Beethoven à jamais ou l'existence de Dieu. Paris: Editions des femmes, 1993.

Theater and Dramatic Works

La Pupille. Cahiers Renard-Barrault, 1971.
Portrait de Dora. Paris: Editions des femmes, 1976. (Reprinted in *Théâtre.* Paris: Editions des femmes, 1986.)
Le Nom d'Oedipe ou le chant du corps interdit. Paris: Editions des femmes, 1978.

La Prise de l'école de Madhubai. Avant-Scène, 1984. (Reprinted in *Théâtre.* Paris: Editions des femmes, 1986.)
L'Histoire terrible mais inachevée de Nordom Sihanouk, roi du Cambodge. Paris: Editions du Théâtre du Soleil, 1985.
Théâtre (Portrait de Dora, La Prise de l'école de Madhubai). Paris: Editions des femmes, 1986.
L'Indiade ou l'Inde de leurs rêves. Paris: Editions du Théâtre du Soleil, 1987.
La Nuit miraculeuse. Film for television. Scenario by Hélène Cixous and Ariane Mnouchkine. *La Sept* (December 1989).
On ne part pas, on ne revient pas. Paris: Editions des femmes, 1991.

Nonfiction: Books

L'Exil de James Joyce ou l'art du remplacement. Paris: Editions Grasset, 1969.
Prénoms de personne. Paris: Editions du Seuil, 1974.
La Jeune Née (with Catherine Clément). Paris: Union Générale des Editions 10/18, 1975.
Un K. incompréhensible: Pierre Goldman. Paris: Christian Bourgeois, 1975.
La Venue à l'écriture (with Annie Leclerc and Madeleine Gagnon). Paris: Union Générale des Editions 10/18, 1977.
Entre l'écriture. Paris: Editions des femmes, 1986.
L'Heure de Clarice Lispector. Paris: Editions des femmes, 1989.

Nonfiction: Individual Essays

"L'Allégorie du mal dans l'oeuvre de William Golding." *Critique* 2339 (April 1966).
"Joyce, la ruse de l'écriture." *Poétique* 4 (1970).
"D'une lecture qui joue à travailler." Preface to a French translation of Lewis Carroll's *Through the Looking-Glass.* Paris: Aubier, 1971.
"La Déroute du sujet ou le voyage imaginaire de Dora." *Littérature et Psychanalyse* 3 (October 1971): 79.
"Une lecture imprudente." *Le Monde,* 5 November 1971.
"Au sujet de Humpty-Dumpty." *Cahiers de l'Herne* 17 (special issue on Lewis Carroll) (1972).
"Poe relu, une poétique du revenir." *Critique* 299 (April 1972): 299.
"Un modèle de modernité." *Le Monde,* 23 June 1972, 16. On Joyce.
"L'Essor de Plus-je." *L'Arc* 54 (1973): 46–52. Special issue on Jacques Derrida.
"La Textremité." *Nouvelle Revue de Psychanalyse* (Spring 1973): 335–50.
"L'Affiche décolle." *Cahiers Renaud Barrault* 83 (1973): 27–37.
"Le Prix Nobel de Littérature à Patrick White." *Le Monde,* 19 October 1973.
"Le Crépuscule des mères." In *Festival d'automne de Paris.* Paris: Gallimard, 1973.
"Le Non-nom" and "Elles volent." Response to "Six questions à Hélène Cixous." *Gramma* (April 1973): 18–26.

"*Electre*: L'Après Médée." In *Le Travail d'Andrei Serban: Festival d'Automne de Paris*. Paris: Gallimard, 1973.
"Les Morts contreparties." Preface to a French translation of James Joyce's *Dubliners*. Paris: Aubier, 1974.
"Le Bon Pied, le bon oeil." *Cahiers Renaud Barrault* 89 (1975): 47–75.
"Finnigans Wake." *Poétique* 26 (1974).
"Le Paradire." *Cahiers Renaud Barrault* 89 (1975): 110–27.
"Le Livre des mortes." *Cahiers Renaud Barrault* 89 (1975): 92–109.
"La Noire vole." *Nouvelle Critique* 82 (March 1975): 47–53.
"L'Ordre mental." Preface to Phyllis Chesler's *Les Femmes et la folie*. Paris: Payot, 1975.
"Le Rire de la Méduse." *L'Arc* 61 (1975): 39–54. Special issue on Simone de Beauvoir.
"La Missexualité." *Poétique* 26 (1976) 383–402. (Reprinted in *Entre l'écriture*. Paris: Editions des femmes, 1986.)
"Un morceau de Dieu." *Sorcières* 1 (January 1976): 14–16.
"La Mode." *Vingt Ans* (June 1976).
"Le Sexe ou la tête?" *Cahiers du GRIF* 13 (October 1976): 5–15.
"Etre femme-juive." *Les Nouveaux Cahiers* 46 (Autumn 1976).
"Une passion, l'un peu moins que rien." *Cahiers de l'Herne* 31 (1976): 326–35. Special issue on Samuel Beckett.
"Aller à la mer." *Le Monde*, 28 April 1977.
"L'Écriture comme placement." In *L'Art de la fiction chez Henry James*. Paris: Klincksieck, 1978.
"O grand-mère que vous avez de beaux concepts." *Des Femmes en Mouvement Hebdo* 1 (9 November 1979): 11–12.
"Poésie e(s)t Politique." *Des Femmes en Mouvement Hebdo* 4 (30 November 1979): 28–33.
"Quant à la pomme du texte." *Etudes Littéraires* [Québec] (December 1980): 412–23.
"Commencer par A." *Des Femmes en Mouvement Hebdo* (21 November 1980).
"La Grâce d'une autre politique." *Le Quotidien de Paris* (April 1981).
"La Poésie comme contrepoison." *Le Nouvel Observateur* (May 1981).
"La Dernière Phrase." *Corps Ecrit* 1 (1981).
"Cahier de métamorphoses." *Corps Ecrit* 6 (1983).
"Suitée de Jérusalem." *Land* (5 June 1983): 36–42.
"Freincipe de plaisir ou paradoxe perdu." In *Le Temps de la réflexion*. Paris: Editions Gallimard, 1983. (Reprinted in *Entre l'écriture*. Paris: Editions des femmes, 1986.) On *Finnegans Wake*.
"Allant vers Jérusalem, Jérusalem à l'envers." *La Nouvelle Barre du Jour* 132 (1983).
"Sonya Rykiel en traduction." In *Sonya Rykiel*. Paris: Herscher, 1984.
"Les Gardiens de notre grandeur." *Le Monde*, 26 May 1985.
"C'est l'histoire d'une étoile." *Roméo et Juliette, Papiers* (1985): 20–23.

"Le Pays des autres." *Revue Opéra* [Brussels] (1986).
"Généalogie." In *Théâtre.* Paris: Editions des femmes, 1986.
"L'Incarnation." In *L'Art du Théâtre* 405. Paris: Actes sud, Théâtre national de Chaillot, 1986.
"Un fils." *Hamlet, Papiers* (1986): 9–15.
"Cela n'a pas de nom." *Le Débat* 41 (1986). On Foucault.
"La Séparation du gâteau." In *Pour Nelson Mandela.* Paris: Gallimard, 1986.
"Portrait de l'Artiste." *Les Cahiers de l'Herne* (1986). Special issue on James Joyce.
"Le Pays des autres." *Réouverture de la Monnaie* [Brussels] (November 1986). Special issue edited by Gérard Mortier.
"Clarice Lispector Titane délicate." *La Quinzaine Littéraire* 484 (April 1987): 10.
"Noir émoi." *Corps Ecrit* 26 (June 1988): 37–43.
"Comment arriver au Théâtre." *Lettre Internationale* 17 (1988), 55–56.
"Marina Tsvetaeva—le feu éteint celle. . ." *Les Cahiers du GRIF* 39 (1988): 87–96.
Rencontres écrites, Mehdi Qotbi [Institut de Monde arabe] (October 1988).
"Je suis plutôt un être de bord." *La Quinzaine Littéraire* 532 (16–31 May 1989): 10.
"Le Sens de la forêt." In *Autour de Julien Gracq.* Paris: Editions José Corti, 1989.
"Théâtre enfoui." *Europe* 726 (October 1989): 72–77.
"Clarice Lispector, Marina Tsvetaeva: Autoportraits." In *Femmes, Women, Frauen,* edited by Françoise van Rossum-Guyon. Amsterdam: Editions Rodopoi, 1990.
"De la scène de l'inconscient à la scène de l'Histoire: Chemins d'une écriture." In *Hélène Cixous: Chemins d'une écriture.* Amsterdam: Editions Rodopoi, 1990.
"L'Auteur entre texte et théâtre." *Hors Cadre* 8 (1990): 33–66.

PRIMARY WORKS: ENGLISH TRANSLATION

Fiction and Theater

Angst. Translated by Jo Levy. London: John Calder, 1986.
The Book of Promethea. Five excerpts. Translated by Deborah Carpenter. *Frank* 6/7 (1987).
The Conquest of the School at Madhubai. Translated by Deborah Carpenter. *Women and Performance* 3 (special feature) (1986).
"Dedication to the Ostrich." Excerpt from *Manne.* Translated by Catherine Franke. *Qui Parle?* (Spring 1989): 133–52.
Inside. Translated by Carol Barko. New York: Shocken Books, 1984.
"*La Jeune Née:* An Excerpt." Translated by Meg Bortin. *Diacritics* (Summer 1977): 64–69.

"The Last Word." Excerpt from *Le Livre de Promethea.* Translated by Ann Liddle and Susan Sellers. *Women's Review* 6 (April 1986): 22–24.
"The Meadow." Excerpt from *La Bataille d'Arcachon. Revue Australienne* (1985).
The Name of Oedipus. Translated by Christiane Makward and Judith Miller. *Contemporary Women's Drama from the French* (forthcoming).
Partie. Excerpt. Translated by K. Cohen. *Tri-Quarterly* 38 (1977): 95–100.
Portrait of Dora. Translated by Sarah Burd. *Diacritics* (Spring 1983): 2–32.
Portrait of Dora, Benmussa Directs. Translated by Anita Barrows. London: John Calder, 1977.
"The Step." From *Le Prénom de Dieu.* Translated by Jill MacDonald and Carole Darring Paul. *French-American Review* (1982).

Nonfiction

"At Circe's, or the Self-Opener." Translated by Carol Bové. *Boundary 2* (1975): 387–97.
"August 12, 1980." Translated by Betsy Wing. *Boundary 2* (1984): 9–39.
"Boxes." Translated by Rosette C. Lamont. In *Centerpoint.* New York: City University of New York, 1977.
"Castration or Decapitation?" Translated by Annette Kuhn. *Signs* (Autumn 1981): 41–55.
"Character of Character." Translated by Keith Cohen. *New Literary History* 5 (1974): 384–402.
The Exile of James Joyce or the Art of Replacement. Translated by Sally A. S. Purcell. London: John Calder, 1976; New York: Riverrun, 1980.
"Extreme Fidelity" and "Tancrede Continues." Translated by Ann Liddle and Susan Sellers. In *Writing Differences: Readings from the Seminar of Hélène Cixous,* edited by Susan Sellers. Milton Keynes, England: Open University Press, 1988.
"Fiction and Its Phantoms: A Reading of Freud's 'Das Unheimliche.'" Translated by R. Denommé. *New Literary History* 7 (1976): 525–48.
Foreword to *Clarice Lispector.* Translated by Verena A. Conley. In *The Stream of Life.* Minneapolis: University of Minnesota Press, 1989.
"From the Scene of the Unconscious to the Scene of History." Translated by Deborah Carpenter. *Future Literary History* (1989): 1–8.
"The Fruits of Femininity." *Guardian,* 16 May 1976.
Introduction to Lewis Carroll's *Through the Looking Glass.* Translated by Marie Maclean. *New Literary History* 13 (1982): 231–51.
"Joyce: The Ruse of Writing." Translated by Judith Still. In *The Post-Structuralist Joyce.* Cambridge: Cambridge University Press, 1984.
"The Laugh of the Medusa." Translated by Keith Cohen and Paula Cohen. *Signs* 1–4 (Summer 1976): 875–93.
The Newly Born Woman. Translated by Betsy Wing. Theory and History of Literature series. Minneapolis: University of Minnesota Press, 1986.

"Poetry Is/and the Political." Translated by Ann Liddle. *Bread and Roses* 2–1 (1980): 16–18.

"The Presence through Writing." Translated by Deborah Carpenter. *Literary Review* (Spring 1987).

"Reaching the Point of Wheat, or a Portrait of the Artist as a Maturing Woman." *New Literary History* 19, no. 1 (Autumn 1987): 1–21.

"Reading Clarice Lispector's 'Sunday before Going to Sleep.'" Translated by Betsy Wing. *Boundary 2* (1984): 41–67.

Readings with Clarice Lispector: Seminaires, 1982–1986. Translated and edited by Verena A. Conley. Minneapolis: University of Minnesota Press, 1989.

"'Sorties': Out and Out: Attack/Ways Out/Forays." In *The Feminist Reader.* Houndmills, England: Macmillan Education Ltd., 1989.

"To Go to the Sea." Translated by B. Kerslake. *Modern Drama* (December 1984).

"Where Is She. . ." and "Sorties." From *The Newly Born Woman.* Translated by Ann Liddle. In *New French Feminisms.* Amherst: University of Massachusetts Press, 1980.

"Writings on the Theatre." Translated by Catherine Franke. *Qui Parle?* (Spring 1989): 120–33.

SECONDARY WORKS

Interviews

Barret, Gisèle. On *L'Histoire terrible mais inachevée de Norodom Sihanouk, roi du Cambodge. Jeu* [Montreal] (October 1985).

Clerval, Alain. On *Souffles. Infoartitudes* (April 1976).

Collin, Françoise. "Quelques questions à Hélène Cixous." *Les Cahiers du GRIF,* no. 13 (1976): 16–20.

Conley, Verena A. "Voice 1." *Boundary 2* (1984): 51–67.

———. "Writing the Feminine: Hélène Cixous." In *Hélène Cixous.* Lincoln: University of Nebraska Press, 1984.

"Conversations." In *Writing Differences: Readings from the Seminar of Hélène Cixous,* edited by Susan Sellers. Milton Keynes, England: Open University Press, 1988.

Coupry, François. "Hélène Cixous ou le rêve de l'écriture." *Libération,* 22 December 1982.

Courtivron, Isabelle de, trans. "Rethinking Differences." In *Homosexualities and French Literature,* edited by Elaine Marks and George Stambolian. New York: Cornell University Press, 1979.

Deleuze, Gilles. "Littérasophie et philosofiture." Emission Dialogues no. 30, edited by Roger Pillaudin. *France-Culture,* 13 November 1973.

"Dossier Jean Genet." *Masques* (Winter 1981–82): 59–63.

"The Double World," "A Realm of Characters," and "Writing as a Second Heart." In *Delighting the Heart: A Notebook of Women Writers,* edited by Susan Sellers. London: Women's Press, 1989.

Finas, Lucette. "L'Etrange traversée d'Hélène Cixous." On *Angst. Le Monde,* 13 May 1977.

Franke, Catherine. *Qui Parle?* (Spring 1989): 152–79.

Gagnon, Madeleine; Philippe Haeck; and Patrick Staramn. On *Le Portrait de Dora. Chroniques* [Montreal] 1 (1977).

Godard, Colette. On *Le Nom d'Oedipe. Le Monde,* 28 July 1977.

Golfier, Bernard. "Le Tragique de la partition." *Théâtre Public* (June 1988).

Hassoun, Pascale; Chantal Maillet; and Claude Rabant. *Patio* 10 (1988).

Hotte, Véronique. "Entretien avec Hélène Cixous." *Théâtre Public,* no. 68 (1986): 22–29.

———. "Une témérité tremblante." *Théâtre Public* (March–April 1986).

Jardin, Claudine. "C'est la culture qui est enfouie dans *Tombe." Le Monde,* 2 June 1973.

Jardine, Alice, and Anne M. Menke. "Exploding the Issue: 'French' 'Women,' 'Writers,' and 'the Canon'?" *Yale French Studies* 75 (1988): 235–38.

Jay, Salim. On *Illa. Mots pour Mots* (1980).

Laurent, Anne. On *La Prise de l'école de Madhubai. Libération,* 30 December 1983.

Lecoq, Dominique. "Les Motions contre l'émotion de l'Histoire." *Politis,* 7 July 1988, 77–88.

Makward, Christiane. "Interview with Hélène Cixous." *Sub-Stance,* no. 13 (1976): 19–37.

Poirson, Alain. "Biographie d'une écriture." *Révolution Magazine,* 31 July 1981.

Quéré, H. "Le Roman aujourd'hui." *Fabula* [Lille] (March 1984).

Rambures, Jean-Louis de. "Je me souviens très bien de mon corps d'enfant." *Le Monde,* 9 April 1976.

Rossum-Guyon, Françoise van. "A propos de *Manne*: Entretien avec Hélène Cixous." In *Hélène Cixous: Chemins d'une écriture,* edited by F. van Rossum-Guyon and M. Diaz-Diocaretz. Amsterdam: Editions Rodopoi, 1990.

———. "Entretien avec Hélène Cixous." *Revue des sciences humaines,* no. 168 (1977): 479–93.

———. *Revue des Sciences Humaines* [Lille] 168 (October–December 1977).

Sellers, Susan. "Hélène Cixous." *Women's Review,* no. 7 (1986): 22–23.

Critical Studies

Alexandrescu, Liliana. "*Norodom Sihanouk*: L'Inachevé comme lecture shakespearienne de l'Histoire contemporaine." In *Hélène Cixous: Chemins d'une écriture,* edited by F. van Rossum-Guyon and M. Diaz-Diocaretz. Amsterdam: Editions Rodopoi, 1990.

Armbruster, Carol. "Hélène-Clarice: Nouvelle voix." *Contemporary Literature* 25 (Summer 1983): 145–57.

Boundary 2 12 (Winter 1984). Special issue on Cixous; edited by Verena Andermatt Conley.

Camelin, Colette. "La Scène de la fille dans *Illa*." *Littérature* 67 (October 1987): 84–101.

Cameron, Beatrice. "Letter to Hélène Cixous." *Sub-Stance* 17 (1977): 159–65.

Conley, Verena Andermatt. *Hélène Cixous.* Toronto and Buffalo: University of Toronto Press, 1992.

———. *Hélène Cixous: Writing the Feminine.* Lincoln and London: University of Nebraska Press, 1984, 1990.

———. Introduction to *Hélène Cixous: Readings.* Minneapolis: University of Minnesota Press, 1991.

———. Introduction to *Reading with Clarice Lispector.* London: Harvester Wheatsheaf, 1990.

———. "Le Goût du nu." *Lendemains* 51 (1988): 120–28.

Cornell, Sarah. "Hélène Cixous's *Le Livre de Promethea*: Paradise Refound." In *Writing Differences: Readings from the Seminar of Hélène Cixous,* edited by Susan Sellers. Milton Keynes, England: Open University Press, 1988.

———. "Hélène Cixous and 'Les Etudes Féminines.'" In *The Body and the Text: Hélène Cixous, Reading and Teaching,* edited by H. Wilcox, Keith McWatters, Ann Thompson, and Linda R. Williams. London: Harvester Wheatsheaf, 1990.

Crecelius, Kathryn J. "La Voix de Tancredi: De Cixous à Sand." In *Hélène Cixous: Chemins d'une écriture,* edited by F. van Rossum-Guyon and M. Diaz-Diocaretz. Amersterdam: Editions Rodopoi, 1990.

Crowder, Diane Griffin. "Amazons and Mothers? Monique Wittig, Hélène Cixous, and Theories of Women's Writing." *Contemporary Literature* 24 (Summer 1983): 117–44.

Defromont, Françoise. "Faire la femme, différence sexuelle et énonciation." *Fabula* 5 (1985): 95–112.

———. "Metaphorical Thinking and Poetic Writing in Virginia Woolf and Hélène Cixous." In *The Body and the Text: Hélène Cixous, Reading and Teaching,* edited by H. Wilcox, Keith McWatters, Ann Thompson, and Linda R. Williams. London: Harvester Wheatsheaf, 1990.

———. "L'Epopée du corps." In *Hélène Cixous: Chemins d'une écriture,* edited by F. van Rossum-Guyon and M. Diaz-Diocaretz. Amsterdam: Editions Rodopoi, 1990.

Deleuze, Gilles. "Hélène Cixous ou l'écriture stroboscopique." *Le Monde,* 11 August 1972, 10.

Duren, Brian. "Cixous' Exhorbitant Texts." *Sub-Stance* 10 (1981): 39–51.

Ertel, Evelyne. "Entre l'imitation et la transposition." *Théâtre Public,* no. 68 (1986): 25–29.

Evans, Martha Noel. "*Portrait of Dora*: Freud's Case History as Reviewed by Hélène Cixous." *Sub-Stance* 11 (1982): 64–71.

Féral, Josette. "The Powers of Difference." In *The Future of Difference,* edited by Hester Eisenstein and Alice Jardine. Boston: G. K. Hall, 1980.

Finas, Lucette. "Le Pourpre du neutre." In *Le Bruit d'Iris.* Paris: Flammarion, 1978, 1981.

Fisher, Claudine Guégan. *La Cosmogonie d'Hélène Cixous.* Amsterdam: Editions Rodopoi, 1988.

———. "Le Vivant de la mort chez Hélène Cixous." *Bérénice: Letteratura Francese Contemporanea* 10 (March 1984): 345–51.

Freeman, Barbara. "Plus corps donc plus écriture: Hélène Cixous and the Mind-Body Problem." *Paragraph* 11, no. 1 (1988): 58–70.

Gallop, Jane. *The Daughter's Seduction.* Ithaca, N.Y., and New York: Cornell University Press, 1984.

Gibbs, Anna. "Cixous and Gertrude Stein." *Meanjin* 38 (September 1979): 281–93.

Hanrahan, Mairéad. "Une porte du *Portrait du soleil* ou la succulence du sujet." In *Hélène Cixous: Chemins d'une écriture,* edited by F. van Rossum-Guyon and M. Diaz-Diocaretz. Amsterdam: Editions Rodopoi, 1990.

Jones, Ann Rosalind. "Inscribing Femininity: French Theories and the Feminine." In *Making a Difference: Feminist Literary Criticism,* edited by Gayle Greene and Coppélia Kahn. London: Methuen, 1985.

———. "Writing and Body: Toward an Understanding of *L'Écriture Féminine.*" *French Studies* 7 (Summer 1981): 73–85.

Jouve, Nicole Ward. "Oranges et sources: Colette et Hélène Cixous." In *Hélène Cixous: Chemins d'une écriture,* edited by F. van Rossum-Guyon and M. Diaz-Diocaretz. Amsterdam: Editions Rodopoi, 1990.

———. "To Fly/to Steal: No More? Translating French Feminisms into English." In *White Woman Speaks with Forked Tongue: Criticism as Autobiography.* London: Routledge, 1991.

Kogan, Vivian. "I Want Vulva! Cixous and the Poetics of the Body." *Esprit Créateur* 25 (Summer 1985): 73–85.

Kolk, Mieke. "La Vengeance d'Oedipe: Théorie féministe et practique du théâtre." In *Hélène Cixous: Chemins d'une écriture,* edited by F. van Rossum-Guyon and M. Diaz-Diocaretz. Amsterdam: Editions Rodopoi, 1990.

Kuhn, Annette. "Introduction to Hélène Cixous's 'Castration or Decapitation?'" *Signs* 7, no. 1 (1981): 36–40.

Lamont, Rosette C. "The Reverse Side of a Portrait: The Dora of Freud and Cixous." In *Feminine Focus: The New Women Playwrights,* edited by E. Brater. Oxford: Oxford University Press, 1989.

LeClézio, Marguerite. "Psychanalyse-poésie: Le Rite de Cixous la Méduse." *Bonnes Feuilles* 9 (Fall 1980): 92–103.

———. "Structures du silence ou délire: Marguerite Duras, Hélène Cixous." *Poétique* 9 (September 1978): 314–24.

Lernout, Geert, *The French Joyce.* Ann Arbor: University of Michigan Press, 1990.

Lie, Sissel. "Pour une lecture féminine?" In *The Body and the Text: Hélène Cixous, Reading and Teaching,* edited by H. Wilcox, Keith McWatters, Ann Thompson, and Linda R. Williams. London: Harvester Wheatsheaf, 1990.

Makward, Christiane. "Structures du silence/du délire: Duras et Cixous." *Poétique,* no. 35 (1978): 314–24.

Marks, Elaine, and Isabelle de Courtivron, eds. *New French Feminisms.* Amherst: University of Massachusetts Press, 1980.

Micha, René. "La Tête de Doras sous Cixous." *Critique* 33 (February 1977): 114–21.

Miller, Judith G. "Jean Cocteau and Hélène Cixous: Oedipus." In *Drama, Sex, and Politics,* edited by J. Redmond. Themes in Drama series, no. 7. Cambridge: Cambridge University Press, 1985.

———. "Contemprary Women's Voices in French Theatre." *Modern Drama* 32, no. 1 (1989): 5–23.

Moi, Toril. "Cixous: An Imaginary Utopia." In *Sexual/Textual Politics.* London and New York: Methuen, 1985.

Mounier, C. "Deux créations collectives du Théâtre du Soleil." In *Les Voies de la création théatrale,* edited by D. Bablet and J. Jacquot. Paris: CNRS, 1977.

Picard, Anne-Marie. "*L'Indiade*: Ariane's and Hélène's Conjugate Dreams." *Modern Drama* 32 (1989): 24–38.

Richman, Michèle. "Sex and Signs: The Language of French Feminist Criticism." *Language and Style* 13 (Autumn 1980): 62–80.

Rossum-Guyon, Françoise van, and Diaz-Diocaretz, eds. *Hélène Cixous: Chemins d'une écriture.* Amsterdam: Editions Rodopoi, 1990.

Running-Johnson, Cynthia. "Feminine Writing and Its Theatrical 'Other.'" In *Women in Theatre,* edited by J. Redmond. Themes in Drama series, no. 11. Cambridge: Cambridge University Press, 1989.

Salesne, Pierre. "Hélène Cixous's *Ou l'art de l'innocence*: The Path to You." In *Writing Differences: Readings from the Seminar of Hélène Cixous,* edited by Susan Sellers. Milton Keynes, England: Open University Press, 1988.

Sandré, Marguerite, and Christa Stevens. "A Bibliography of the Works of Hélène Cixous." In *Hélène Cixous: Chemins d'une écriture,* edited by Françoise van Rossum-Guyon and Myriam Diaz-Diocaretz. Amersterdam: Editions Rodopoi, 1990.

Sankovitch, Tilde A. "Hélène Cixous: The Pervasive Myth." In *French Women Writers and the Book: Myths of Access and Desire.* Syracuse, N.Y.: Syracuse University Press, 1988.

Savona, Jeannette Laillou. "In Search of Feminist Theatre: Portrait of Dora." In *Feminine Focus: The New Women Playwrights,* edited by E. Brater. Oxford: Oxford University Press, 1989.

Sellers, Susan, ed. *Writing Differences: Readings from the Seminar of Hélène Cixous.* Milton Keynes, England: Open University Press, 1988.

Sherzer, Dina. "Postmodernist Feminist Fiction." In *Representations in Contemporary French Fiction.* Lincoln and London: University of Nebraska Press, 1986.

Sihach, Morag. "Their 'Symbolic' Exists, It Holds Power—We, the Sowers of Disorder, Know It Only Too Well." In *Between Feminism and Psychoanalysis,* edited by Teresa Brennan. London and New York: Routledge, 1989.

———. *Hélène Cixous: A Politics of Writing.* London and New York: Routledge, 1991.

Slama, Béatrice. "Entre amour et écriture: *Le Livre de Promethea.*" In *Hélène Cixous: Chemins d'une écriture,* edited by F. van Rossum-Guyon and M. Diaz-Diocaretz. Amsterdam: Editions Rodopoi, 1990.

Sprengnether, Madelon. "Enforcing Oedipus: Freud and Dora." In *The (M)other Tongue: Essays in Feminist Psychoanalytic Interpretation,* edited by Shirley Nelson Garner, Claire Kahane, and Madelon Sprengnether. Ithaca, N.Y.: Cornell University Press, 1985.

Stanton, Domna. "Difference on Trial: A Critique of the Maternal Metaphor in Cixous, Irigaray, and Kristeva." In *The Poetics of Gender,* edited by N. K. Miller. New York: Columbia University Press, 1986.

———. "Language and Revolution: The Franco-American Disconnection." In *The Future of Difference,* edited by Hester Eisenstein and Alice Jardine. Boston: G. K. Hall, 1980.

Stevens, Crista. "Hélène Cixous: Portraying the Feminine." In *Beyond Limits,* edited by L. Brouwer et al. Groningen, the Netherlands: University of Groningen, 1990.

Still, Judith. "A Feminine Economy: Some Preliminary Thoughts." In *The Body and the Text: Hélène Cixous, Reading and Teaching,* edited by H. Wilcox, Keith McWatters, Ann Thompson, and Linda R. Williams. London: Harvester Wheatsheaf, 1990.

Sudaka, Jacqueline. "Avec Hélène Cixous." *Les Nouveaux Cahiers* 46 (automne 1976): 92–95.

Van Rossum-Guyon, Françoise, and Myriam Diaz-Diocaretz, eds. *Hélène Cixous: Chemins d'une écriture.* Amersterdam: Editions Rodopoi, 1990.

Wilcox, Helen; Keith McWatters; Ann Thompson; and Linda R. Williams, eds. *The Body and the Text: Hélène Cixous, Reading and Teaching.* New York: St. Martin's Press, 1990.

Willis, Sharon. "Hélène Cixous's *Portrait de Dora*: The Unseen and the Un-Scene." *Theatre Journal* 37 (1985): 287–301.

———. "Mis-translation: *Vivre l'orange.*" *Sub-Stance* 16 (1987): 76–83.

Index

The Author

Lynn Kettler Penrod is professor of French in the Department of Romance Languages at the University of Alberta, where she teaches twentieth-century French literature, children's literature in French, women's writing in French, and literary translation. Her books include *An Annotated Bibliography of Canadian Children's Literature in French* and *Expériences Littéraires*, and she has published articles on Hélène Cixous, Simone de Beauvoir, Christiane Rochefort, Michel Tournier, J. M. G. Le Clézio, and George Sand.

The Editor

David O'Connell is professor of foreign languages and chair of the Department of Foreign Languages at Georgia State University. He received his Ph.D. in 1966 from Princeton University, where he was a National Woodrow Wilson Fellow, the Bergen Fellow in Romance Languages, and a National Woodrow Wilson Dissertation Fellow. He is the author of *The Teachings of Saint Louis: A Critical Text* (1972), *Les Propos de Saint Louis* (1974), *Louis-Ferdinand Céline* (1976), *The Instructions of Saint Louis: A Critical Text* (1979), and *Michel de Saint Pierre: A Catholic Novelist at the Crossroads* (1990). He is the editor of *Catholic Writers in France since 1945* (1983) and has served as review editor (1977–79) and managing editor (1987–90) of the *French Review*.